P9-EEE-410

Low-Maintenance
GARDENING

Sunset Books
Vice President, Sales: Richard A. Smeby
Editorial Director: Bob Doyle
Production Director: Lory Day
Art Director: Vasken Guiragossian

Low-Maintenance Gardening was produced by:
Editor: Fiona Gilsenan
Art Director: Robin Weiss
Senior Editor: Tom Wilhite
Assistant Editor: Claudia Blaine
Photo Editor: Melinda Lawson Anderson

Consultants: Scott Atkinson, Robert Kourik, Karen Kienholz Steeb, RJ Turner Jr.
Writers: Mia Amato, John and Jeri Cretti, Damon Hedgpeth, Bob Hornback,
    Madeleine Keeve, Jim McCausland, Laura Tringali, Lance Walheim
Researcher: Barbara Brown
Copyeditors: Barbara J. Braasch, Evan Elliot, Carol Whiteley
Proofreaders: Desne Border, Angela Gennino, David Sweet
Indexer: Bayside Indexing Service

Computer Production: Phoebe Bixler, Deborah Tibbetts
Illustrators: Ken Niles, Mimi Osborne, Marina Thompson
Maps: Debra Lambert
Production Coordinator: Patricia S. Williams

Our thanks to the following designers for allowing their work to be shown in this
book: Laurie Callaway (Palo Alto, CA), Linda Chisari (Del Mar, CA), Lisa Herbert,
H & H Horticulture (Stinson Beach, CA), Susie Dowd-Markarian and Jay Tripathi,
Gardenworks Inc. (Healdsburg, CA), Jordan Jackson (Seattle, WA), Rick LaFrentz
(Menlo Park, CA), Kim M. Haworth (Brisbane, CA), Joni Prittie (Monterey, CA),
Robert Trachtenberg, Garden Architecture (San Francisco, CA), Bernard Trainor,
Botanika (Palo Alto, CA)

First printing September 1998
Copyright © 1998, Sunset Publishing Corporation, Menlo Park, CA 94025.
First edition. All rights reserved, including the right of reproduction in whole
or in part in any form. Library of Congress Catalog Card Number: 98-86297.
Hardcover edition: ISBN 0-376-03513-7. Softcover edition: 0-376-03512-9.

Printed in the U.S.A.

Cover *Jerry Pavia.*
A sea of drought-tolerant plants lines a path.

Facing page *Michael S. Thompson.*
White agapanthus.

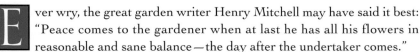

Foreword

Ever wry, the great garden writer Henry Mitchell may have said it best: "Peace comes to the gardener when at last he has all his flowers in reasonable and sane balance—the day after the undertaker comes."

Yet we, the living, want gardens. Not only do they make us proud of our homes, they put us in touch with nature, delight us with their sights and smells, and provide us with fresh produce and seasoning for our kitchens. They draw wildlife and provide safe havens where our children can play. In many parts of the West, we are blessed with weather that allows year-round outdoor entertaining and recreation. And western gardeners can grow a dazzling number of plants whose origins can be traced to far-flung places.

Too often, however, we fail to make our gardens work for us. We plant flowers that remind us of our childhoods—even though that may have been half a continent away in a completely different climate. We are seduced by exotic specimens at the nursery, only to transplant them where they receive too much sun or too little water.

Sometimes we forget that the garden is always changing: plants grow, weeds sprout, pests move in, and the seasons turn, bringing more sun or rain than we expected. We get busy, and the roses don't get deadheaded. We go on vacation, and forget to have the sprinklers turned on. We overplant in hopes that our gardens might look like those featured in magazines—then we run out of the time and energy to look after them properly.

This book is intended to help you avoid these pitfalls by creating a garden you can live with. For almost every time-consuming chore, there's an easy-care alternative—whether it be planting smarter, designing better, or watering more efficiently. In these pages, you'll find recommendations for hundreds of trouble-free plants, plans that simplify design, and imaginative ways to bring color and personality into your garden. The key is proper planning and a regular schedule of straightforward tasks. After all, your garden is there to be enjoyed, not endured.

Table of Contents

Planning Your Garden

Planting Your Garden

Caring for Your Garden

PLANNING YOUR GARDEN

"If you tend a garden for the joy of it, you don't want to be a slave to it. The gardeners who are successfully lazy are the ones who have planned effectively: the layout of the garden, the choice of plants, and a schedule of seasonal jobs and regular maintenance which, timed properly, saves later grief."

Linda Tilgner
The Lazy Gardener

1
Getting Started

Standing on the threshold of a new property is exciting, but it can also be intimidating. How can you transform a bare or overgrown lot into the garden of your dreams? How much will it cost? Can you do it yourself? How can you design a garden that will meet the changing needs of your family? And once you've established your garden, how will you find the time and expertise to keep it healthy and beautiful?

Just as you don't need to be an interior designer to decorate your home's interior, you don't need to be a landscape architect to design a garden. The first step is to evaluate your property and assess your own needs, then to identify regional conditions that may influence your garden plans. If you don't feel confident tackling the job of garden design you can save time and avoid mistakes by using professionals —especially if your property presents challenges such as steep slopes or poor drainage. See pages 232–233 for information on working with professionals.

Your Property

A low-maintenance garden design starts with an understanding of the conditions on your property. The next step is to choose an overall style you like and then to develop a set of goals for building the garden. The real work—constructing a deck, digging a flower bed where there once was bare concrete, planting your favorite trees and shrubs—should not be rushed, as thoughtful hardscape design and the right choice of plants are the main means of reducing maintenance.

Begin with some careful evaluation. If you're redesigning your garden, what elements should be retained? Sometimes a single high-care problem—a large, demanding lawn, for example—can be remedied without changing the rest of the garden design.

Look around the garden for existing clues that indicate a need for different features—worn spots in a ground cover may suggest a route for a new path, for instance. Be observant: if only your front yard gets full sun, put the rose garden there, not in back. But most of all, be creative. If the soil in one part of the garden is poor, pave it over or build raised beds; if the afternoon wind makes outdoor seating uncomfortable, think about relocating a patio, or planting a windbreak of trees. Don't let preconceived ideas stand between you and the garden you really want.

What have you got? Evaluate all existing structures and systems, including the house style and architecture, underground electrical lines and outlets, and water or irrigation lines. Examine hardscape, too, with a critical eye. Just because a patio or path is literally "made of stone" doesn't mean you can't tear it out or redesign it for easier cleaning or better traffic flow. Note planting areas, and whether you want to keep them.

How's the weather? Climatic influences in the garden include precipitation, sun and shadow (which change considerably throughout the year), fog patterns, and microclimates (pockets where the climate may be slightly different). If you're new to the area, ask local residents about seasonal events such as wind; look at mature trees and windbreaks for a "lean" that indicates wind direction and intensity.

From the ground up. Your soil greatly influences how your plants grow and determines which ones are best suited to your garden. Soil depth and compaction will also affect plant health, as will the presence of any diseases, such as oak root fungus. To find out more on evaluating and improving the soil in your garden, see pages 187–189.

The view from here. From several viewpoints (front door, back door, windows upstairs and down) look out over your surroundings, including the neighbors' property, distant views, power lines, and any neighboring structures that affect light or privacy. Also check paperwork for the locations of property lines, setback requirements, and homeowner's association rules, if any. Look for slopes or high areas, and damp, poorly draining spots.

Plants. Don't try to plant heat-lovers in the woods or create an English garden in the desert. Observe your local flora—you'll have more success if you fill your garden with the type of plants that thrive naturally in your area. When reviewing the Plant Selection Guides in Chapters 4 & 5, always note the Sunset zone recommendations and the sun and water needs of each plant.

Your Garden

Transforming your garden from bare dirt to blooming greenery doesn't happen overnight. Careful planning and preparation are key. The facing page gives an overview of the process.

When determining your needs, ask yourself and your family how the garden will be used. Do you frequently entertain or dine outdoors? Do you have active children who need a place to play? Or do you prefer the garden to be a quiet spot for relaxation? What time of day are you most likely to enjoy the garden? Are you away for long stretches of time? The answers to these questions will help you draw up a "wish list" of garden features.

If you are having trouble visualizing what a prospective garden plan might look like, mock up a fake version of the real thing. Tall stakes can stand in for trees or for elements such as fountains or sculpture. Large pieces of cardboard can indicate paving or decks. Strings and stakes can outline paths and garden "rooms." Leave the "stage set" in place for a few days to see how it influences traffic patterns, views, privacy, and access; you'll soon see whether your plan needs adjustment.

This coastal garden in California had to be easy to care for—its owners are weekend occupants. To preserve the ocean view from the upper deck of the house, no plants could be taller than 10 ft.—and they had to tolerate seaside conditions. In addition to the deer that had made this previously vacant lot their home, the site was also a leach field, which meant that only deer-resistant plants with non-invasive roots could be used. The result is a garden that blends into the natural landscape and requires no more ongoing maintenance than a clean-up every four months. Ornamental grasses, New Zealand flax, smoke tree, and native California plants such as manzanita provide interest and texture. Brown drain rock constitutes an informal path that curves through the garden to a simple teak bench; the muted color of the path blends with the plants and doesn't show fallen leaves. The garden is shown here 4 years after being planted.

FIVE STEPS TO A NEW GARDEN

1. **Look at what you've got.** The preceding pages explained how to evaluate your property, but remember that any living and lived-in garden will need some tending. Make a complete list of all the routine care your garden currently requires (see Chapter 9, "Maintaining Your Garden"), including weekly as well as once or-twice monthly chores. Then, as best you can, tally the hours per week or month you expect to spend working in your new garden. If the total strikes you as too high, adjust your design accordingly.

2. **Figure out what you want.** This is the fun part. Decide what kind of garden you want. Herbs? Flowers? A lawn for touch football or badminton? A shady patio? A dog run? Look at the photos and plans in this book and in magazines. Rent some gardening videos, if you like, for inspiration, or contact your local garden club or horticultural society and inquire about garden tours in your area.

3. **Make a plan.** After writing a "wish list," review your property to discover where you might put the features you want. If you decide to design your garden yourself, the easiest way to proceed is to draw the outlines of your property on graph paper, then use sheets of tracing paper on which to sketch different possible designs. If you work with a professional designer or architect, a full plan will be provided for you, but it's still a good idea to present your initial ideas on paper.

4. **Install the hardscape.** If you have no experience with construction, hire landscaping help. Soil grading and drainage are key elements when installing new paving or terracing, and are an absolute must if you want a trouble-free patio or retaining wall. Choose long-lasting materials such as decay-resistant woods, and consider automated irrigation and lighting systems. Chapter 3, "Building Your Garden," walks you through the basics of hardscape design.

5. **Choose easy-care plants.** Trees, shrubs, hedges, and ground covers are the stalwart plants for easy-care gardens. Scout for rugged alternatives to traditional plantings—native ferns, ornamental grasses, and succulents that thrive in western gardens. Chapter 4 ("The Ornamental Garden") and Chapter 5 ("The Edible Garden") include Plant Guides, as well as suggested plantings for different situations.

California

A t first glance, California seems a gardener's paradise. With natural beauty that ranges from snow-capped mountains to sunny beaches, it's possible to grow thousands of different plant species, many of which are known elsewhere only as house plants.

But, of course, California has many climates and many styles. In the northern reaches, conditions are more closely related to the Pacific Northwest. In the Southeastern part of the state, the garden is a desert. Along the coast, gardeners are beset by fog patterns that turn the seasons upside down.

Water conservation is an everyday concern in California. The varied terrain and its weather cycles regularly produce droughts of several years' duration, mudslides caused by heavy winter rains, wildfires born in dry, windy weather, and occasional earthquakes.

Spanish missionaries imported the Mediterranean plants that are now so much at home in contemporary gardens: palms, olives, citrus, and grapes. Later immigrants, arriving from the Gold Rush through the growth of California as an agricultural heartland, brought with them gardening styles from their own homelands. In the 1950s, noted San Francisco landscape architect Thomas Church defined a quintessentially Californian style of outdoor living that included the use of hardscape and native plants in garden design. These principles define much of low-maintenance gardening today.

California is often considered two separate entities: Northern California, which contains the inland zone 14 and the mild coastal zones 15–17, is characterized by moderate winters and dry summers. Southern California has warmer coastal zones from 18–24, but also contains high- and low-desert regions that more closely resemble the Southwest (10–13). Further inland, zones 7–9 are found in the valleys, and the coldest western zones (1–2) are located in the high-mountain regions. To successfully select plants, gardeners in California must pay special attention to the climate zone ratings in the Plant Selection Guides in Chapters 4 & 5.

CLIMATE & SOIL

Most of California's climate is considered Mediterranean, but two high mountain ranges and the Pacific coastline affect its gardening conditions. Below the snow line, winter is a mild, rainy season that stretches from October to May. Spring, summer, and early fall are typically rainless, with temperatures that are moderate, chilly (closer to the coast), or torrid (in sheltered valleys). Further inland, extreme temperatures occur in both winter and summer. And while southern valleys may experience only 1 or 2 inches of rainfall per year, 20–30 feet of snow is not rare in California's mountains. Near the coastline, the likelihood of winter frost decreases.

Native soils are generally fast-draining and mineral-rich, though clay strata (caliche), rocks, and alkalinity may be natural conditions. And the considerable growth of new housing developments throughout the state means that many gardeners start with less-than-perfect soil conditions, after topsoil has been bulldozed away.

There are few plants listed in the Plant Selection Guides in this book that are not at home somewhere in California — from the cacti and other desert plants of Southern California to the wildflowers of Marin county to the hardy shrubs of the high mountains.

FAVORITE CALIFORNIA PLANTS*

Arctostaphylos uva-ursi 'Point Reyes'
POINT REYES MANZANITA

Cactus

Camellia japonica

Ceanothus
WILD LILAC

Citrus 'Improved Meyer'
'MEYER' LEMON

Cupressus sempervirens 'Stricta'
ITALIAN CYPRESS

Cymbidium
CYMBIDIUM ORCHID

Erigeron karvinskianus
SANTA BARBARA DAISY

Festuca elatior hybrids
TALL FESCUE

Fraxinus angustifolia 'Raywood'
RAYWOOD ASH

Helictotrichon sempervirens
BLUE OAT GRASS

Lavandula
LAVENDER

Narcissus
DAFFODIL

Pelargonium
GERANIUM

Pennisetum setaceum 'Rubra'
PURPLE FOUNTAIN GRASS

Penstemon
BEARD TONGUE

Phoenix canariensis
CANARY ISLAND DATE PALM

Phormium tenax
NEW ZEALAND FLAX

Podocarpus macrophyllus
YEW PINE

Polystichum munitum
SWORD FERN

Rosa
ROSE

Sequoia sempervirens
COAST REDWOOD

*Most of these regional favorites can be found in the Plant Selection Guides in Chapters 4 & 5.

Pacific Northwest

The Cascade Range defines much of Northwest gardening. This great, volcano-studded spine of mountains divides the area from British Columbia to California into two climates. To the west, the ocean air keeps most of western Oregon and Washington damp and heavily forested. The soil is acidic, the winters are chilly (but rarely harsh), and the shade is abundant, so gardeners take their cues from nature, planting ferns, rhododendrons, maples, evergreens, dogwoods, woodland flowers, and even moss lawns. With its wet winters and dry summers, the climate also suits Mediterranean plants and there is hardly a better place to grow maples, flowering cherries, azaleas, camellias, and evergreens associated with Asian gardens. Combined with a rich farming tradition, the regional garden style has deep roots on three continents.

Moving east, the high Cascade crest squeezes most of the rain and snow out of the storms that sail by, leaving the gardens of eastern Washington and Oregon drier, hotter in summer, and colder in winter. An open landscape blends sagebrush and wine grapes, cherry orchards and ponderosa pines. In east-side towns, lilac-scented gardens spread out from under shade trees, bright annuals border perfect bluegrass lawns, and Russian olives form shelter belts that allow vegetables and rose gardens to thrive—all this is possible, as long as there's sufficient water to sustain it.

Although the Pacific Northwest is considered a rainy place, Seattle, Washington receives only 10 in. of summer rain—far less than Boston or New York—which makes for a long, mild summer-through-fall growing season. In fact, the region encompasses several distinct climate zones: The cold, high-mountain zones (1–3), and the marine-influenced, warmer zones to the west (4–7). Consult the Plant Selection Guides in Chapters 4 & 5 for plants that thrive in these areas.

CLIMATE & SOIL

Though the west side of the mountains receives plenty of rain—50 inches is common in the lowlands, with 100 inches or more along the coast—this precipitation is seasonal—80 percent of it falls in winter.

Because of all that rain, west-side soil is on the acid side—perfect for everything from blueberries to rhododendrons, and acceptable (or easily correctible with lime) for most other garden plants. Soils around Puget Sound are mostly glacial till—stony conglomerations of clay and sand with generally low fertility—while those in western Oregon's most populated river valleys (the Columbia, Willamette and Rogue chief among them) are deep, rich, and on the heavy side. East of the Cascades, soil pH is in the slightly acid to slightly alkaline range.

West of the mountains, the growing season runs from March through October, when the harvest finishes up and plants shut down for winter. The last frost comes in May most places, and first fall frosts come in late October or early November. Only in Southern Oregon are the summers hot. In winter, minimum temperatures usually remain above freezing. On the east side, the growing season usually runs from April through September. Hot days are typical in summer as are sub-freezing temperatures in winter.

FAVORITE NORTHWEST PLANTS*

Acer circinatum
VINE MAPLE

Acer palmatum
JAPANESE MAPLE

Aquilegia formosa
WESTERN COLUMBINE

Cercidiphyllum japonicum
KATSURA TREE

Chrysanthemum maximum
SHASTA DAISY

Clematis montana
ANEMONE CLEMATIS

Cornus kousa
KOUSA DOGWOOD

Cosmos bipinnatus

Galium odoratum
SWEET WOODRUFF

Hamamelis intermedia
WITCH HAZEL

Helleborus
HELLEBORE

Iris sibirica
SIBERIAN IRIS

Lilium
LILIES, ASIATIC OR L/M HYBRIDS

Narcissus
DAFFODIL

Pachysandra terminalis
JAPANESE SPURGE

Papaver nudicaule
ICELAND POPPY

Polystichum munitum
SWORD FERN

Rhododendron

Romneya coulteri
MATILIJA POPPY

Rosa
ROSES, INCLUDING RUGOSAS

Thymus praecox arcticus
CREEPING THYME

Trachycarpus fortunei
WINDMILL PALM

* Most of these regional favorites can be found in the Plant Selection Guides in Chapters 4 & 5.

Southwest

The American Southwest is defined for gardeners by two conditions: heat and dryness. These, however, are moderated by a vast landmass that begins in western Texas, runs through New Mexico, Arizona, southern Nevada, and Utah, and into the deserts of Southern California.

The region's rich horticultural tradition began in the seventeenth century when the land was settled by the Spanish. Self-reliant gardens were the only ones that could survive this outpost culture. Today, despite cities, suburbs, and vast, irrigated agricultural areas, the Southwest remains one of the country's great open spaces. Eternal vistas, endless sky, and the elegant simplicity of the desert inspire local gardeners, as do the mountains, whose jagged peaks factor into almost every landscape.

But Southwest style moves beyond the vernacular. Tropical collections, Asian themes, formal landscapes, and rustic, natural—even woodland—designs are all possible in the Southwest. The trick lies in choosing plants that can survive the heat and dryness of the region. Fortunately, other dry floral kingdoms—Australia, the Mediterranean, South Africa, and parts of South America—offer a bounty of plant material, as does the Southwest itself with universally popular native plants ranging from airy gaura and coral bells to sculptural ocotillo and graceful mesquite.

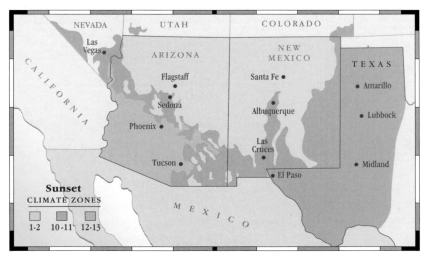

Sunset
CLIMATE ZONES

1-2   10-11   12-13

CLIMATE & SOIL

Blue skies and sunny days are typical in the Southwest, but low rainfall and steady evaporation mean that only heat-tolerant plants can thrive without some coddling. Planted windbreaks and other design elements can create microclimates even within the smallest garden; the ubiquitous courtyard is a perfect example. Walls and high trees screen and shelter the space from wind and sun; careful underplantings increase humidity and reduce evaporation. Protective hardscaping helps, too—such as overhead structures that protect from the sun or walls that provide cooling shade or, conversely, reflect heat.

Southwest soils tend to be compacted and dry. Because the soil doesn't drain well, salts can't leach away, which creates alkaline conditions. What's missing is organic material—decomposed vegetative matter. Diligent amending and mulching of dense desert soils is the first step toward improving drainage and soil composition, but Southwest gardeners may have more success choosing plants that are adapted to the region's natural conditions.

FAVORITE SOUTHWEST PLANTS*

Agave

Albizia julibrissin
SILK TREE

Antigonon leptopus
QUEEN'S WREATH

Bougainvillea

Buddleia davidii
BUTTERFLY BUSH

Caesalpinia pulcherrima
RED BIRD OF PARADISE

Carnegiea, Opuntia
CACTUS

Citrus

Ferocactus
BARREL CACTUS

Fouquieria splendens
OCOTILLO

Gaura lindheimeri
GAURA

Lavandula
LAVENDER

Nerium oleander
OLEANDER

Parkinsonia aculeata
MEXICAN PALO VERDE

Penstemon eatonii
FIRECRACKER PENSTEMON

Perovskia 'Blue Spire'
RUSSIAN SAGE

Plumbago auriculata
CAPE PLUMBAGO

Ratibida columnifera
MEXICAN HAT

Salvia greggii, S. farinacea
AUTUMN SAGE, MEALY-CUP SAGE

Syringa
LILAC

Verbena

Washingtonia robusta
MEXICAN FAN PALM

Wisteria

Zinnia

Most of these regional favorites can be found in the Plant Selection Guides in Chapters 4 & 5 (pages 74–145).

Several microclimates exist within the desert. Zones 1 and 2 have cold winters and short growing seasons. Zones 10 and 11, the high deserts, have enough winter chill for deciduous fruits but not enough to rule out hardy palms. Zone 12 has a longer growing season—February through November. Zone 13 contains the subtropical deserts of the Southwest, with the longest, hottest summer. Yearly rainfall also reflects the region's diversity: 3 in. in Yuma, Arizona, 11 in. in Tucson, and 14 in. in Santa Fe, New Mexico. Consult the Plant Selection Guides in Chapters 4 & 5 for plants that are well-suited to these different climate zones.

Rocky Mountains

The Rocky Mountains are blessed with abundant sunshine, relatively dry winters (except in the high country), and low humidity that saves plants from many diseases and pests. On the other hand, mountain gardeners must cope with drying winds, high summer heat, and unpredictable frosts in early fall and late spring. Hail storms can devastate trees, flowers, and vegetable gardens. On the eastern slope of the Rocky Mountains, heavy, wet snows fall often in late spring or early fall. Deciduous landscape plants that are in full leaf or in their peak of spring bloom may undergo a natural, but severe, pruning (a phenomenon coined "limb-breaker season").

But local gardeners are a resourceful lot. Windbreaks and heavy mulches make it possible to grow many plants that would otherwise perish from the fluctuating temperatures, wind, low humidity, and the low winter sun that can burn the trunks of young trees.

Because the land features and gardening conditions vary—from mountain canyons to urban canyons—no single style predominates. In this region of contrasts, plant choices range from mountain natives to exotic imports, Mediterranean lavender to Russian sage. Gardeners are free to express their individual tastes, just as long as they try to understand the conditions in which they garden.

Rocky Mountain climate zones represent a diversity of growing conditions. Zone 1 is categorized by frigid temperatures and short growing seasons; in the lower elevations, zone 2 has more erratic snowfall and drying winds. In the "banana belts" of zone 3, winters are comparatively mild. At the other extreme, zones 10 and 11 represent the high desert regions, including parts of Arizona and New Mexico. Winter minimum temperatures range from 32°F to 25°F. Consult the Plant Selection Guides in Chapters 4 & 5 for plants that do well in these very different climate zones.

CLIMATE & SOIL

The combinations of fluctuating temperatures, low humidity, drying winds, and difficult soil types influence how well plants adapt to the region. In elevations above 7,000 feet, winters are cold, and the snow can stay on the ground for several weeks or all winter long, depending upon exposure. Growing seasons tend to be shorter in the high country. In the highest elevations, frosts can come during the summer months, and the growing season ranges from 50 to 70 days (compared with 150 days in the high plains).

Most of the populated areas of the Rocky Mountain region have heavy, clay soils with poor aeration. This reduces the ability of plants to replenish water that is lost through low humidity. Adding more water to the soil further complicates the problem by waterlogging the roots—yet plants must be adequately watered so that they don't dry out due to low humidity and dessicating winds. Because little can be done to change these conditions the best solution is to improve and mulch the soil, plant windbreaks, or garden in raised beds.

FAVORITE MOUNTAIN PLANTS*

Abies concolor
WHITE FIR

Acer platanoides
NORWAY MAPLE

Acer rubrum
RED MAPLE

Amelanchier
SERVICEBERRY

Asclepias tuberosa
BUTTERFLY WEED

Buddleia davidii
BUTTERFLY BUSH

Cercocarpus
MOUNTAIN MAHOGANY

Coreopsis verticillata 'Moonbeam'

Dianthus barbatus
SWEET WILLIAM

Echinacea purpurea
PURPLE CONEFLOWER

Fraxinus americana 'Autumn Purple',
Fraxinus pennsylvanica
ASH

Gleditsia triacanthos inermis
THORNLESS HONEYLOCUST

Hemerocallis hybrids
DAYLILIES

Hosta

Iris, Bearded & Siberian

Juniperus scopulorum
ROCKY MOUNTAIN JUNIPERS

Lilium
LILIES, HYBRID, ASIATIC & TIGER

Lupinus hybrids
LUPINE

Mahonia

Paeonia lactiflora and hybrids
PEONY

Penstemon barbatus
BEARA TONGUE

Picea pungens 'Glauca'
COLORADO BLUE SPRUCE

Pinus aristata
BRISTLECONE PINE

Sedum telephium 'Autumn Joy'

Tilia
LINDEN

*Most of these regional favorites can be found in the Plant Selection Guides in Chapters 4 & 5.

2

Low-Maintenance Gardens

What makes a garden low maintenance? As these photographs show, it's not just boring expanses of paving or pachysandra. The gardens and plantings pictured here are varied, colorful, and creative—and they share other qualities, too. First, the best gardens start with good "bones"—the underlying design and structures that make the space work for its inhabitants. Second, they are in harmony with their surroundings, which gives the garden a sense of regional style and allows it to work with nature rather than against it. (The garden at right, for instance, has no demarcation from the desert beyond; it melds perfectly into its environment.) Finally, a successful garden depends on careful plant selection. You must choose types that have the ability to thrive in less-than-ideal conditions. Keep these points in mind as you look through this chapter for ideas and inspiration.

Above & right *Designing for color over several seasons can be a challenge. In this Northwest garden, long-lived bulbs make it simple. Above, spring-blooming* Scilla siberica *are dormant in summer, when montbretia* (Crocosmia crocosmiiflora) *sends out its orange flowers. In the picture at right the hydrangea is sending out new growth after its once-yearly pruning; rhododendrons, perfectly suited to the climate, need only after-bloom deadheading. A casual jumble of rocks, a weathered stump, and a recycled concrete wall are the hardscape elements that anchor the scene. Atop the wall, free-blooming evergreen candytuft* (Iberis sempervirens) *adds greenery even when its white flowers are not in bloom.*

Left Though similar, these two designs are deceptively different. Gravel is a versatile hardscape material, but keeping it litter-free and fastidiously raked (top) can be a daily chore. Boulders used as accents can be left unadorned (bottom); covered with moss, they require regular watering. A guide to choosing materials for paths and patios starts on p. 42.

Below, left and right Thoughtful plant selection is the key to reduced maintenance: these two combinations illustrate that principle. On the right, grasses, succulent Sedum telephium 'Autumn Joy', and perennial Russian sage will give long-lasting color with minimal watering and only occasional grooming. The combination at left is pretty, but the tulips require painstaking lifting and chilling and blue forget-me-nots (Myosotis sylvatica) aren't reliable in warmer zones and can invade the garden in temperate regions. For the best easy-care plants, turn to The Ornamental Garden, which starts on p. 76.

Left *Naturalistic garden plans combine casual materials and plantings for a garden that blends into the surrounding landscape. Here, an unstructured pathway and peeled board fence are surrounded by a loose arrangement of fescue and carefree perennials, including red poppies, purple penstemon, and yellow sundrops, which punctuate the design with color. A drought-tolerant garden plan is given on p. 174.*

Left *Foliage can provide both color and texture in Asian-influenced gardens. This combination of evergreen shrubs, Japanese maples, and shade-loving ornamental grasses has plenty of variety. Low-growing ground cover softens the paving stones. For an Asian-inspired garden plan, see p. 166.*

Right *Formal gardens usually require too much clipping, raking, and other grooming to be low maintenance. But formality can be suggested with symmetrical arrangements and traditional materials. Here, easy-care lavender cotton, lamb's ears, Santa Barbara daisy, and catmint surround an old-fashioned birdbath ringed with flagstone. Look on p. 165 for a formal entryway plan.*

Left *In the desert, the easiest gardens eschew water-thirsty lawns and mixed borders. Instead, hardscape materials are combined with drought-tolerant plants. Lantana, cactus, and penstemon are all good choices. The red geraniums, which require more water and grooming, are reserved for containers. A southwestern courtyard plan can be found on p. 169.*

27

Right *Mediterranean-inspired gardens combine long-blooming, unthirsty plants, such as* Limonium *and lavender, with equally drought-tolerant trees (here, an olive and a cordyline). Artfully placed containers and clean architectural lines were inspired by the early missions.*

Below *Even the profuse abundance of a cottage garden can be achieved with less labor if the border is filled with no-fuss artemesia, cosmos, penstemon, butterfly bush, and grasses. Mulching and drip irrigation, however, are a must for busy combinations such as this.*

Above *Contemporary designs are well-
suited to simple sculpture and painted
walls that bring form and color into a
plant-free garden "room." In the foreground, violet lantana echoes the colored
wall within.*

Left *Woodland gardens work well in
shady, damp places. This one combines
maples, orange montbretia, ferns, and
ground-cover sedum. These plants all
grow slowly and, when given the right
conditions, rarely suffer from diseases
or pests. The shady environment and a
mulch of wood chips keep weeds at bay.*

Above, left *Abundant use of hard-scape—paved surfaces, walls, boulders, and furniture—significantly reduces maintenance. Integrating those elements with the house architecture and choosing plants that blend with the colors of the hardscape unify the design.*

Above, center *Variations in level can diversify a design and help meet the differing water needs of plant groupings. The color of the house contrasts beauti-fully with the sky. The low walls and selectively placed plantings make this desert garden quietly interesting.*

Right *The bountiful plantings in this front yard have been carefully chosen. Undemanding shrubs like barberry, ground-hugging conifers, ferns, Sedum telephium 'Autumn Joy', and rudbeckia can be left in place for years. A well-mulched drip irrigation system provides each of the plants with the correct amount of water.*

Left This border of coniferous shrubs is filled with plants that require little pruning or grooming. The lawn is kept edged and is watered with an underground sprinkler system. An elaborate arbor needs no adornment. Citrus is well-suited to containers, which can be protected in colder climates.

Below An alternative to an expanse of lawn is a variety of paving materials over a large area. This series of patios ascends a slight grade to the house, and contains a simple water feature, plus several planting areas for easy-care choices such as the penstemon in the foreground.

31

Above, left *Certain plants are indis-pensable staples of a low-maintenance garden. The carefree bloom of Santa Barbara daisy, santolina, and catmint leave the gardener time to tend the more demanding roses in the background.*

Above *Daylilies are another reliable no-fuss plant in any climate zone. Here, they brighten a stone staircase with their sunny, repeat blossoms.*

Left *In a wet climate, a simple covering of a single plant, such as moss, can bring unexpected vibrancy to a pathway. Pink-flowered azaleas provide colorful accents.*

Above Succulents, cacti, and pink-flowered verbena provide beautiful shapes and textures in dry-climate gardens. A planting mound slightly raised above the pathways assists drainage. Most of the variety in this arrangement of succulents comes from the different forms and colors of the foliage.

Left Paving needn't be unadorned. Thyme happily creeps between the crevices of this flagstone patio, bringing fragrance to the seating area. In the foreground is a border of penstemon, buckwheat, pinks, and other perennials. None of these plants require much water, fertilizing, or grooming.

Clockwise from left *More than any other part of the garden, mixed borders require careful planning and plant selection, so give them a position of prominence in the garden. At left is a mix of white-flowered iris and silver artemesia bordered by white pansies and sweet alyssum. A clever twist on formality is provided by container-grown boxwood and an edging of lamb's ears (above). At right and above, right, are two simple pathways framed with creative combinations of ornamental grasses and perennials. Chapter 4 (pp. 76–133) contains planting plans for similar easy-care beds and borders.*

Clockwise from above *Variegated agave, snow-in summer, and marigolds* (Tagetes lemmonii) *mix yellows and greens. Lady's-mantle, pink-flowered chives, lamb's ears, New Zealand flax, and tufted ornamental grasses line a pathway. Daylilies and variegated* Miscanthus sinensis *dominate a mixed border. Long-blooming lavender and Santa Barbara daisy top a stone wall. A burgundy-red Japanese maple and a sword fern* (Polystichum munitum) *provide a contrast of opposite colors. Japanese blood grass* (Imperata cylindria 'Rubra') *and deciduous* Fothergilla major *put on a vibrant autumn show.*

All these combinations provide contrasting but complementary colors, shapes, and heights. What shouldn't conflict are the cultural needs of plants that are grouped together—their water, sun, and soil preferences. The lists of easy-care plants in Chapters 4 & 5 (pp. 76–145) will help guide your choices.

Clockwise from right A 'river' of
pebbles winds through ground-cover
ajuga and sedum, iris, and agapanthus.
Santa Barbara daisy spills over a wall;
lobelia and pelargonium are planted at
its base. Licorice plant (Helichrysum
petiolare) mounds gracefully beside a
teak bench. A boxwood hedge contains a
single flowering azalea.

Mixing hardscape and plants in such
simple combinations can be very effective
and doesn't require complex planning.
You can always build on your original
idea by adding more plants or sculpture.
The Decorative Garden (pp. 146–161)
shows ways to bring additional color
and form into the garden with artworks,
containers, and paint.

3
Building Your Garden

When landscape architects and designers talk about the "bones" of the garden, they are referring not only to the overall layout but to the structures and "hardscape"—paths, decks, walls, raised beds, and so on—that define that layout. These bones will remain even as different plants grow or are replaced and, if the design is well-conceived and flexible, elements of the garden can eventually be converted to suit your family's changing lifestyle.

The hardscape delineates areas of use and it helps define the garden's style. The materials you choose, whether brick, stone, wood, or concrete, should be durable and they should be in keeping with your home's architecture. Always select the best materials you can afford; they'll look better, last longer, and require less maintenance than cheaper ones. And remember that a hallmark of good design is the limited use of different building materials in the same garden; in this case, less variety leads to greater visual harmony.

Paths & Patios

Garden walkways and patios work best when they not only look good, but fill other roles as well. Paths can create flow through sections of the garden; link diverse elements, such as raised beds, flower borders, and play areas, into a unified whole; and camouflage areas of the property where plants won't easily grow. Likewise, a well-designed patio encourages a variety of activities, from entertaining to relaxing.

It's likely that your property offers logical sites for both paths and patios. A path may connect exterior doors or utility areas, or suggest a route from the house through the garden. Generally, a patio is most convenient when it can be accessed easily from the kitchen, living room, or main bedroom. Still, don't limit yourself to obvious choices. To try out a location you're not sure about, outline the proposed shape of the path or patio with garden hoses or planks and live with the layout for a few days. You'll soon see whether it works for you.

Above all, don't forget that paths and patios are utilitarian surfaces and should be sturdy enough to bear heavy traffic. If the ground in your area freezes in winter, you'll need some special construction techniques. For advice that will—or won't—lead you down the garden path, review the tips on materials and construction that follow.

Pathways that follow a direct route may be the most practical in a small garden. Formal paving materials, such as brick, are well suited to such a linear route.

Winding its way through the garden, a curved path invites walkers for leisurely strolls. Natural materials such as wood chips and stones work well in such informal settings.

Changes in grade may call for some clever tricks with geometry. Diagonal walkways and mixed materials emphasize garden "rooms" and make small spaces appear larger.

PERFECT PATHWAYS

Make it match. Choose a paving style and material that complement your house. Meandering gravel or bark-chip paths suit informal gardens; a geometric masonry walk, is more formal.

Don't skimp on width. Wider sections encourage lingering while narrower areas hasten travel. Allow 2 ft. for a person to walk alone, 3 ft. for a person with a wheelbarrow, and 5 ft. for two people ambling side by side. As plants will spread into gravel paths, make the paths at least 3 ft. wide.

The right night light. If you plan nocturnal strolls, line paths with low-voltage lights. They are easy to install, prevent injury, and discourage intruders.

Play with perspective. Visually deepen a small area by gradually tapering the width of a straight path from the midpoint to the end. Likewise, pavers set on a diagonal will add visual depth.

Keep it tidy. Edge the path to boost eye appeal as well as to keep loose materials in and unwelcome plants out. Bricks, boards, timbers, and redwood benderboard work well, as do commercial plastic or aluminum edging strips (see p. 53).

Incorporate a surprise. A path is most interesting when it alternately reveals and conceals special plantings, a piece of sculpture, a small bench, or a special view. And a path that winds up a hillside to a secluded overlook is a treat for children.

Complementary style. Strips of lightweight fabric are suspended over this patio (top), providing light shade without the work called for by most climbing vines. Easy-care hedges create a backdrop of greenery; artwork and containers add variety. A vividly colored seating area (bottom) conceals seated guests from the street behind. The same acrylic house paint was used for house walls and the bench-wall; flagstone paving and a few carefully chosen specimen plants soften the stricter contemporary lines and angles of the bench construction.

PATIO POINTERS

Stand alone. A pretty patio accented with containers or small raised beds can form the centerpiece of a low-maintenance garden design. Best of all, a patio doesn't need watering, weeding, or babying over the winter.

Outside in. Install large glass doors or picture windows with a patio and garden view. Further merge the outdoors and indoors by using the same type of paving (or pattern) on the patio and on the floor of the adjoining indoor room.

Face lift. Resurface a concrete slab with brick, pavers, or stone, provided the slab is structurally sound. Or hire a contractor to treat or stain it, to add color or texture. If the concrete is in less than perfect shape, you can build over it with a low wood deck.

Break out of the box. Curves will loosen a garden design and help blend the patio with its surroundings. An angled patio can visually deepen the yard.

Comfort zones. Plan seating areas out of the wind and bright sun. Never plant trees that can shed litter over a seating area (see p. 80).

Cover up. Deciduous plantings provide shade in summer and, when their leaves are gone, permit welcome rays on crisp winter days.

Dress up. Build in planting pockets for scented thyme, add sculpture or mosaic tiles, or create a small water feature (see pp. 70–73).

CONCRETE COSMETICS

Shapely. Though often typecast as cold and forbidding, with the proper forms and reinforcement, concrete can conform to most shapes, including that of giant stepping stones. Building supply stores sell ready-made plastic forms and ready-mix concrete for do-it-yourselfers.

Textured. Seeded aggregate (colorful pebbles embedded before poured concrete dries) adds texture and traction. Or you can set larger river rocks and fieldstones into the wet concrete to lend interest.

Patterned. Concrete can be lightly smoothed or heavily brushed when wet, resulting in subtle patterns. Likewise it can be stained, or chemically colored with pigments, to create variegated or translucent effects.

Pickled. In another popular treatment, handfuls of rock salt are cast into wet concrete. When the salt melts, it leaves small holes—and an unusual texture—behind.

Recycled. If all else fails and you simply must get rid of an old concrete slab, consider breaking it into stone-shaped sections and reusing the pieces in paths and walls in the same way you might incorporate pieces of newly purchased stone.

PAVING MATERIALS

Garden structures made of brick, pavers, or stone are good-looking, durable, and easy to maintain. When simply set in sand, these materials impart a casual air; a symmetrical mortared installation has a more formal attitude. With hundreds of sizes, styles, and colors to choose from, you're sure to find something to suit your eye, home, and price range.

If you lack experience working with these materials, stick with a simple design. Many stones are precut in square or rectangular shapes, making them easy to lay in a grid pattern. Bricks and pavers are also easy to install, provided your design doesn't require much trimming to shape. Where possible, choose a sand-bed installation rather than a mortared one—it's much more forgiving of design flaws.

Cast concrete "bricks," colored in classic terracotta as well as other hues, have become increasingly popular as substitutes for the real thing because they are generally less expensive. Ready-mix concrete laid in small amounts into a special form to resemble stone, tile, or brick can be an easy and economical option for do-it-yourselfers.

When choosing a material, safety and practicality are as important as appearance, installation, and cost. Some materials—such as glazed tiles—become slippery when wet and the uneven surfaces of some stones could trip unwary guests or frolicking children. Porous materials, such as some types of flagstone, are poor choices for eating areas or for areas near fruit trees, as they absorb stains readily and permanently.

Blue stones. *The surface of these square-cut stones is slightly uneven, and they are staggered around the inside corner; both factors help to make the path less formal than many stone pathways. Sedges spill onto the pathway but won't grow too big, silver-toned plants match the paving, and a gravel mulch helps keep weeds at bay.*

LOOSE MATERIALS

Walkways made from gravel, bark chips, or other natural materials are quick, easy, and economical to build. The uneven texture and natural colors of meandering paths made from these materials blend naturally with the garden surroundings. If you use gravel or crushed stone (see pp. 48–49), you get the bonus of superior drainage; never again will you have to slog through mud on wet days. And, if underlaid with weed-suppressive material, you can prevent most weeds from gaining a toehold.

Loose materials work well for small seating areas, too, but don't build your main patio area (or the walkway to the main entrance) from these materials. Their uneven surfaces can make chairs and tables tippy, not to mention the difficulties they present to guests in high-heeled shoes.

The downside of using loose materials for paths is that they require periodic maintenance to retain their good looks. The key to a successful path is a well-packed substrate, but even so, loose materials can eventually work down into the soil or get scattered from the path by exuberant walkers and must be replenished. In addition, gravel requires some raking to keep it neat, and you will also have to pick stray pieces out of neighboring planting beds or lawn areas. All paths made from loose materials collect leaves in autumn, and since you can't brush them clean, you'll need to sweep them off with a leaf blower or carefully rake their surfaces.

Narrow sections of lawn also make lovely paths, but grass can be a fairly high-maintenance surface because it has to be fertilized, weeded, and mowed (see page 101). Plus, it won't grow as well in shade as in sun and, if you neglect careful edging, the grass will soon spread into your borders.

STEPPING OUT

Stepping-stone paths need not be made of stone—large wooden rounds, precast concrete pavers, or site-built concrete pavers all are functional and charming. Follow the same guidelines for paths in general (see page 42) when laying out a stepping-stone walkway. Choose pieces that are at least 12 inches across in any direction for stable, comfortable walking, and place the pieces close enough to allow comfortable strides. When using natural stones, make sure they are thicker than ¾-inch if you're going to lay them in a sand base. Otherwise, they could flip up when stepped upon or crack under excessive weight. Stones with a gritty texture offer the best traction when wet.

Winding lane. This combination of grasses and stone is well made despite its casual air. Benderboard edgings keep pebbles in place. The flagstones are almost flush with the smaller stones, preventing trip-ups. Rosemary growing around a boulder and Mexican feather grass (Stipa tenuissima) *echo the blue and beige tones of the pathway.*

LAYOUT & PREPARATION

The easiest way to outline a curved path is with pulverized limestone or colored chalk, or two garden hoses. (Periodically measure between the edges to make sure the width of the path doesn't vary along its length—unless that is your intention.) Mark a straight path by stretching strong cord between stout stakes. Remember to add the width of the edging material you plan to use to your calculations.

Any path or patio calls for some site excavation. This is probably the hardest part of the job, especially if you run up against large rocks and roots, or have to transplant trees and shrubs. The depth to which you excavate depends upon what—and how—you are building. For a walkway made from gravel, crushed stone, or bark chips, you can simply dig out the soil to the correct depth (about 4 inches for bark chips, 2 inches for gravel or crushed stone, plus 1 inch for a sand bed) and pour in the loose material until it is level with the surrounding area. Excavation is a bigger job for a path or patio made of bricks, pavers, or stone. In general, setting these materials in sand is best for do-it-yourselfers; concrete work is more demanding because there's little room for error. Unless you've chosen a highly porous top material, such as gravel, plan on sloping the path or patio slightly to one side for drainage, or build it with a slight crown in the center to allow runoff.

Landscape fabric or plastic sheeting suppresses weed growth and separates substrate materials. For a gravel path (top), first put down edgings, then lay the fabric. Pour decomposed granite or sand over the fabric and tamp it down to a uniform 1-inch thickness. Lay at least 2 inches of gravel over the path. A typical brick, stone, or paver installation in a frost-free area starts with a layer of heavy-duty landscaping fabric over the soil. This layer is then topped by a 2-in. sand bed. The surface materials are set into the bed, then more sand is worked between the joints to hold the pieces in place. In areas of poor drainage and in frost zones, start with a 2- to 8-in. gravel base to allow water to run off (bottom), then add the landscaping fabric and sand bed.

BUILDING YOUR GARDEN

RAMPS & STEPS

To a great extent, step design is dictated by yard slope. On long slopes, the entire path can become a series of wide ramplike steps. But on steep terrain, where a lengthy set of steps may be both dangerous and uncomfortable to navigate, retaining walls can reshape levels, which can then be linked with shorter runs of steps.

Constructing steps from the same material used for the path unifies the landscape; using different materials adds contrast. Both railroad ties and 6-by-6 pressure-treated timbers make simple, rugged garden steps. (Wooden and masonry stairs are best used for entryways.) Steps have two components: the flat part, called the tread, and the vertical part, called the riser. Ideally, risers should measure between 5 and 8 inches; tread depth should be between 11 and 15 inches. All risers and treads in any one flight of steps should be uniform in size.

It's trickier to design and construct a ramp than it is to build stairs, so you might want to leave this job to an expert. A drop of a foot or two between the entrance and the ground will allow a simple straight ramp, but a greater drop will likely demand the incorporation of one or more turns. As slip-resistant ramps are a must, rough-textured concrete is a better surfacing choice than wood, which can become slippery when wet.

Sweeping steps. Forming a broad S-curve up a slope, this 4-by-4 timber staircase makes the climb less steep (above, top). A strip of lawn is kept mowed on either side of the stairway, but the turf grass must be kept from encroaching onto the steps. For wheelchair access, a ramp should follow a gentle slope and have no impediments (above, left), qualities that also allow comfortable foot passage. A creative combination of stones and brick leads to a concrete pathway (above), showing that a mixture of materials can be attractive and original. Low-growing thyme creeps around the stones.

SHOPPING FOR SUPPLIES

You'll have a far greater choice of boulders, gravel, river rock, and other paving supplies if you seek out a stoneyard or wholesale supplier. There you can choose, bag, and load your own materials for much less than you would pay at a building-supply store or garden center. To find one in your area, look in the Yellow Pages for 'Masonry Supplies' or 'Landscaping Equipment and Supplies.' Many of these companies will also deliver bulk supplies to your home. Another option is to seek out local quarries, where you can sometimes negotiate with the owner or manager to purchase their stone products, especially fines, at rock-bottom prices.

When shopping for paving materials, consider color, sheen, texture, and size. Be sure to take home samples just as you would paint chips. Like paint, gravel color will seem more intense when covering a large area, and it can look considerably different when wet, or as the light changes.

River rock and smooth pea gravel have naturally water-worn, smooth surfaces. Sharp-edged gravel is collected or mined from natural deposts; crushed rock is mechanically fractured and graded to a uniform size. 'Fines' are the finely-ground remnants of quarried rock; they are often much cheaper than larger sizes of the same material. Another useful material is decomposed granite, a grainy, claylike substance that packs well—it is often used in desert gardens.

The names of gravel and stone are often, but not always, clues to their origin, and their availability varies from one location to another. Decomposed granite, for instance, can only be found in certain parts of the West. Due to the costs of transporting rock, locally quarried materials are usually the best choice for your garden; not only are they less expensive, but they are more likely to harmonize with the surrounding landscape.

Sample rocks and gravel.
Outer ring: white dolomite and ¼-in. granite.
Square corners: blue and gray fines.
Middle circle, clockwise from top: Salmon Bay
mix, ¾-in. quartz, Aqua Cove mix, ¼-in. quartz.
Center circle: red lava.

Raised Beds

Raising the garden above the ground can solve some of a gardener's most frustrating problems. Because you fill the beds with good soil to begin with, you're spared the backbreaking labor of trying to improve hard or heavy soil. You can customize drip irrigation and soil amendments for each bed, depending on what you want to grow. You can protect plants from hungry critters by installing wire mesh beneath the bed or netting above—and by elevating plantings along play areas, driveways, and paths you also protect them from being kicked or run over. Raised beds also add beauty and height to a flat landscape, and the variation from ground to bed level makes small gardens appear larger. And if you need easy access to your plants, either due to a disability or simply to eliminate bending and stooping, you can design your beds with a wide cap on which to sit and garden in comfort.

A simple timber-framed raised bed can incorporate a lattice screen (above, left) to shade young vegetables or to support climbing vines. Dry stone walls (left) drain well and suit succulents or herbs, which can be tucked in the crevices between stones. Beds can showcase a specimen plant on a patio, such as this Japanese maple (above), or provide a place for plants that have special soil or watering needs.

SIZE & SHAPE

Raised beds can be almost any size, but if you build them more than 4 feet wide, you'll have trouble reaching the middle from either side. For beds that will double as benches, a good height is 18 inches. Taller beds make good accents, but keep in mind that the higher the bed, the more expensive it will be to construct and fill. To save money and improve drainage, you can fill beds taller than 18 inches with a bottom layer of stone, sand, or gravel. Build freestanding beds as long as you like, within reason: several smaller beds offer more design flexibility than a single large one. Beds that run along the length of a wall or fence can be any length; the bed can even vary in height and width. To put gardening chores within easy reach of a wheelchair, beds should be about 16 inches high and never wider than 4 feet. They can be rectangular or U-shaped, with the opening in the U just wide enough for a chair.

Beds are often built in geometric shapes because they are constructed from wood, but other materials allow greater latitude with design. Meandering beds give an illusion of space and their less structured look works well with informal architectural styles. A bed built to follow the contour of uneven terrain—starting low at one end and growing higher at the other—blends beautifully with a sloping landscape. If you plan to use a bed as a retaining wall, keep in mind that walls over 2 feet high require a permit in most municipalities and anything over 4 feet high needs to be designed by an engineer.

BUILDING BEDS

You can locate a raised bed just about anywhere it will receive enough sun for the plants you wish to grow. This means about 6 hours per day for most warm-season vegetables (such as tomatoes) and other sun-worshippers. If you'll be hand-watering, don't stray too far from a water source, as soil in raised beds dries out faster than it does in the ground. An automatic watering system is the best way to cut back on maintenance: soaker hoses, perforated plastic sprinkle hoses, and drip-type irrigation systems (see pages 190–195) all direct water exactly where—and when—it's needed.

It's easiest and quickest to make raised beds from wood—you can knock together a simple bed in less than an hour. Use rot-resistant woods such as redwood, cedar, cypress, or pressure-treated lumber rated for ground contact. Avoid any wood that's been treated with pentachlorophenal or creosote, because these chemicals can leach into the soil. Brick beds are harder to construct—and you must build a concrete footing for them to rest on—but if your landscape features brick pathways, patios, or edgings, this can be a way to unify your garden design. (Another option is to construct a sturdy, low bed with 2-by-6 lumber and then use bricks around the outside of the bed, inserted into the soil at an angle, as an edging material.) Beds made of flat stones or pieces of broken concrete suit informal gardens; if you keep the height low, you won't need to mortar the pieces together. Commercial modular masonry systems, available in various styles and weights, are convenient for small, freestanding raised beds and entryways, especially as they can be easily formed into curves. Most use cast "lips" or interlocking pins to hold the walls together so the pieces fit like a puzzle.

RAISING BETTER BEDS

Catch some rays. To maximize the amount of sun plants receive, orient rectangular beds with their long sides running north and south.

Make it sturdy. For wooden beds, use 1½-in.-thick (or thicker) lumber. Because the corners are the weak links, either lag screw them together or beef them up with pieces of 4 by 4s nailed to the insides of the corners. Beds longer than 12 ft. need support to keep them from bowing outward, so nail the side boards to posts sunk midway along their lengths.

Long-lasting. Extend the life of a wooden bed by lining the interior walls with polyethylene sheeting or builder's felt. A coat of paint or stain that matches the exterior of the house will unify the landscape and help protect the wood.

Nice and roomy. If you're building multiple beds, make paths between them at least 2 ft. wide.

Keep critters out. If gophers are a problem in your area, protect your plants by lining raised beds with wire (see p. 223).

Top up with topsoil. If your garden soil is fairly good, fill raised beds with a mix of equal parts of soil and organic matter such as compost. Don't bother using poor soil—use planting mix or topsoil instead. (Look in the Yellow Pages under Topsoil for companies that sell soil in bulk. Many will deliver to your home.)

Deep drainage. Before filling the bed, place 3 to 4 in. of the new soil in the bottom and mix it into the ground as best you can. This will aid drainage and create a transition zone between the two soils.

Big eaters. Plants grown in raised beds (or any containers) need more frequent applications of fertilizer, particularly nitrogen. It's easiest to mix in a time-release fertilizer at planting time (see p. 189).

Border beds. *These beds have all been constructed against a boundary—either a fence or a wall—in ways that complement the structures' style and materials. The plaster wall in this garden (above and right) zigzags and steps up several levels as a decorative element in its own right; the bed is planted with tall ocotillo, white-flowered lantana, and golden barrel cactus. A mixed border fills the low brick bed at right; the wooden fence provides a backdrop for colorful perennials such as blue pincushion flower (Scabiosa). Stacked stone walls are an extension of the stairs (below, right) and are high enough to allow fragrant rosemary to spill over the sides; tall irises rise up behind.*

ON THE EDGE

Neat, crisp edgings define garden spaces and add contrast to paths, low beds, and areas of lawn. To various extents, edgings can also keep plants in and grass and weeds out. Because of the unmortared joints between them, bricks and pavers, while pretty, are less reliable weed-stoppers than continuous materials such as wooden boards or commercial rubber or metal edgings.

Where the edging will abut the lawn, think about how you're going to trim the grass where it meets the edging. If the edging is higher than your mower deck can clear, you're setting yourself up for a tedious running appointment with a string trimmer. Sometimes the best edging of all in this case is nothing more than a beveled edge between the lawn and the garden. It's free, easy to maintain, and simple to create. Just slice 4-inch-deep cuts along the bed with a flat-edged shovel, then force the soil back into the bed to create an angle of about 45 degrees.

Clockwise from top, left. An edging may be as simple as a beveled edge between lawn and bed. Supple branches, such as bamboo or willow, can be fashioned into an edging that defines the transition from pathway to plantings. Flexible plastic edging material prevents turf grass from spreading into adjoining plantings. A loosely laid collection of stones matches the informal style of a gravel path.

Fences & Walls

Fences and walls can transform a garden into a secure, attractive retreat from the outside world. When well designed, they provide privacy, screen out wind and noise, and "edit" unpleasant views. Fences serve many of the same functions as walls, but are generally less formal in appearance, easier to build, and, when you calculate labor costs, less expensive. What fences can't do is create the air of permanence that a wall imparts to a garden.

Almost all fences are composed of three parts: posts (vertical pieces), rails (horizontal pieces), and boards that are attached to the rails. The durability of a fence depends on the stability of its posts, so these must be securely installed, a process that usually requires the use of concrete (see page 63). Walls have special requirements, too, especially for foundations, and they may require steel reinforcement. If the wall is more than 3 feet high or you live in an area of seismic activity, you may require approval by an engineer; your local building department can tell you more.

Fencing in or out. *The amount of privacy required for each space will influence the location and style of a fence or wall, but remember that solid, high structures can visually dominate a space. A high stuccoed or plastered wall such as this (top) clearly defines the garden's entry. Where privacy is not an issue, wooden screening can be a visual barrier, allowing the passage of light and air while suggesting the division of "outdoor rooms" within the garden itself — separating play areas from planting beds, for instance. Here, 6-by-6 posts are tied together with horizontal rails. Each upright rests on a stone pad to prevent rot; low-growing black mondo grass is planted in front.*

STYLE & SUBSTANCE

Probably the most popular fencing material is wood, and for good reason: the stylistic versatility it offers is unmatched by any other type of fencing. But aluminum paneling, ornamental iron, and chain-link fencing have their fans, too—though you'll probably want to camouflage the latter with a combination of vines (see page 60) or by weaving wooden strips through the links. Whatever your choice of fencing, coordinate it with the style, materials, and scale of the house. A dainty picket fence around a massive stone house would look ridiculous, but it might be just the thing for a small Craftsman-style or shingled home.

Walls should also coordinate with existing garden structures. Among typical wall materials are masonry units (brick, concrete block, and adobe), uncut stone, and poured concrete. In general, masonry units are the easiest to assemble because they are all the same size, and they offer plenty of design possibilities. You can choose a decorative pattern for laying the courses, vary the thickness, or combine different materials. Building an attractive, structurally sound stone wall takes more artisanship. Poured concrete is the most labor-intensive choice. Most of the work of concrete goes into constructing and stabilizing the forms that contain the concrete; the actual "pour," for better or worse, is accomplished quickly. Concrete can be poured in many shapes and textures, but consult a contractor if you have never worked with the material before, or if the wall will be more than a few feet high. Likewise, concrete block that is to be covered with a coating of plaster or stucco may require the skills of an expert.

Wood is a highly versatile fencing material. The classic white picket fence can be dressed up with decorative posts and a built-in seat (left). Another familiar sight, the split-rail fence (center), is particularly suited to gardens that border open spaces. Wood can easily be colored with an exterior-grade paint, but remember that as plantings grow, touch-ups become more difficult. This high fence (right) incorporates panels of contrasting color, allowing views from all sides while still clearly defining the space.

Style setters. *The gate above—of bamboo poles affixed to a sturdy wood frame—both suggests solidity and suits the garden's Asian style. The double gate at top right is lighter weight, inviting entry into informal landscapes rather than promoting privacy. The simple wire gate and fence at lower right have been disguised with woven flexible twigs; a similar technique can disguise chain-link fencing, but be sure to use durable branches such as willow.*

Remember that a gate is usually the first structure encountered in the garden, so it can set the tone of your landscape: a charming, low, picket gate invites guests in, while a high, solid gate guards the privacy and safety of those within. Gates can be used to create access, to frame a view, or to make a design statement in tandem with a fence or wall. You can either build the gate in a style and material that matches the fence or choose a contrasting material or design, such as a wooden gate within flanking plaster or brick columns. Let the height of the fence determine the height of the gate.

Don't forget that gates can also be placed within the garden, to break up garden "rooms," secure children's play yards, or conceal work or storage areas.

Fence dressers. The classic cottage-style painted fence (below, left) makes an excellent backdrop for a lacy drift of summer annuals such as cosmos. Matching the gate details to those of the front door ties the design to that of the house. Anemone clematis is draped over a simple 2-by-2 in. square picket fence (below); heavy posts and rails are needed to support this vigorous vine (see p. 60).

GREAT GATES

Width. The minimum opening is 3 ft., but adding an extra foot allows more gracious passage. Definitely make the opening 4 ft. wide if you anticipate having to pass through with wheelchairs, tricycles, wheelbarrows, mowers, or other equipment. Divide a gate that will span over 4 ft. into two parts, to avoid sagging.

Bracing. Support wooden gates with a diagonal brace that runs from the upper corner of the gate's latch side to the lower corner of its hinge side. A sag rod or turnbuckle run along the opposite diagonal will further fortify the gate against sagging.

Posts. Gates take a beating, so they must be supported by stout posts set in a concrete footing. (In areas of frost, the footing must extend below the frost line; see p. 62.) Set wooden posts on a base stone in a layer of gravel. The gravel improves drainage and prevents the concrete from settling under the bottom of the post, where it can seal in moisture and hasten decay.

Swing. On wooden gates, leave about ½-in. of clearance between the fence posts and the gate so the gate will swing freely even if the fence settles with age.

Hardware. Choose a strong latch and hinges that can stand up to the weight of the gate. It's better to select hardware that is too hefty than too flimsy. Plan to attach both hinges and latches with long galvanized screws that won't pull out, and use galvanized hardware or decorative wrought iron painted with weather-resistant paint.

Masonry. Attach a heavy gate to a brick, block, or mortared stone wall with special masonry hinges. These hinges are placed in the mortar joints; the extra support they give is ideal for wrought-iron gates or any gate battered by high winds.

Decks & Arbors

Decks expand your outdoor living space—at reasonable cost. Your deck can be a complex multilevel structure that defines areas for dining, reading, or sunbathing, or it can be a simple freestanding platform nestled in a quiet corner of the yard. Any deck can smooth out bumps, tame slopes, and ride over drainage problems that might make a patio impractical, and, where space allows, decks and patios can be combined to replace high-maintenance garden features.

Decks may be almost any shape. Most require some concrete work for footings, but deck construction isn't inherently complicated. Low, rectilinear decks are easiest to build, and even they can be embellished with built-in benches and other features.

Unless privacy is the point, the deck should be sited so that it's easily accessible from a public room. Also try to determine when the deck will be in the sun or shade and the direction of prevailing winds—you may have to tweak the site plan or add an arbor or other overhead structure for protection. If you don't feel confident evaluating the microclimates in your garden, consult a landscape architect or contractor.

Arbors and other overhead structures offer climate control, define zones of use, direct foot traffic, and mask unsightly features. But the structure must be stout enough to support the weight of any plants and, to minimize maintenance, choose plants that require little coddling (see page 60).

Up and up. *Levels, stairs, and platforms transform a deck into a multi-functional structure, providing access to the house, as well as seating and planting areas. The all-in-one approach, as shown here, can make the deck a centerpiece of even a small or steep garden, which simplifies design and maintenance.*

Extra, extra. Design additional features before deck construction begins. Clever railings (left) turn a simple deck into a design statement. A built-in fountain recirculates water to a small bowl surrounded by plants (below). Don't let a tree get in the way of a deck—build around it and surround it with planters (bottom). Just be sure to line wooden planters with water-proof material (such as heavy-duty 6-mil plastic) and provide for adequate drainage.

How big? Your deck should be able to hold essential furniture and cooking accessories and still have enough room for people to move around. Just make sure the deck fits within the required setback allowance from your lot lines. On a tight lot, a narrow wraparound deck is a good choice.

Cold feet. Poured concrete footings rest on a gravel bed and support the posts. In cold areas, they must extend below the frost line (see p. 62).

What wood? Decks are always made from wood. Pressure-treated wood is the best choice for posts and under-pinnings. Redwood or cedar are the usual choices for decking, railings, and stairs, but another option for nonstructural components is wood polymer lumber (see p. 61).

Pick a pattern. Decking is usually 2-by-4 in. or 2-by-6 in. lumber. Because the decking design can affect the substructure, pick your pattern before beginning construction. Generally, more complex decking patterns require smaller joist spans and, thus, can complicate framing.

Railings all around. These can be made from metal, wood, safety glass, or a combination of materials. Low decks may not require a railing; check your local building code. Here, too, decide how you're going to attach the railing to the deck before you start building.

What's up? A built-in overhead can affect the structure of the deck, so plan for it during design. Always check overhead rafter (or joist) spans with your building department.

Fancy features. Extras such as built-in storage benches, lighting, small water features, planters, and even counter spaces for outdoor cooking transform a deck from a simple fea-ture to a garden centerpiece. And maintenance is simplified by having everything close at hand.

Use these perennial vines to adorn overheads. Most take full sun and are drought tolerant once established.

Bougainvillea (zones 22–24, or protected) Evergreen, to 40 ft. Vibrant bracts in many colors.

Cissus antarctica KANGAROO TREEBINE (zones 16–24) Evergreen, to 10 ft.; climbs gracefully by tendrils. Good for containers, small gardens.

Clematis montana ANEMONE CLEMATIS (zones 1–6, 15–17) Give regular water. This "queen of the climbers" grows to 20 ft. or more, with massive display of lightly fragrant, pink flowers in early spring.

Gelsemium sempervirens CAROLINA JESSAMINE (zones 8–24) Give regular water. Evergreen; grows to 20 ft. with bright yellow, fragrant trumpets from Feb.–Apr. (All parts poisonous.)

Hardenbergia violacea 'Happy Wanderer' (zones 8–24) Evergreen 1–10 ft.; flowers pinkish purple, in late winter.

Jasminum polyanthum PINK JASMINE (zones 5–9, 12–24) Evergreen to 20 ft., dark foliage and fragrant pink flowers, late winter through summer. Cut back each year.

Lonicera hildebrandiana GIANT BURMESE HONEYSUCKLE (zones 9, 14–17, 19–24) Glossy evergreen leaves; fragrant tubular flowers in summer, white then yellow. To 50 ft.; cut out older stems if needed.

Lonicera sempervirens TRUMPET HONEYSUCKLE (zones 3–24) Semi-evergreen; to 50 ft. Bluish foliage and bright orange to red trumpet-shaped flowers attract hummingbirds. Berry-like red fruit in fall. Prune yearly to control size and shape. 'Sulphurea' has yellow flowers.

Pandorea jasminoides BOWER VINE (zones 16–24) Evergreen; to 30 ft. with glossy leaflets and white or pink flower clusters June–Oct.

Aging gracefully. Both these sturdy overheads use weathered wood to blend into the surroundings. At left, a framework of beams and prefabricated lattice panels are all that is needed to shade this small seating area. A house-attached arbor (below) cools both the patio and the rooms within the walls.

BUILDING MATERIALS

Recycled Materials Lumber made from a combination of wood and plastic is becoming a popular alternative to solid wood for decking and other nonstructural applications. The reason is simple: the material promises not to crack, splinter, rot, sustain insect damage, or require refinishing. The downside? Wood polymer lumber is more expensive than solid wood. If you prefer the real thing, there are endless ways to incorporate recycled wood in the garden. Whether it's an arbor constructed from salvaged redwood barn beams (right), a fence of unpeeled logs, or a living trellis of branches, "found" wood can be used in almost any landscape to craft a memorable design.

Wood Redwood and cedar are beautiful, strong, naturally weather- and rot-resistant—and expensive. To save money, use these woods where they can best be appreciated—for decking, railings, benches, arbors, and the like. Substitute pressure-treated lumber, Douglas fir, or western larch where the wood won't show, or where you plan to paint or stain it.

Unfinished redwood and cedar weather to a patina that some find attractive, but you can treat wood with sealants, water repellents, or stains that protect and beautify them. Don't use clear surface finishes such as polyurethane on outdoor structures because they wear quickly and are difficult—sometimes impossible—to recoat. Different finishing products advise different recoating timetables. Carefully follow the directions on the product label both initially and later, when recoating.

Metals Metals are used primarily to construct arbors, trellises, railings, and gates. Depending on how you use metals, they can give your house and yard an elegant contemporary look (right), blend almost invisibly into the view, or add romance and a feeling of history. Strength isn't usually an issue when the posts of the structure are well supported (see page 62), but in the case of arbors and trellises the metal must be sturdy enough to support not only its own weight, but also the weight of the mature vines it will carry.

OVERHEAD ADVANTAGE

Calculate shade. A southern exposure without trees could mean that your deck needs sun protection most of the day. Decks on a house's east or west side will need only partial sun protection.

Match styles. The design of any overhead structure should take its cue from the architectural style of the house. The structure needn't be built from the same materials as the house, but unless you're very sure of your design expertise, blend rather than contrast the arbor with its surroundings.

Aim high. To make sure an overhead structure won't block desirable views from either the deck or the house, raise the roof structure to at least 7 ft. above the finished deck floor. (Local building codes may specify heights.)

Arch design. Simple arbor frames or archways are similar in construction to overhead sunshade frames, but they are generally less enclosed, making them perfect for covering a walkway, enhancing a gateway, or framing a garden view. Many catalogs and garden centers sell such metal or wooden items.

Be secure. An arbor won't stand up to much if it isn't securely positioned in the ground or on a concrete slab (see p. 62).

Colorful climbers. Vines soften the lines of a structure, subdue glare, and provide privacy. The nine perennials listed on the facing page typically perform well with minimum pruning and maintenance. Vines in full leaf can cast intense shade, so space overhead sunshade boards generously so you won't block winter sunshine after deciduous vines die back, or vigorous vines are cut back.

Outdoor Seating

A prime reason for constructing a low-maintenance garden is to spend time enjoying and admiring it, so it's worth investing some effort choosing comfortable, durable garden furniture from which to do so. Outdoor items come in various materials and a host of styles. Some seating comes straight from a gardener's imagination in the form of artfully arranged boulders, stones, or wooden planks. If you're shopping for seating, you'll be faced with choices that run the gamut from informal Adirondack chairs to stately Mission-style benches.

Once you've decided between rustic and elegant, further narrow your choices by considering price. Typically, wooden furniture is more expensive than its resin or metal cousins. It can also require more maintenance—wood weathers to various shades of gray, and may dry and split unless treated with sealer, stain, or another finishing product. As you shop, you'll probably come across furniture made from teak, cedar, and redwood, but you may also find pieces crafted from jarrah, Honduran cedar, and jatroba. All are good choices for outdoor furniture.

Two seaters. *These sets of armchairs show how furniture can be well matched to its surroundings. The Southwest courtyard, top, houses rustic "stick" chairs that stand up to sun; the grassy garden, below, features few plants, but striking red Adirondacks have high visual impact. You can extend the life of wooden outdoor furniture by painting with sealant or covering in inclement weather.*

When buying wood furniture, pay close attention to the joinery between parts. A good joint—where a chair leg or arm meets the seat, for example—looks nearly seamless. And it is strong: it gives a chair or bench the strength needed to withstand weight and lateral movements. For extra fortification, some joints are reinforced at critical points with brass hardware or wood dowels. Comfort is another issue when buying wood furniture that won't be covered with cushions. Shaped seats, angled backrests, and softer woods all make a chair easier to sit in, but as comfort is subjective, always "test-sit" a piece of furniture before you buy it.

Built-in benches on decks supplement portable outdoor furniture and free floor space for other uses. They can be built into wide steps, integrated with deck railings, or used as transitions between different levels of a deck. Benches have good storage potential, too: all a bench needs to turn it into a storage trunk is a hinged top and enclosed sides. But remember, because certain benches tie into the understructure of the deck, decide what you need at the design—not the building—stage of deck construction.

MAINTENANCE & UPKEEP

Try to wash outdoor furniture at the beginning of each outdoor season. Special outdoor cleaners are available for furniture and cushions, or you can use a solution of mild detergent and water. Glass cleaner works well for plastic resin furniture. Marine stores sell cushions and covers for outdoor use; if you purchase cotton cushion covers, throw them in the washing machine when needed and store them indoors during bad weather. Of course, if you live in a severe-weather climate, consider covering your furniture or storing it indoors during the winter months.

BEYOND TEAK

Synthetic wicker. Made of cellulose, resin, or latex-coated fibers, synthetic wicker looks and feels much like the real thing, but it can stand up to harsh weather without losing its looks or strength.

Genuine wicker. Natural-fiber wicker and rattan are less durable than synthetics. They're suited to sheltered spots, or should be covered or brought indoors in bad weather.

Metal. If your budget won't allow wrought iron, try the lighter-weight cast aluminum or steel lookalikes. Enameled or powder-coated aluminum-frame furniture is another option—it's durable, lightweight, and rustproof.

Plastic. Resin seating is inexpensive and requires only a quick wash every now and then. Because they can usually be stacked, plastic chairs and chaises are handy if space is limited.

Built-ins. A brick wall-seat encloses an outdoor dining area (above); elegant metal table-and-chair sets can be dressed up for dinner. A simple solution to stump removal (right): carve the remaining trunk into a low seat. Include a drainage hole to prevent rot and add cushions for comfort.

Ways with water. *Papyrus rises grace-fully in the margins of this still pool (above, left). Carefully laid flagstone and gravel suggest running water. Equally attractive as a dry stone creek (above), this waterway is surrounded by drought-resistant plants such as Mexican evening primrose, fescue, and lavender. A simple bamboo and granite fountain (left) is in harmony with surrounding materials.*

Simple but soulful. Pan, half hidden by foliage (below). A traditional Vappa (bottom, left), set into a stone wall. A pump recirculates water from a basin below through tubing behind the wall. Homemade wall fountain of punctured drain pipe (bottom, right).

In these gardens, it is the greenery surrounding the water feature that brings color to the scene, rather than fish or more-fussy aquatic plants.

PLANTING YOUR GARDEN

"When a reasonable attempt at growing something fails . . . you can gracefully accept the fact that, for whatever reason, this particular plant does not seem to thrive in your particular environment. So what? It's not like there aren't thousands of others to choose from. No one ever won an argument with nature."

Tom Christopher and Marty Asher
The 20-Minute Gardener

4

The Ornamental Garden

I t's virtually impossible to imagine the garden without plants. In fact, for most of us, plants *are* the garden. But many will reward only the most dedicated gardener with perfect bloom and abundant growth; these plants demand regular grooming, staking, watering, pruning, spraying, and other care. Fortunately, other types don't. The Plant Selection Guides in this chapter give recommended easy-care plants for Western gardens. Some sections also list plants that might not thrive in every garden but do very well in certain situations. When choosing plants for your garden, start with the more permanent ones, which include the trees, shrubs, ground covers, and lawn, if any. Then fill in raised beds and borders with combinations of ornamental and edible plants. To make your selections even simpler, we've included planting plans for different plant types and each area of the garden.

Trees & Shrubs

A treeless garden looks unfinished; it lacks boundaries and interest overhead. More than any other plant, trees define the landscape—think of the Northwest's quaking aspens, or the gnarled cypresses perched along California's coast. So select trees that establish your garden's style. Along with pathways and structures, trees and shrubs form the "backbone" of the garden. Because they are long-term investments, choose them with care.

Some plants prefer dappled light under trees, but many don't—especially turf grasses, so install groundcovers or naturalize some bulbs. The temperature under a good shade tree's canopy can be up to 10 degrees lower than its surroundings, or higher by the same amount when it's cold; take advantage by placing a seating area beneath.

Although there's a distinction made between shrubs and trees, the difference is not always clear. Generally shrubs are under 20 feet, multitrunked, and hold their branches closer to the ground—but there are exceptions. Once they move away from the house foundation, shrubs have varied roles to play in the garden—from members of a mixed border to specimens in their own right.

If you buy a brand-new home, the developer may install large trees to give the garden an established look. In older gardens, unless it has historic value, an aging or diseased old tree may not be worth the cost of its upkeep and should be professionally removed.

SHAPELY SHRUBBERY

Columnar *Tall, narrow trees lend a geometric look to even small, formal gardens. Use singly as accents, to flank entranceways, or in rows.*

Rounded *Large, lollipop-shaped tree has a single trunk and a full, rounded crown at maturity. Rounded trees are ideal form for deciduous shade trees.*

Spreading *Trees with extended side branches also make good shade trees; some hold their branches in layered tiers, such as dogwood* (Cornus).

Irregular *An irregularly shaped tree can be interesting, but is best suited to a naturalistic or informal garden. Junipers and cypress are good examples.*

Conical *The pyramid shape of needle evergreens has uniformly spaced branches. When planting, allow room for maturing trees to spread lower branches.*

Weeping *Trees with naturally pendulous branches make fountainlike accents; larger specimens may be placed to arch over a lawn or water feature.*

Narrowly oval *Less formal than columnar types, these trees add grace and height without excessive shade. Place together for a windbreak.*

Shrubby *Trees with multiple trunks and several branches that extend from the base, low to the ground. Placed in a row, these make good screens.*

Pretty in pink. Tabebuia impetiginosa *often blooms not once but twice during the year, in late winter and again in fall—and it tolerates neglect. Colorful flowering trees make good accents, especially in front gardens, patios, or entryways.*

TREE TALK

Arborist. Landscape expert specializing in tree maintenance, including pruning, pest and disease control, and removal. Should be licensed and certified by state and industry boards; look in Yellow Pages under 'Tree' or ask at a local nursery.

Canopy. The full height and extent of a tree's upper branches. Shade trees have a dense, rounded, or spreading canopy.

Conifer. A tree that produces its seeds in cones, has needlelike leaves, or foliage with soft scales. Most, but not all, are evergreen.

Crown. A tree's head of foliage.

Drip line. The area of active root growth of a mature tree or shrub; generally coincides with its canopy.

Deciduous. A tree or shrub that produces new leaves in spring and drops them in autumn or winter, revealing bare limbs. The leaves often change color before they drop.

Evergreen. A tree or shrub that does not drop all its leaves in winter, though older foliage may fall periodically. May be broad-leafed or needle-leafed (includes most conifers).

Shade tree. A large tree with a dense canopy that effectively blocks heat and light. Shadows cast northward of a shade tree are always longer than those to the south.

Specimen tree. A rare or particularly attractive tree due to its flowers, age, foliage color, interesting fruits, or form. Place alone to showcase these qualities.

Understory. The area underneath the canopy of a tree. The delicate leaves of understory species suffer when exposed to sun and wind.

Windbreak. Densely branched and planted trees, usually evergreen, placed on the north or windy side of a property to block the flow of cold or drying winds.

A tree for the smaller backyard or patio is one that knows its limits. It has no rampant roots and no sticky pollen or messy fruits to litter a patio, pathway, or deck. It grows big enough to create some shade, but never so tall that it threatens a roofline or overpowers the scale of a garden scene.

If you don't mind sweeping a few leaves, deciduous trees work well. Where winters are mild, consider shady, broad-leafed evergreens and don't overlook small palms for a tropical effect. Here are a few choices:

Acacia podalyrifolia
PEARL ACACIA

Acer palmatum 'Atropurpureum'
RED JAPANESE MAPLE

Agonis flexuosa
PEPPERMINT TREE

Amelanchier canadensis
JUNEBERRY, SHADBLOW

Chionanthus retusus
CHINESE FRINGE TREE

Hakea laurina
SEA URCHIN

Koelreuteria paniculata
GOLDENRAIN TREE

Olea europaea 'Swan Hill'
FRUITLESS OLIVE

EASY-CARE TREES & SHRUBS

The ideal low-maintenance tree has been described as one that "grows quickly to 30 feet and then stops." Most tree descriptions give the ultimate height and spread of a tree but, as most trees outlive the gardeners that plant them, choose fast-growing species for quick effect, or purchase an older tree. Those sold in 15-gallon or 24-inch boxes are likely to be about four years older and twice the height of the same species sold in a 5-gallon can. A landscape architect or contractor can help you find and install these larger trees.

The trees and shrubs in these Plant Selection Guides have been chosen for their ability to resist disease and insects and because their roots will not lift paving or lie in wait for unsuspecting mower blades. They'll tolerate a wide range of soil types, and they shed no messy bark, berries, or other excessive debris. In many cases, these trees require little additional water after the first year or two—those are listed with a "Drought Tolerant" symbol.

Keep in mind that every tree does shed: deciduous trees drop their leaves in autumn, while evergreens continually lose some old foliage. The choices given here produce debris that quickly disintegrates or, like the ginkgo, drop their leaves or seedpods in a few day's time, so raking is not a prolonged chore.

To save yourself the work of continual shaping and pruning, it's best to choose a tree or shrub with the growth pattern you prefer (see page 78), and allow it to develop into its natural form. Some plants require little pruning; others benefit from deadheading or an annual tidying with shears, primarily to keep them healthy and to increase their bloom. Large trees should only be pruned by a professional arborist. For more information on routine tree and shrub care, see pages 212–214.

Special effects. Trees and shrubs offer more than green leaves; those with tinted foliage such as this smoke tree (above, right) can blend into color schemes. The twisted branch pattern and spreading canopy of native desert mesquite (Prosopis) is expansive, yet casts only light shade below (right).

EASY-CARE EVERGREEN TREES FOR WESTERN GARDENS

	Botanical name COMMON NAME	Sun & Water/ Zones	Height/ Spread	Leaves	Flowers/Fruit	Comments
SMALL	*Acacia podalyriifolia* PEARL ACACIA	☼ ○ ◐ / 8, 9, 13–24	10–20 ft. by 12–15 ft.	Roundish, 1½ in. long, silvery gray, soft and satiny to touch	Light yellow, fluffy, in long clusters, Nov.–Mar.	Dense chubby shape, excellent for patio. Good winter color. Prune after flowering to keep compact (see p. 213)
	Chamaecyparis obtusa 'Gracilis' SLENDER HINOKI CYPRESS	☼ ◑ ◐ / 4–6, 15–17	To 20 ft. by 3 ft.	Deep green, blunt, thick, and closely set on branches	Small brown cones	Needs good drainage. Best with some protection from wind. Slow growing, graceful. Occasional blast of water from hose will clear out mites and remove dead foliage
	Cordyline australis	☼ ○ ◐ ◐ / 5, 8–11, 14–24	20–30 ft. by 8–10 ft.	Sword-shaped, 3 ft. long by 2–5 in. wide	Fragrant, small, creamy white clusters in late spring	Looks like a palm tree. Grows fastest in deep soil
	Drimys winteri WINTER'S BARK	◑ ● ◐ / 8, 9, 14–24	25 ft. by 8 ft.	Bright green, leathery, elliptical, fragrant, 5–10 in. long	Small clusters of jasmine-scented white flowers in winter and spring	Dignified, multistemmed, with beautiful mahogany bark. Needs good drainage. Prune only to shape
	Eriobotrya deflexa BRONZE LOQUAT	☼ ◑ ◐ / 8–24	15–20 ft. by 15 ft.	Shiny, pointed, narrow, 5–10 in. Bright copper color when new, dark green when mature	Garlands of creamy white, fragrant flowers in spring	Fast growing tree with spreading shape
	Eucalyptus spathulata NARROW-LEAFED GIMLET	☼ ○ ◐ / 5, 6, 8–24	6–20 ft. by 4–8 ft.	Ribbonlike, 2–3 in. long	Cream and gold, opening in summer	Small, erect, multitrunked. Tolerates little water and poor drainage, but is flammable; good desert plant. Prune in winter, if needed
	Hakea laurina SEA URCHIN, PINCUSHION TREE	☼ ○ / 9, 12–17, 19–24	To 30 ft. by 15 ft.	Narrow, 6-in., gray green, often with red margins	Showy clusters in late fall look like round crimson pincushions with golden pins	Good small patio tree, but stake when young (see p. 201)
	Leptospermum laevigatum AUSTRALIAN TEA TREE	☼ ○ ◐ / 14–24	Slow to 30 ft. by 30 ft.	Oval, green to gray green, to ½ in. wide, 1 in. long	Small white flowers in spring	Prefers well-drained, slightly acid soil. Casual-looking, with shaggy bark
	Melaleuca nesophila PINK MELALEUCA	☼ ○ ◐ ◐ / 13, 16–24	To 15–30 ft. by 15–20 ft.	Gray green, thick, roundish, to 1 in.	Mauve, fading to white; long period of bloom	Tolerates sea coast; poor, rocky soil; desert heat. Interesting, gnarled shape. Thick, spongy bark
	Schefflera actinophylla QUEENSLAND UMBRELLA TREE	☼ ◑ ◐ / 21–24 (16–20, protected)	To 30 ft. by 20 ft. or more	Giant, dark green, made up of 7–16 large leaflets	Horizontal clusters that change from greenish yellow to pink to dark red. Tiny dark purple fruit	Underplant with ferns for tropical effect. Head back branch tips occasionally to keep compact (see p. 213)
	Trachycarpus fortunei WINDMILL PALM	☼ ◐ / 4–24	30 ft. by 9 ft.	3 ft. across, on toothed, 1½-ft. stalks	Tiny bluish fruits	The classic fan-leafed palm. Can grow quickly. Trim fronds if shabby (see p. 217)
	Tristania laurina	☼ ○ ◐ / 19–24	Slow to 10 ft. by 5 ft.	To 4 in. long, usually narrow	Clusters of small yellow flowers in late spring or early summer	Formal looking, with dense, rounded crown. Peeling mahogany-colored bark
MEDIUM	*Acacia baileyana* BAILEY ACACIA	☼ ◐ ◐ / 7–9, 13–24	20–30 ft. by 20–40 ft.	Feathery, blue-gray leaves	Flowers yellow, in many clusters, fragrant, in Jan.–Feb.	Good on slopes. Spreading shape
	Agonis flexuosa PEPPERMINT TREE	☼ ◐ / 15–17, 20–24	To 25–35 ft. by 20–25 ft.	Narrow, willowlike, to 6 in. long. Peppermint scent when crushed	Small, white, in June	Graceful, weeping form. Tolerates neglect, poor soil. Picturesque in a lawn—or plant near a seating area to enjoy fragrant leaves
	Arbutus unedo STRAWBERRY TREE	☼ ◑ ◐ ◐ / 4–24	8–35 ft. by 8–35 ft.	Dark green, red stemmed, 2–3 in. long	Clusters of strawberry-like fruit and small, white, urn-shaped flowers in fall and winter	Rounded shape. Best in well-drained soils. A. 'Marina' (for Zones 8, 9, 14–24) is similar, but with larger leaves and rosy pink flowers in fall
	Brahea armata MEXICAN BLUE PALM	☼ ○ / 10, 12–17, 19–24	40 ft. by 6–8 ft.	Silvery blue, almost white	Conspicuous creamy flowers hang on long stalks	Formal-looking slow grower. Pretty desert palm
	Eucalyptus nicholii NICHOL'S WILLOW-LEAFED PEPPERMINT	☼ ○ ◐ / 5, 6, 8–24	40 ft. by 40 ft.	Light green, narrow, 3–5 in. long	Small white flowers, mostly in summer	Weeping and graceful, with peppermint-scented leaves and deeply furrowed, reddish-brown bark. Flammable; plant away from house

☼ Full sun; ◑ Part shade; ● Full shade; ○ Drought tolerant; ◐ Little water; ◐ Regular water; ◐◐ Ample water. To find your climate zone, see pages 14–21.

Botanical name COMMON NAME	Sun & Water/ Zones	Height/ Spread	Leaves	Flowers/Fruit	Comments
Eucalyptus polyanthemos SILVER DOLLAR GUM	☼ ◯ ◌ 5, 6, 8–24	20–60 ft. by 10–20 ft.	Young leaves gray green, oval or round, lengthening with age	Creamy white, in 1-in. clusters in spring and summer	Grows almost anywhere except wet places. Slender and erect, sways beautifully in wind. Flammable; plant away from house. Prune in winter if needed
Geijera parviflora AUSTRALIAN WILLOW	☼ ◯ ◌ 8, 9, 12–24	25–30 ft. by 20 ft.	3–6 in. long, narrow, medium green	Small creamy flowers in early spring, early fall	Graceful rounded shape. Prefers well-drained soil and some summer water. Casts light shade
Melaleuca linariifolia FLAXLEAF PAPERBARK	☼ ◯ ◌ 9, 13–23	To 30 ft. by 35 ft.	Bright green or bluish green, 1¼-in.-long leaves are stiff, needlelike	Fluffy spikes of small white flowers in summer look like snow on branches	Stake young plants (see p. 201). Older ones develop attractive umbrella shape. Interesting, shedding white bark
Metrosideros excelsus NEW ZEALAND CHRISTMAS TREE	☼ ◯ ◌ 17, 23, 24	To 30 ft. by 30 ft.	On young plants, smooth and glossy; on older ones, dark above, white beneath	Dark scarlet, in big clusters, May–July	Branches heavily from ground up. Water through first two dry seasons only. Best near coast
Olea europaea 'Swan Hill' OLIVE	☼ ◯ 8, 9, 11–24	Slowly to 30 ft. by 25–30 ft.	Willowlike, deep green	Fruitless	Unlike fruiting olives, bears no fruit and has little or no pollen. Graceful, classic Mediterranean tree. Smooth gray trunks become gnarled with age. Thin each year to enhance branch pattern (see p. 213)
Pinus contorta BEACH PINE, SHORE PINE	☼ ◯ ◌ 5, 15–17	To 30 ft. by 20–35 ft.	Dark green needles	Light yellow-brown cones	Not at its best in hot, dry areas. Takes interesting, irregular shape in windy areas
Tristania conferta BRISBANE BOX	☼ ◯ ◌ 19–24	To 30–60 ft. by 20–40 ft.	4–6 in. long, oval, leathery, bright green	White to creamy, ¾ in. wide, in clusters in summer	Takes almost any soil, but young plants get better start in good soil. Upright form, rounding with age
Umbellularia californica CALIFORNIA LAUREL	☼ ◑ ◯ ◌ 4–10, 12–24	To 20–25 ft. by 20–25 ft.	2–5 in. long, ½–1 in. wide, yellow green and glossy on top, dull light green beneath	Tiny yellow flowers in spring; followed by olivelike, inedible fruit	Grows best in deep soil with ample water, but tolerates many conditions. Stays neat looking, eventually becoming broad and dense
LARGE *Calocedrus decurrens* INCENSE CEDAR	☼ ◑ ◯ ◌ 1–12, 14–24	To 75–90 ft. by 40 ft.	Rich green, fragrant foliage in flat sprays	Small brown cones	Adaptable western native. Dense form
Castanospermum australe MORETON BAY CHESTNUT	☼ ◌ 18–22	To 50–60 ft. by 50 ft.	Large, shiny, dark green, divided into leaflets	Bright red and yellow, in stiff, 8-in. spikes	Upright and spreading, spectacular in flower
Cedrus atlantica ATLAS CEDAR	☼ ◯ 2–23	To 60 ft. by 30 ft.	Bluish green needles less than 1 in. long	Interesting cones remain on branches longer than most conifers	Open, angular growth in youth; pinch back tips on young trees to keep bushy (see p. 214). Beautiful tufted foliage; interesting cones
Cryptomeria japonica JAPANESE CRYPTOMERIA	☼ ◌ 4–9, 14–24	To 80 ft. by 40 ft.	Soft bright green foliage turns brownish purple in cold weather	Roundish red-brown cones, ¾–1 in. wide	Graceful and soft-looking conifer. Fast growing in youth
Pinus thunbergiana JAPANESE BLACK PINE	☼ ◯ ◌ All zones	20–100 ft. by 50 ft.	Needles, bright green, stiff	Brown, 3-in.-long cones	Broad, conical shape. Hardy and adaptable. Needs some water in desert
Podocarpus gracilior FERN PINE	☼ ◑ ◌ 8, 9, 12–24	To 60 ft. by 40 ft.	Narrow, 2 in. long, soft, blue green; new growth fresh green	Inconspicuous	Growth habit varies, but soft and delicate looking, often with graceful, dropping branches. Slow-growing. Pest free
Quercus ilex HOLLY OAK, HOLM OAK	◑ ◯ ◌ 4–24	40–70 ft. by 40–70 ft.	To 3 in. long, dark green on upper surface, yellowish or silvery below	Small acorns	Tolerates wind and salt air. Good street tree
Sequoia sempervirens COAST REDWOOD	☼ ◑ ◌ 4–9, 14–24	70–90 ft. by 14–30 ft.	Small, pointed narrow; medium green on top, grayish underneath	Small, round 1-in.-long cones	Conical shape. Good near lawns, or anywhere where it gets water. Fertilize when young. Unlikely to reach giant proportions in garden
Washingtonia robusta MEXICAN FAN PALM	☼ ◌ ◑ 8, 9, 11–24	To 100 ft. by 20 ft.	Large, tough, fan-shaped fronds spread at top, hang near bottom, with reddish streak on undersides	Long tracks of small white flowers, followed by tiny fruits	Fast growing, with compact crown and slender trunk. Signature Los Angeles palm

☼ **Full sun**; ◑ **Part shade**; ● **Full shade**; ◯ **Drought tolerant**; ◌ **Little water**; ◉ **Regular water**; ◈ **Ample water.**   To find your climate zone, see pages 14–21.

EASY-CARE DECIDUOUS TREES FOR WESTERN GARDENS

	Botanical name COMMON NAME	Sun & Water/ Zones	Height/ Spread	Leaves	Flowers/Fruit	Comments
SMALL	*Acer circinatum* VINE MAPLE	☼ ◐ ● / 1–6, 14–17	5–35 ft. by 5–15 ft.	Leaves 2–6 in. wide, light green, turning scarlet or yellow in fall	Tiny reddish purple flower clusters in Apr.–May	Graceful vinelike tree for shady corners. Select in fall to ensure good color. Water deeply once per season in addition to regular water
	Acer ginnala AMUR MAPLE	☼ ◐ ○ ● / 1–9, 14–16	20 ft. by 15 ft.	Three-lobed, toothed leaves brilliant red in fall	Small fragrant, yellow, in spring	May develop several trunks. Does well in cold, windy areas, even in poor soil
	Acer griseum PAPERBARK MAPLE	☼ ◐ ● / 1–9, 14–21	To 25 ft. by 20 ft.	Leaves divided into 3 leaflets, turning bright red in fall	Inconspicuous red flowers, then showy winged seeds	Beautiful peeling reddish bark, vibrant fall color. Plant as specimen tree
	Acer palmatum JAPANESE MAPLE	☼ ◐ ● / 1–10, 12, 14–24	Slow to 20 ft. by 20 ft.	Delicate leaves 2–4 in. long with scarlet, orange, or yellow fall color	Tiny flowers in spring followed by two-winged fruits	Graceful, slow-growing tree invaluable in Asian, woodland gardens. Protect from wind, overhead irrigation water. Don't disturb roots. Full sun in Zones 16, 17, 21–24. Countless varieties available in wide range of sizes and leaf colors
	Chionanthus retusus CHINESE FRINGE TREE	☼ ● / 2–9, 14–24	To 20 ft. by 20 ft.	Broad leaves 1–4 in. long.	Small panicles of pure white flowers cover tree in June–July	Tolerates pollution. Good specimen tree. Request male trees for larger flowers, no fruit
	Chitalpa tashkentensis CHITALPA	☼ ● / 3–24	20–30 ft. by 20–30 ft.	Long, narrow leaves	Pink or white flowers, frilly, trumpet-shaped, May through fall	Multitrunked; fast growing. Beautiful large flowers on a tough tree
	Cornus kousa KOUSA DOGWOOD	☼ ◐ ● / 3–9, 14, 15, 18, 19	20–25 ft. by 15–20 ft.	Medium green leaves with rusty brown hairs at base turn yellow and scarlet in fall	Profuse, creamy, white, in late spring. Red strawberry-like fruit in Oct.	Interesting year-round. Natural shape is shrubby, with horizontal spreading branches
	Elaeagnus angustifolia RUSSIAN OLIVE	☼ ◐ ○ ● / 1–3, 7–14, 18, 19	To 20 ft. by 20 ft.	Willowlike, silvery gray leaves	Small very fragrant yellow flowers followed by small fruit	Dislikes humid summers. Plant in well-drained soil. Good as specimen tree or hedge
	Parrotia persica PERSIAN PARROTIA	☼ ○ ● / 4–6, 15–17	30 ft. by 15–30 ft.	Lustrous dark green leaves, 3–4 in. long, turn orange, then pink, then scarlet in fall	Flowers with red stamens appear in spring before leaves	Excellent fall color. Multitrunked; slow growing
	Prunus serrulata JAPANESE FLOWERING CHERRY	☼ ● / 2–7, 14–20	15–30 ft. by 10–25 ft.	Long slender leaves turn yellow or tawny yellow in fall	Flowers white, pink, or rosy pink in spring	Many varieties available—choose when in flower. Plant in deep, well-drained soil. Good in raised beds, for gardening under
	Tabebuia impetiginosa PINK TRUMPET TREE	☼ ● / 15, 16, 20–24	Fast to 25–30 ft. by 20–25 ft.	Dark green, divided into leaflets, sometimes evergreen	Trumpet-shaped flowers, lavender pink with white and yellow markings, in late winter, late summer to fall	Rounded, spreading shape, good for flower display, as patio tree
MEDIUM	*Acer davidii* DAVID'S MAPLE	☼ ◐ ○ ● / 1–6, 15–17, 20, 21	20–35 ft. by 20 ft.	Glossy green leaves, 2–7 in. long, oval; bronze in spring and yellow, orange, or purple in fall	Clusters of greenish yellow flowers in spring	Shiny green, silver-striped bark interesting in winter. Give deep watering monthly during first two summers
	Aesculus carnea RED HORSECHESTNUT	☼ ○ ● / 1–10, 12, 14–17	40 ft. by 30 ft.	Dark green leaves divided fanwise	Hundreds of 8-in. plumes of soft pink to red flowers	Striking flower show Apr.–May. Rounded shape casts deep shade. Seeds slightly toxic
	Calodendrum capense CAPE CHESTNUT	☼ ○ ● / 19, 21–24	25–40 ft. by 25–40 ft.	Light to medium green, oval, to 6 in. long	Profuse spikes of rosy lilac flowers held high above foliage, May–July	Slow growing, with spreading shape. Plant out of wind. Prefers heavier, not sandy, soil
	Cercidiphyllum japonicum KATSURA TREE	☼ ◐ ● ●● / 1–6, 14–16, 18–20	To 40 ft. by 35 ft.	Nearly round, 2–4 in. long, dark blue green above and grayish beneath, with tints of red	Inconspicuous	Usually has multiple trunks, spreading shape. Handsome, hardy tree with fresh-looking foliage. Prefers rich soil and protection from hot sun and drying winds
	Cercidium floridum BLUE PALO VERDE	☼ ○ ● / 10–14, 18–20	Fast to 30 ft. by 30 ft.	Tiny leaflets appear briefly, then bluish green branchlets remain	In spring, covered with 2–4-in.-long clusters of yellow flowers	Interesting desert tree that attracts birds. Falling seed capsules create some litter

☼ **Full sun**; ◐ **Part shade**; ● **Full shade**; ○ **Drought tolerant**; ◐ **Little water**; ● **Regular water**; ●● **Ample water.**

To find your climate zone, see pages 14–21.

Botanical name COMMON NAME	Sun & Water/ Zones	Height/ Spread	Leaves	Flowers/Fruit	Comments
Erythrina coralloides NAKED CORAL TREE	☼ ○ ◐ 12, 13, 19–24	To 30 ft. by 30 ft.	8–10-in. leaves emerge in May–June, then turn yellow and drop in late fall	Fiery red blossoms on tips of naked twisted black-thorned branches Mar.–May	Interesting branch structure. Prune in Jan., making cuts to open inner growth, but don't cut branch tips (see p. 213). Flood once per month in dry season
Jacaranda mimosifolia JACARANDA	☼ ◐ 12, 13, 15–24	25–40 ft. by 15–30 ft.	Fernlike leaves drop in Feb.–Mar.	Clusters of lavender-blue flowers in summer. Roundish flat seed capsules follow	Does best in hot, sunny spots out of wind. Stately spreading form; spectacular in bloom
Koelreuteria bipinnata CHINESE FLAME TREE	☼ ◐ 8–24	20–40 ft. by 20–40 ft.	Long leaflets, dark green above and lighter beneath, turn yellow in Dec.	Small, yellow, in summer, followed by orange, red, or salmon fruit capsules	Very spreading shape. Good patio, shade tree
Koelreuteria paniculata. GOLDENRAIN TREE	☼ ○ ◐ ● 2–21	20–35 ft. by 10–40 ft.	Leaves to 15 in. long, divided into small leaflets	Long yellow clusters in summer. Buff to brown fruit in fall	Head back awkward growth (see p. 213). Needs regular water in youth. 'Kew' or 'Fastigiata' is erect and narrow
Nyssa sylvatica SOUR GUM, TUPELO, PEPPERIDGE	☼ ◐ ● 3–10, 14–21	30–50 ft. by 15–25 ft.	Dark green, glossy, to 5 in. long, turning hot, coppery red in fall	Flowers inconspicuous, followed by blue-black fruit that is attractive to birds	Excellent for fall color. Slow to moderate growth into interesting picturesque shape with age
Prosopis glandulosa torreyana HONEY MESQUITE	☼ ○ ◐ 10–13	Fast to 30 ft. by 35 ft.	Tiny bright green leaflets	Small greenish yellow, in spring and summer; followed by beanlike pods	Typically multitrunked. Spreading canopy casts light shade. Water monthly for faster growth in first two summers. Also called TEXAS MESQUITE
Sapium sebiferum CHINESE TALLOW TREE	☼ ● 8, 9, 12–16, 18–21	35 ft. by 30 ft.	Roundish leaves taper to point; excellent yellow or red fall color	Tiny yellow flowers; grayish white fruit with waxy coating	Naturally shrubby shape. Select tree while in fall color
Sophora japonica JAPANESE PAGODA TREE	☼ ◐ ◐ All zones	To 40 ft. by 40 ft.	Dark green, 6–10-in. leaves divided into many leaflets	Long open clusters of yellowish white flowers, July–Sept.	May not flower for first few years. 'Regent' is a vigorous form that flowers earlier. Good spreading shade tree. Flowers can stain paving
LARGE *Celtis occidentalis* COMMON HACKBERRY	☼ ◐ All zones	50 ft. by 40 ft.	Leaves oval, bright green, 2–5 in. long, emerging in late spring, turning yellow in autumn	Small berrylike fruits loved by birds	Rounded crown. Deep rooted, so can be planted near paving. Takes wind, heat, pollution
Ginkgo biloba MAIDENHAIR TREE	☼ ○ ◐ 1–10, 12, 14–24	To 50 ft. by 35 ft.	Broad fan-shaped light green leaves turn brilliant gold in fall	Yellowish seeds to 1 in. long	Plant male trees only; females produce ill-smelling fruit. Water regularly until about 20 ft. tall, then little water needed. Requires staking when young (see p. 201). Stately with age
Larix decidua EUROPEAN LARCH	☼ ● 1–9, 14–17	30–60 ft.	Bright grass-green needles turn brilliant yellow before dropping	Attractive small cones	Slender, graceful conical tree that attracts birds
Pistacia chinensis CHINESE PISTACHE	☼ ○ ◐ 4–16, 18–23	To 60 ft. by 50 ft.	Leaves with paired leaflets 2–4 in. long, with scarlet, crimson, orange, or yellow fall color	Inconspicuous flowers. Fruit on female trees bright red, turning dark blue	Very little water once established. Stake in youth (see p. 201)
Quercus coccinea SCARLET OAK	☼ ◐ All zones	60–80 ft. by 60–80 ft.	Leaves bright green, to 6 in. long, turning scarlet in autumn	Inconspicuous flowers. Acorns ½ in. across	Deep rooted. Shade is not too dense for understory plantings
Quercus phellos WILLOW OAK	☼ ◐ 1–4, 6–16, 18–21	To 50–90 ft. by 50–90 ft.	Leaves resemble willow leaves; turn yellowish before falling	Inconspicuous flowers. Acorns ¼ in. across	Delicate foliage, but may hang on through winter in warm climates
Quercus shumardii SHUMARD RED OAK	☼ ◐ 4–9, 12, 14–17	60–80 ft. by 60–80 ft.	Bright green leaves, to 6 in. long, turn red to yellow in fall	Inconspicuous flowers. Acorns ½–1 in. across	Similar to scarlet oak. Tolerates acidic, poorly drained soil
Zelkova serrata 'Village Green' JAPANESE ZELKOVA	☼ ● 3–21	To 60 ft. by 60 ft.	Leaves similar to elm, turning rusty red in fall	Inconspicuous flowers	Give young trees deep watering. May need to thin in youth (see p. 213). Graceful, vigorous, with excellent fall color

☼ **Full sun;** ◐ **Part shade;** ● **Full shade;** ○ **Drought tolerant;** ◐ **Little water;** ● **Regular water;** ◐ **Ample water.** **To find your climate zone, see pages 14–21.**

EASY-CARE EVERGREEN SHRUBS FOR WESTERN GARDENS

Botanical name COMMON NAME	Sun & Water/ Zones	Height/ Spread	Leaves	Flowers /Fruit	Comments
Abelia grandiflora GLOSSY ABELIA	☼ ◑ ● ● 5–24	To 8 ft. by 5 ft.	Glossy, dark green, oval leaves, may turn bronze in fall	Flowers white to light pink, profuse in summer and fall	To keep open, arching shape, cut a few stems to ground in late winter
Callistemon citrinus LEMON BOTTLEBRUSH	☼ ● 8, 9, 14–24	To 10–15 ft. by 10–15 ft.	Narrow leaves coppery when new, then vivid green	Bright red, 6-in.-long bottlebrush flowers most of the year	Massive shrub—good for background. Prune out dead wood once per year (see p. 213). Tolerates heat, cold, adverse soils. Many varieties available
Camellia japonica	◑ ● ● ● 4–9, 12, 14–24	8–15 ft. by 8–15 ft.	Thick, lustrous, broadly oval leaves	Flowers 3–6 in., white, pink, red, and variegated combinations in late fall through spring, depending on variety	Plant out of wind in good soil. Mulch and water regularly until established. Fertilize after bloom with acid plant food. Pick up fallen flowers; prune only to open up dense shape (see p. 213)
Carpenteria californica BUSH ANEMONE	☼ ◑ ○ ● 5–9, 14–24	3–6 ft. by 4–5 ft.	Leaves thick, narrow, dark green above, whitish beneath	Fragrant white flowers to 3 in. wide, May–Aug.	Upright and spreading, with formal look. Beautiful flowers. May get pests (see pp. 220–221)
Ceanothus (shrub forms) WILD LILAC	☼ ○ ● 1–9, 14–24	Size varies by species	Most have small, glossy, dark green leaves	Covered with mildly fragrant flowers in spring, white through many shades of blue	Most are sprawling and need plenty of room. Pinch new growth (see p. 213) to control shape. Short lived (to 10 years), but fast-growing
Cistus ROCKROSE	☼ ○ ● 7–9, 12–24	2–6 ft. by 2–6 ft.	Most have furry to crinkly dark green to gray-green leaves	Flowers white, pink, reddish purple, with heavy bloom in spring	Require excellent drainage. Pinch young plants; cut out oldest stems once a year (see p. 213)
Coleonema BREATH OF HEAVEN	☼ ◑ ● ● 7–9, 14–24	5 ft. by 5 ft.	Needlelike, fragrant leaves	Covered in tiny white or pink flowers in winter and spring	Plant in light, fast-draining soil. Rounded upright shape. Also called *Diosma*
Fatsia japonica JAPANESE ARALIA	◑ ● ● 4–9, 13–24	5–8 ft. by 5–8 ft.	Glossy, dark, fanlike leaves, to 16 in. across, on long stalks	Round clusters of small white flowers in fall, then black fruit	Dramatic and versatile. May get snails and slugs (see pp. 220–221)
Fremontodendron californicum COMMON FLANNEL BUSH	☼ ○ 7–24	6–20 ft. by 6–20 ft.	Leaves dark green above, feltlike beneath	Lemon yellow, saucer-shaped flowers, May–June	Upright, sprawling western native. Needs excellent drainage—good for hillsides. Flowers and stems can irritate skin
Garrya elliptica COAST SILKTASSEL	☼ ◑ ● 5–9, 14–21	To 10–25 ft. by 10–25 ft.	Branches densely covered with leaves to 2½ in., dark green above and gray beneath	Clustered flower tassels Dec.–Feb., followed by purplish fruit on female plants	Dense and spreading. 'Evie' and 'James Roof' have unusually long catkins. Makes casual screen or specimen
Gaultheria shallon SALAL	◑ ● ● ● 3–7, 14–17, 21–24	2–10 ft. by 2–10 ft.	Round, glossy bright green leaves 2–4 in. long	Clusters of tiny white or pink bell-shaped flowers in Mar.–June. Black fruit attractive to birds	Smaller in sun, larger in shade. Likes acid, woodsy soil. May spread by underground shoots. Occasional pruning keeps it dense (see p. 213)
Grevillea rosmarinifolia ROSEMARY GREVILLEA	☼ ○ 8, 9, 12–24	To 6 ft. by 5 ft.	Narrow, dark green, 1½-in. needlelike leaves	Unusual, spiderlike flowers, red and cream, in fall and winter	Dense, compact form. Takes heat and aridity. Many other species available
Heteromeles arbutifolia TOYON	☼ ◑ ● 5–24	6–10 ft. by 6–10 ft.	Thick, leathery, glossy, dark green leaves 2–4 in. long	Small white clusters, June–July, followed by bright red berries	Dense, upright western native, good for specimen, screen, or hillside planting
Juniperus chinensis 'Torulosa' (J. c. 'Kaizuka') HOLLYWOOD JUNIPER	☼ ◑ ○ ● All zones	To 15 ft. by 10 ft.	Branches thickly clothed with rich green needlelike foliage	None	Very irregular shape, so use as specimen. *J. chinensis* has columnar form. Hundreds of other species in a variety of shapes, sizes, and colors
Leptospermum scoparium NEW ZEALAND TEA TREE	☼ ○ ● 14–24	3–10 ft. by 3–9 ft.	Tiny, dark green, pointed	Many white to pink flowers, spring or summer	Upright, rounded form; blends well with other drought-tolerant shrubs. Give summer water only for first few years. Many varieties available, including 'Gaiety Girl' (pink, to 5 ft.), 'Helene Strybing' (deep pink, 6–10 ft.), 'Ruby Glow' (red, 6–8 ft.), and 'Snow White' (2–4 ft.)
Leucophyllum frutescens TEXAS RANGER	☼ ● 7–24	6–8 ft. by 6–8 ft.	Small silvery leaves	Deep purple flowers at various times, often after showers	Slow growing, good for desert. Several varieties available, with flowers violet to white

☼ **Full sun;** ◑ **Part shade;** ● **Full shade;** ○ **Drought tolerant;** ● **Little water;** ● **Regular water;** ●● **Ample water.**

To find your climate zone, see pages 14–21.

Botanical name / COMMON NAME	Sun & Water/ Zones	Height/ Spread	Leaves	Flowers /Fruit	Comments
Loropetalum chinense	☼ ◐ ● / 6–9, 14–24	3–5 ft. by 5–8 ft.	Leaves light green, soft, 1–2 in. long	Flowers, white to greenish, composed of clusters of twisted narrow petals, appear year-round, but most heavily in Mar.–Apr.	Neat, compact shape, with elegantly tiered branches. Likes rich, well-drained soil. 'Rubrum' has mixed green and purplish leaves, pink flowers. 'Razzle Dazzle' has plum foliage, hot pink flowers
Mahonia aquifolium OREGON GRAPE	☼ ◐ ● ○ / 1–21	To 6 ft. by 3 ft.	Leaves 4–10 in. long, with spiny oval leaflets, dull to glossy green, ruddy in youth	Yellow flowers in 2–3-in. clusters in Mar.–May, followed by edible blue-black fruit	Tall, erect shape. Cut any awkward stems to ground; they will be quickly replaced. Treat at first sign of pest damage (see pp. 220–221)
Myrtus communis TRUE MYRTLE	☼ ◐ ○ / 8–24	To 5–6 ft. by 4–5 ft.	Leaves glossy, bright green, pointed, 2 in. long, pleasantly aromatic	White, sweet-scented, ¾-in.-wide flowers in summer, followed by blue-black berries	Rounded form. Good for informal screen. Needs good drainage. Dwarf and variegated forms available. Prune to open interior (see p. 213)
Nandina domestica HEAVENLY BAMBOO	☼ ◐ ○ ◕ / 5–24	Slow to 6–8 ft. by 3–4 ft.	Leaves divided into many leaflets, pink to soft green to bronzy red to purple	Flowers pinkish or creamy white in loose clusters in late spring or summer. Fruit follows if several plants are grouped together	Needs some shade in hot regions and does best in rich soil. Form is upright and vertical, but overall look is lacy and delicate. Cut oldest canes to the ground in late winter (see p. 213)
Nerium oleander OLEANDER	☼ ○ / 8–16, 18–24	8–12 ft. by 8–12 ft.	Narrow leaves are dark green and leathery	Flowers 2–3 in. across, clustered at branch ends—white, yellow, pink, salmon, or red	Broad and bulky—prune in early spring to control size and form (see p. 213). Leaves and flowers are poisonous; smoke from burning branches causes severe irritation
Osmanthus fragrans SWEET OLIVE	☼ ◐ ○ ◕ / 8, 9, 12–24	To 10 ft. by 10 ft.	Leaves glossy, medium green, oval, to 4 in. long	Flowers inconspicuous but fragrant, mostly in spring and early summer; throughout year in mild-winter areas	Broad compact form. Young plants best in some shade. In Zones 12 and 13, grow in eastern or northern exposure. Suffers in areas with salty irrigation water
Pieris japonica LILY-OF-THE-VALLEY SHRUB	◐ ● / 4–9, 14–17	To 9–10 ft. by 9 ft.	Mature leaves glossy, dark green, to 3 in; new growth bronzy pink to red	Drooping flower clusters, white to dark pink, attractive even in bud, opening Feb.–May	Prefers acid soil; apply slow-release fertilizer and give twice-yearly flooding. Remove spent flowers (see p. 213). Upright, dense, tiered growth. Leaves and nectar are poisonous
Pinus mugo mugo MUGHO PINE	☼ ○ / All zones	Slow to 4 ft. by 4 ft.	Needles dark green	Cones 1 in., tawny to dark brown	Low and mounding. Good drainage important. Not at its best in desert
Pittosporum tobira TOBIRA	☼ ◐ ○ ◕ / 8–24	To 6–15 ft. by 6–15 ft.	Leaves shiny, dark green, 2–5 in. long	Creamy white, fragrant flowers in clusters in early spring; round green fruit follows, opening to reveal attractive orange seeds	Dense, attractive foliage and pleasingly upright form. Good for screens. 'Wheeler's Dwarf' is a 2-ft. miniature, excellent for foreground. Aphids and scale may attack (see pp. 220–221)
Prunus laurocerasus 'Zabeliana' ZABEL LAUREL	☼ ◐ ● / 3–9, 14–21	To 6 ft. by 6 ft.	Narrow, leathery, dark green leaves, 3–7 in. long	Creamy white flower spikes in summer; small black fruit in late summer and fall	Branches angle upward and outward. Good low screen or big foundation plant. Prune to shape (see p. 213)
Rhamnus californica COFFEEBERRY	☼ ◐ ○ ◕ / 4–24	3–15 ft. by 3–15 ft.	Leaves shiny, dark green, paler beneath	Small flowers. Attractive berries are green, then red to black	'Eve Case' is dense and compact, to 4–8 ft. tall and wide. Prune only to control shape (see p. 213)
Raphiolepis indica INDIA HAWTHORN	☼ ◐ ○ ◕ / 8–10, 12–24	2–5 ft. by 2–5 ft.	Glossy, leathery, medium green leaves	Flowers white to pink, appearing profusely late fall to late spring	Pinch branch tips yearly (see p. 213). May get fungus (see p. 230). Many varieties available
Rhododendron RHODODENDRON, AZALEA	◐ ◕ ◕◕ / Best in 4–6, 15–17	Vary by species	Vary	Great variety in flower size and color; mostly trumpet shaped, in clusters	Best in Northwest. Need rich, acid, well-drained soil or acidic fertilizer. Visit a local nursery to determine best ones for your area
Sarcococca ruscifolia	◐ ● ◕ ◕ / 4–9, 14–24	4–6 ft. by 3–7 ft.	Glossy, deep green leaves, 2 in. long	Flowers small, white, highly fragrant, followed by red fruit	Slow-grower that takes deepest shade. Interesting shapes
Viburnum davidii	◐ ● / 4–9, 14–24	1–3 ft. by 3–4 ft.	Leaves glossy, dark green, deeply veined, to 6 in. long	White flowers, followed by metallic turquoise fruit	Use in foreground with other acid-soil-loving plants. May get pests (see pp. 220–221)

☼ **Full sun**; ◐ **Part shade**; ● **Full shade**; ○ **Drought tolerant**; ◖ **Little water**; ◕ **Regular water**; ◕◕ **Ample water.**

To find your climate zone, see pages 14–21.

EASY-CARE DECIDUOUS SHRUBS FOR WESTERN GARDENS

Botanical name COMMON NAME	Sun & Water/ Zones	Height/ Spread	Leaves	Flowers /Fruit	Comments
Berberis thunbergii JAPANESE BARBERRY	☼ ◐ ○ ◔ All zones	To 4–6 ft. by 4–6 ft.	Small, roundish leaves, deep green, turning yellow, orange, and red before falling	Bright red berries along branches, fall through winter	Dense foliage on arching, spiny branches. *B. t.* 'Atropurpurea', with bronzy to purplish red foliage all summer; *B. t.* 'Crimson Pygmy', with bright red leaves, grows to only 2 ft. high. Thin in late winter (see p. 213)
Buddleia davidii BUTTERFLY BUSH, SUMMER LILAC	☼ ◐ ◔ ◓ ● All zones	To 8 ft.	Dark green above, whitish beneath, narrow and tapering, 4–12 in. long	Spikes of small, fragrant, lilac flowers with orange eye in midsummer	Needs good drainage. Cut back in winter for fresh spring growth. Very attractive to butterflies
Callicarpa bodinieri BEAUTYBERRY	☼ ◐ ◔ 3–9, 14–24	6 ft. by 6 ft.	Long, narrow leaves turn pink or orange to purple in fall	Small purple flowers followed by attractive violet berries	Graceful, arching shrub; cut back almost to ground in late winter (see p. 213). 'Profusion' bears heavy fruit
Caesalpinia gilliesii BIRD OF PARADISE BUSH	☼ ◔ 8–16, 18–23	6–10 ft. by 6–10 ft.	Deciduous in cool winters. Fernlike foliage and gray bark	Beautiful summer flowers, yellow with red stamens, attract hummingbirds	Fast grower. In hot summers, water deeply once a month. Pods and seeds cause illness
Cercis occidentalis WESTERN REDBUD	☼ ○ 2–24	10–18 ft. by 10–18 ft.	Small blue-green leaves turn light yellow or red in fall	Brilliant magenta flowers in spring, followed by attractive seedpods	Regular water in first 1–2 years to speed growth. Excellent for dry hillsides, as focal point
Chaenomeles FLOWERING QUINCE	☼ ◓ 1–21	2–10 ft. by 2–10 ft.	Shiny green leaves, narrow, 2–3 in. long	Flowers 2 in. wide in white, pink, orange, or red, on bare stem	Most spread irregularly and have thorns. Good barrier plant. Thin after bloom (see p. 213)
Clethra alnifolia SUMMERSWEET	☼ ◐ ◔ 2–6	To 10 ft. by 10 ft.	Dark green leaves are 2–4 in. long, narrow, toothed, in May	Spikes of tiny white flowers at branch tips in late summer	Forms slowly growing clumps. Grows best in acid, well-drained soil. Pink forms available
Cotinus coggygria SMOKE TREE	☼ ○ ◔ All zones	To 15 ft. by 15 ft.	Roundish leaves 1–3 in. long, bluish-green in summer, yellow to red in fall	Flowers tiny, but stalks cover tree with fuzzy "smoke" effect	Rounded shape. At its best in poor rocky soil with fast drainage. 'Purpureus' and 'Royal Purple' have purple to wine leaves
Euonymus alata WINGED EUONYMUS	☼ ◐ ◔ 1–9, 14–16	To 10 ft. by 10 ft.	Dark green leaves turn rich rose-red in fall	Small flowers followed by few bright orange-red fruits	Background, screen, or specimen; looks good against dark evergreens
Fothergilla major	◐ ◔ ◓ 3–9, 14–17	9 ft. by 6 ft.	Oval, 4-in.-long leaves turn yellow to red in early fall	White brushlike flowers emerge with leaves in spring	Erect shrub that provides excellent fall color
Hamamelis intermedia WITCH HAZEL	☼ ◐ ◔ 4–7, 15–17	15 ft. by 20 ft.	Leaves 5–6 in. long, dark green, roundish, turn yellow to red in fall	Yellow to orange flowers appear before leaves	Big spreading shrub gives color in fall and spring. Many varieties available. If shrub becomes too dense, thin out old wood after bloom (see p. 213)
Hibiscus syriacus ROSE OF SHARON	☼ ◓ 1–21	10–12 ft. by 8–10 ft.	Medium-sized leaves with 3 lobes	Flowers in summer, 2½–3 in. across, white, pink, red, rose, purple, or blue	Compact when young, spreading with age. Double-flowered varieties produce less fruit. Prune hard each year in late winter (see p. 213)
Hydrangea quercifolia OAKLEAF HYDRANGEA	◐ ● ◔ 1–22	6 ft. by 6 ft.	Oaklike leaves up to 8 in. long, deep green, turning bronze to crimson in fall	Large open clusters of white flowers in June	Broad and rounded. To keep below 3 ft., prune to ground in early spring, but this limits bloom (see p. 213)
Ribes sanguineum glutinosum PINK WINTER CURRANT	☼ ◐ ○ ◔ 4–9, 14–24	5–12 ft. by 6–10 ft.	Leaves 2½ in. wide, light to medium green	Flowers white to deep pink, hanging in clusters in early spring	Fast growing, with upright to spreading shape. Informal, but spectacular in bloom
Spiraea japonica	☼ ◐ ◔ 1–11, 14–21	2–6 ft. by 2–6 ft.	Light green leaves, oval and pointed, saw-toothed	Flowers in various shades of pink, in wide, flat clusters at branch tips in summer	Upright grower. 'Little Princess', to 20 in. tall, has pink blooms over a long period. 'Shirobana', 3 ft. tall, has white, pink, and red flowers
Vitex agnus-castus CHASTE TREE	● ○ 4–24, best in 13–24	15–20 ft. by 10–15 ft.	Dark green leaflets are handsome	Spectacular lavender to navy blue spikes that cover the shrub from July–Oct.	Tolerates poor soils, little water. Fast grower. White 'Alba' and pink 'Rosea' available

☼ Full sun; ◐ Part shade; ● Full shade; ○ Drought tolerant; ◔ Little water; ◓ Regular water; ◓◓ Ample water.

To find your climate zone, see pages 14–21.

Rugged Hillside

A steep, south-facing hillside seems like a difficult spot in which to create a garden, but there is a low-maintenance alternative to expensive terracing and irrigation: plant a variety of drought-tolerant, evergreen flowering shrubs. Apply a 3-inch layer of mulch to all unplanted areas to keep down weeds and conserve moisture. In this selection the irises near the path will need a monthly soaking during the dry season, but the other plants will thrive without summer water after their first year. The color show lasts from early spring until midsummer. Plant choices for three regions are given below.

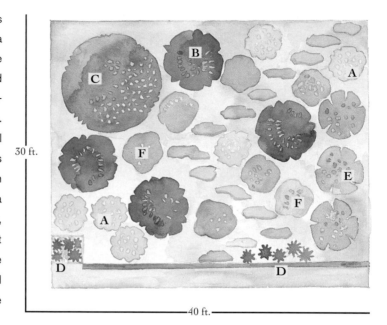

Carpenteria californica
BUSH ANEMONE

Fremontodendron 'California Glory'
FLANNEL BUSH

Rosmarinus officinalis 'Prostratus'
DWARF ROSEMARY

THE PLANTS

A. *Carpenteria californica* (6)
  BUSH ANEMONE

B. *Ceanothus* 'Dark Star' (4)
  WILD LILAC

C. *Fremontodendron*
  'California Glory' (1)
  FLANNEL BUSH

D. *Iris douglasiana* (13)
  DOUGLAS IRIS

E. *Ribes sanguineum glutinosum*
  'Spring Showers' (3)
  PINK WINTER CURRANT

F. *Rosmarinus officinalis*
  'Prostratus' (7)
  DWARF ROSEMARY

For a Northwest Garden
A. *Mahonia aquifolium* (6)
  OREGON GRAPE

B. *Ceanothus thyrsiflorus* (4)
  BLUE BLOSSOM

C. *Cercis occidentalis* (1)
  WESTERN REDBUD

D, E, F. *as above*

For a Southwest Garden
A. *Cistus salviifolius* (4)
  SAGELEAF ROCKROSE

B. *Salvia clevelandii* (4)

C. *Acacia pendula* (1)
  WEEPING ACACIA

D. *Lavandula angustifolia* (9)
  ENGLISH LAVENDER

E. *Tristania laurina* (3)

F. *Santolina chamaecyparissus* (7)
  LAVENDER COTTON

Shady Boardwalk

A small, shady backyard is transformed by the addition of a simple raised walkway made of redwood. A variety of ferns, from the small and delicate five-finger fern to the imposing Tasmanian tree fern, lend an exotic feeling of lushness. Rhododendrons and azaleas are vibrantly colored in spring, when the leaves of the deciduous Japanese maples are fresh. In winter, the graceful maple branches provide visual interest. These plantings suit a moist site with slightly acidic, woodsy soil.

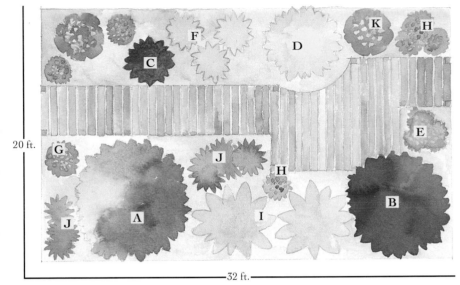

Acer palmatum 'Ever Red'
JAPANESE MAPLE

Nephrolepis cordifolia
SOUTHERN SWORD FERN

Rhododendron 'Lem's Cameo'

THE PLANTS

A. *Acer palmatum* 'Bloodgood' (1)
JAPANESE MAPLE

B. *Acer palmatum* 'Burgundy Lace' (1)
JAPANESE MAPLE

C. *Acer palmatum* 'Ever Red' (1)
JAPANESE MAPLE

D. *Acer palmatum* 'Sango Kaku' (1)
CORAL BARK MAPLE

E. *Adiantum aleuticum* (3)
FIVE-FINGER FERN

F. *Asplenium bulbiferum* (3)
MOTHER FERN

G. *Azalea* 'Constance' (3)

H. *Azalea* 'Sherwood Orchid' (3)

I. *Dicksonia antarctica* (2)
TASMANIAN TREE FERN

J. *Nephrolepis cordifolia* (6)
SOUTHERN SWORD FERN

K. *Rhododendron* 'Lem's Cameo' (2)

Roses

There's no question that roses demand attention, but their flowers are so beloved that many gardeners find them worth the effort. If you choose to have roses, be prepared to spend some extra time selecting, planting, and caring for them. Follow the guidelines given here and on pages 200–201 (planting) and page 215 (pruning).

Choosing the right rose for your area is essential. Roses that mildew in Portland may thrive in San Diego. Consult the lists on pages 92–93, but your own neighborhood may be the best guide. Look for healthy, attractive specimens—they'll likely do well in your own garden, too.

SORTING OUT ROSES

The classification of roses can be bewildering, but it's important to know what you're getting. Simply put, the three main groups are the modern roses (hybrid teas, grandifloras, floribundas, polyanthas, miniatures, climbing roses, and shrub roses); old roses (albas, centifolias, damasks, gallicas, Chinas, moss roses, Bourbons, damask perpetuals, hybrid perpetuals, Noisettes, and teas); and the wild species and their hybrids.

The best known of these are modern hybrid teas, which bear large, usually full-petaled flowers, mostly one to a long stem. They are favorites for cut flowers and generally grow 3 to 6 feet high. Floribundas are shrubby roses that produce large clusters of flowers. Most bloom over a long period and are excellent, easy-care landscape plants. They generally grow 3 to 6 feet high, but can be upright or spreading. Grandifloras are a diverse group of roses with flowers born singly or in clusters. They most resemble hybrid teas in form but can be larger and more vigorous growing. Miniature roses have small leaves and tiny flowers. They grow anywhere from 12 inches to 4 feet high and are ideal for containers or as edgings. Climbers need to be tied to a strong support like an arbor or trellis to stay upright. They grow 8 to 20 feet high.

ROSE RULES

Buy big. Look for plump, healthy bare-root plants in winter, (or order bare-root from mail-order sources in late winter for delivery at planting time in your region). Choose trouble-free varieties from the list on the following pages. Look for roses numbered 1 or 1½, with three living canes on each plant. During the growing season, container-grown plants allow a better choice in selection, as you can evaluate bloom color and fragrance.

Perfect planting. Although some experts advise letting roses adapt to your soil, it's generally recommended to loosen the soil to a depth of two feet and amend with rich organic matter, such as compost. Add lime if the soil is acidic.

Shine on. Roses need at least six hours of full sun during their growing season. Don't plant in shade or canes will grow spindly and weak.

Fresh air. Good air circulation is crucial for warding off diseases such as mildew, black spot, and rust. Set out bushes so they'll be at least one foot apart when mature.

Mulch is a must. Maintain a 1–3 in. circle of mulch around roses, leaving a 3-in. circle of open soil around each plant's trunk.

Pest prevention. To stave off pests such as scale, spray stems with horticultural oil (see p. 231) during the dormant season. Include a fungicide to help prevent diseases.

Cut to size. Prune roses according to your zone when new leaf buds begin to swell in late winter or early spring. Shear them to a lower height or prune arching shrubs by thinning out old, grayish canes, crossing stems, and any dead branches. Some roses need only light, occasional pruning. For more information, see p. 215.

Not too wet. Water roses deeply during the first year and directly after the first bloom. Set drip emitters on '1 gph' or 'high' for one hour, twice a week, three times a week during hot weather. But water well-established roses only once a week.

Pest patrol. It's wise to inspect roses for pests once a week. Look for aphids, ants crawling on stems, leaves sticky with aphid honeydew, or webbing near leaf stems (caused by spider mites or leaf-chewing caterpillars). For treatments, see pp. 224–225.

Growing hips. Stop snipping blooms by Halloween in mild winter areas, mid-August in cold-winter areas, to allow roses to form their fruits (called hips). This helps them enter their dormant phase for a healthy winter rest. Rake away fallen leaves and debris, which may harbor overwintering insects and diseases.

Shrub roses are a catch-all category. They vary in size and form, and include hybrid musks, David Austin's English roses, ground cover roses, and hardy Canadian roses.

Old-fashioned roses, also called old, antique, heirloom, or heritage roses are shrubby (4 to 8 feet) and can be tough as nails. Many can be discovered in old cemeteries, still blooming despite decades of neglect. On the downside, most bloom once a year, but their green foliage (and thorns) still make them useful as backdrops, boundary hedges, and fence coverings.

ROUGH AND READY RUGOSAS

Rugosa roses are easily identified by their pleated, or leathery, leaves, which help protect them from insect damage and foliage diseases. Harsh conditions, such as sub-zero temperatures, drying winds, and salt spray do not diminish their deep green foliage, abundant blooms, and ample fall hips.

These roses are not for the formal garden, for their bloom is intermittent and they grow in a sprawling fashion more suited to hillsides and casual terraces. Wild at heart, rugosas are at their best in full sun and well-drained soils. They rarely need spraying with chemicals or feeding with fertilizer. Those listed below are suitable for most areas of the West.

Rambling rose. Many climbing roses, including 'Kathleen', need only enough pruning to keep them in shape. They'll happily scramble over fences, walls, even roofs. Deadheading faded flowers will prolong bloom.

RUGOSAS FOR WESTERN GARDENS

'Basye's Purple Rose' Bushy upright plant with gray-green foliage; fragrant, velvety, deep purple blooms with stamens edged in gold. 4–6 ft. by 4 ft.

'Blanc Double de Coubert' Pure white flowers with petals loosely arranged, 2–3 inches across. This bushy old variety can be used as a background shrub for screening, growing quickly to an ultimate height of 5 ft. by 6 ft. Good for containers.

'Charles Albanel' Spreading plant with bright green foliage; semidouble medium-red flowers have strong fragrance. 4 ft. by 4 ft.

'Corylus' Shiny, bright green, wrinkled leaves; fragrant silvery-pink blooms; bright orange hips. 4 ft. by 4 ft.

'Delicata' Compact, bushy plant with wrinkled foliage and extremely fragrant semidouble lilac flowers with creamy yellow stamens. 3 ft. by 3 ft.

'Pink Robusta' Magnificent glossy, disease-resistant foliage; semidouble pink flowers good for cutting; always in bloom. 7 ft. by 7 ft.

'Purple Pavement' Wrinkled foliage on rounded shrub; fragrant semidouble crimson-purple flowers with gold stamens. 3 ft. by 3 ft.

'Rose à Parfum de l'Hay' Vigorous, bushy plant without the rugose foliage; large, fully double cherry red flowers (no hips). 5 ft. by 5 ft.

'Scabrosa' Very fragrant 5-inch-wide single crimson blooms; huge hips which birds love. 6 ft. by 4 ft.

'Snow Owl' Compact plant with rugose foliage; white blooms tinted with lilac.

'Thérèse Bugnet' Upright growth with a hint of rugose foliage; fragrant old-fashioned-looking, ruffled double lilac flowers. 5 ft. by 4 ft.

For Southern California, also try **'Belle Poitevine'** (6 ft. by 5 ft. with soft pink flowers), **'Linda Campbell'** (6 ft. by 8 ft. with red flowers), **'Rugosa Magnifica'** (6 ft. by 5 ft. with purplish red flowers), **'Topaz Jewel'** (5 ft. by 5 ft. with yellow flowers).

HYBRID TEAS

'Duet' Lovely blend of large, pink, sometimes ruffled flowers. Light fragrance. Tall, vigorous with deep green leaves. One of the better landscape hybrid teas. Good as cut flower, for hedges.

'Honor' Beautifully formed, double, clear white blossoms. Light fragrance. Tall, with dark green leaves. Best flower form where summers are cool. Fine cut flower.

'Olympiad' Large, bright red, double with a delicate fruity scent. Tall, upright with dense foliage. Best red rose for cool climates, but widely adapted. Good hardiness. Excellent cut flower.

'Pascali' Abundant, double, brilliant white blooms. Light fragrance. Vigorous, upright, dense foliage. Long-time favorite. Good choice for Mountain regions.

'Peace' Double blooms are bright yellow edged pink. Light, fruity fragrance. Medium size with dark glossy leaves. One of the most popular roses. Good cut flower.

'Sheer Elegance' Rich light pink, double blooms. Light fragrance. Medium size with glossy, dark green foliage. Particularly good in the Northwest.

'Voodoo' Large, double orange and yellow blooms with a hint of scarlet. Strong fruity fragrance. Vigorous, upright, with deep green foliage. Best color with warm summers, in Southwest and Southern California; withstands heat well.

FLORIBUNDAS

'Apricot Nectar' Abundant clusters of large, apricot-orange blooms with strong fragrance. Upright, bushy with dark green leaves. Good repeat bloom. Nice cut flower.

'Class Act' Beautiful clusters of clear white blooms. Light fragrance. Vigorous, rounded shrub with clean-looking foliage. Consistent performer with long bloom period.

'Europeana' Large clusters of lightly fragrant crimson blooms. Medium size, rounded habit. Best in Southwest, can mildew elsewhere.

'Iceberg' Large clusters of clear white flowers, sometimes tinged pink in cool weather. Nice fragance. Vigorous, upright plant with dark green leaves. Free-blooming and easy to care for. One of the most useful landscape roses.

'Livin' Easy' Large, apricot blooms with fruity fragrance. Medium size and very glossy, deep green leaves. Widely adapted. Good hedge.

'Sarabande' Orange-red blooms with showy yellow stamens. Light fragrance. Compact, spreading habit with glossy leaves. Lower growing than other floribundas. Nice edging.

'Simplicity' Medium pink blooms in large clusters. Little fragrance. Tall, upright bush, clean looking foliage. Generous bloom over a long period. Great hedge.

'Sunsprite' Glowing lemon yellow blooms, often with wavy petals. Strong fragrance. Compact form with shiny, dark leaves. Seems always in bloom.

GRANDIFLORAS

'Gold Medal' Golden yellow blooms, rich fragrance. Tall, upright, with deep green foliage. Generous bloom. Good cut flower.

'Shreveport' Blend of salmon pink and orange. Large, double. Mild fragrance. Tall with shiny, dark green leaves. Generous bloom. Best color in fall. Excellent cut flower.

'Tournament of Roses' Large clusters of dependable pink flowers. Light fragrance. Medium size, upright, with glossy leaves.

CLIMBING ROSES

'Altissimo' Huge, deep red single blooms (5 to 7 petals) with showy yellow stamens. Slight fragrance. Manageable growth to about 10 ft. high. Deep green foliage. Reliable bloomer with stunning character.

'Cl. Iceberg' Often rated the finest climbing white rose. Sport of floribunda 'Iceberg' (see left). To 15 ft.; repeat bloom.

'Dortmund' Bright red, single blooms with a bright white center. Moderately fragrant. 10–12 ft. high. Shiny dark green leaves.

'Improved Blaze' Clusters of cup-shaped, red blooms. Light fragrance. Vigorous to 12–15 ft. high. Medium green, shiny leaves. The most popular climber.

'Joseph's Coat' Clusters of blossoms change from yellow to orange to red. To 12 ft., with glossy foliage.

SHRUB ROSES

'All That Jazz' Bright orange flowers with 5 to 10 petals. Slight fragrance. Tall, upright plant with deep, glossy green leaves. Hardy and very easy to grow.

'Baby Blanket' Light pink flowers. Light fragrance. Low growing to about 2 to 3 feet high and twice as wide. Makes a nice ground cover. Generous bloom.

'Bonica' Delicate clusters of small pink blooms. Moderate fragrance. Tall, arching growth to at least 4 ft. high. Glossy, deep green foliage. One of the Meidiland roses. Hardy. Useful as a hedge.

'Carefree Beauty' Masses of large pink blooms. Mild fragrance. Upright shrub with compact habit. Dense, bright green foliage. Tough plant. Hardy.

'Carefree Delight' Single pink flowers with a bright white center. Slight fragrance. Spreading mound with dark green leaves. Generous bloom. Hardy.

'Carefree Wonder' Bright pink flowers with a white center. Light fragrance. Upright mound reaching 4–6 ft. high. Glossy, dark green leaves. Free blooming and hardy.

'Flower Carpet Pink' Large sprays of dark pink flowers. Light fragrance. Low spreading plant with shiny, dark green foliage. Useful as a ground cover. One of the Flower Carpet series; other varieties have white and light pink blooms.

'Morden Centennial' Clusters of clear pink blooms. Light fragrance. Vigorous bush with dark leaves. One of a series of extremely hardy roses from Canada (most have Morden in the name). Generous bloom even in coldest areas.

'Prairie Dawn' Glowing pink blooms. Light fragrance. Compact, slightly spreading plant. One of a series of very hardy roses (most have Prairie in their name) for cold winter climates.

'Ralph's Creeper' Clusters of orange red blooms. Moderate fragrance. Low, spreading plant, reaching 2–3 ft. high and twice as wide. Fine ground cover.

'Scarlet Meidiland' Large clusters of ruffled, bright red flowers. Slight fragrance. Vigorous, spreading plant. Hardy. Good repeat bloom. Excellent ground cover. One of a series of shrub roses, most which have Meidiland in their name. Some are useful as hedges, others ground covers. All need room to grow.

DAVID AUSTIN ENGLISH ROSES

'Abraham Darby' Flowers are blend of coppery apricot, yellow, and warm pink; strong, fruity fragrance. Good repeat bloomer. 5 ft. tall; in warm-winter climates can be used as climber.

'Bonica' Clear pink flowers in clarge clusters. Reliable repeat bloom. Dark glossy leaves. Arching canes form 5-ft. mound.

'Graham Thomas' Flowers rich butter yellow with strong fragrance. Repeat bloomer. Arching fountain-like shrubs; cactus-green foliage. Robust growth to 5 ft.

'Fair Bianca' White, fully double flowers with strong old-rose fragrance. Grows to 3 ft. tall, with prickly stems and dark foliage.

OTHER ROSES

'Cécile Brunner' (polyantha) clusters of pale pink flowers; light fragrance. Also known as the Sweetheart Rose. Climbing and white forms available. One of the most popular roses.

'Kathleen' (hybrid musk) Pink, single blooms turn lighter as they open; followed by orange hips if not deadheaded. Vigorous to 8 ft; dark green foliage.

Rosa banksiae LADY BANKS' ROSE Evergreen climber (deciduous in cold climate). Strong growth to 20 ft. or more. Shower or small yellow or white flowers in spring. Stems thornless.

'Sombreuil' (hybrid tea) Clusters of creamy-white flowers blushed with pink. Strong fragrance. Small-scale climber or container rose with lacy, fernlike foliage. Long bloom.

'Souvenir de la Malmaison' (Bourbon) Tissue-pink, double flowers; intense perfume. Small-scale or container rose.

'The Fairy' (polyantha) Small, profuse pink flowers. Dense, spreading bush; can be used as ground cover.

'Zéphirine Drouhin' (Bourbon) Bright pink, semi-double fragrant flowers. Long-blooming. Thornless stems; to 10 ft. high.

Hedges

All hedges consist of shrubs planted closely together, but there the similarities end. Sheared once a year, small-leafed evergreens can form low edgings in a formal bed or knot garden (such as the one on page 165); fast growers can be left high and dense to buffer noise or form a sturdy wind barrier. Within the garden itself, hedges serve as living walls, subtly directing traffic, concealing a work, play, or seating area, or forming a permanent background for a mixed planting bed.

A really annoying privacy problem might seem to call for a fast-growing, leafy hedge but remember that many plants, when crowded, can become unhealthy. Instead of replacing dead shrubs to fill gaps, plan for selective removal, taking out every other shrub in a closely spaced hedge as it grows.

Consult the Guide on the facing page for a selection of plants that make fine hedges with a minimum of fuss. The guidelines on page 214 will show you how to do a once-yearly trimming to keep your hedges in shape. Too-eager fertilizing will only create the need for extra trimming, so feed your hedges just enough to keep them healthy. When making your selection, remember that only evergreens will give you year-round privacy and protection from wind.

Drawing a line. *Between the native oak woodland and a rough lawn, this low-growing, casually trimmed* Westringia fruticosa *marks a distinct boundary without seeming obtrusive.*

Simply red. *Photinia fraseri sends out russet-tinged new growth that can be trimmed for arrangements. Beyond that, this sturdy, dense hedge requires only a once-yearly shearing to keep its shape.*

KEEP THEM IN . . . OR OUT

Armored plants. Shrubs armed with spiky thorns or scratchy foliage can do double duty by keeping out four-footed or two-footed intruders. Dauntless plants that require minimal maintenance include natal plum, barberry, holly, rugosa roses, yucca, and many juniper species.

Kid keepers. Within your garden, soft but densely shrubby plants can help prevent children or pets from wandering where they shouldn't. Easy-care choices include boxwood, Japanese privet, azalea in shady spots (see p. 86), and drought-loving germander or santolina (see p. 143).

Gentle reminder. Sweetly scented or flowering shrubs create a wall of fragrance and color encouraging guests to keep within bounds. Roses or lavender will ably serve the purpose, or try silverberry, rosemary, or pineapple guava.

Be neighborly. Use common sense when setting out plants near property lines. Neighbors have a legal right to prune any branches that extend over their side of the line, so set out young hedge plants at least a foot within the property line so they don't grow onto your neighbor's land, or choose plants that can take a shearing in stride.

Botanical name COMMON NAME	Evergreen/ Deciduous	Sun & Water/ Zones	Height/ Spread	Leaves	Flowers/Fruit	Comments
Buxus sempervirens COMMON BOXWOOD, ENGLISH BOXWOOD	Evergreen	☼ ◐ ● ◖ 3–6, 15–17	15–20 ft. by 10–15 ft.	Medium-size, oval, dark green	Tiny and inconspicuous	Clip or leave to form a billowy mass. *B. s. 'Suffruticosa'*, TRUE DWARF BOXWOOD, slower growing to 4–5 ft. *Buxus microphylla* japonica, JAPANESE BOXWOOD, (8–24), better adapted to hot, dry climates and alkaline soils
Carissa macrocarpa NATAL PLUM	Evergreen	☼ ◖ 22–24	7–10 ft. by 7–10 ft.	Lustrous, small, emerald green	Fragrant, white, all year; edible red fruit	Thorns on branch tips make this a good barrier plant. Looks best unpruned
Dodonaea viscosa 'Purpurea' PURPLE HOP BUSH	Evergreen	☼ ○ ◖ 7–9, 12–24	12–15 ft. by 12 ft.	Willowlike, bronzy green to purplish red, to 4 in. long	Flower clusters insignificant, but creamy to pink seedpods are attractive	Plant 3 ft. apart for clipped hedge or 6 ft. for unpruned screen. Native Arizona green form for Zones 10–13, is hardier, good in desert. May get scale (see pp. 230–231)
Elaeagnus pungens SILVERBERRY	Evergreen	☼ ◐ ◖ ● 4–24	6–15 ft. by 6–15 ft.	Gray-green, 1–3 in. long, with wavy edges and rust-colored dots	Small, yellow to white, fragrant, in fall	Large and sprawling. Variegated forms available, with silver to gold to yellow leaves. Good barrier plant
Escallonia rubra	Evergreen	☼ ◐ ● 4–9, 14–17, 20–24	6–15 ft. by 3–10 ft.	Ovate, dark green, glossy, 1 in. long	Red or crimson, in clusters during warm months	Takes coastal wind and sun, but not alkaline soil. Remove one-third of old wood each year (see p. 213)
Feijoa sellowiana PINEAPPLE GUAVA	Evergreen	☼ ◖ 7–9, 12–24	18–25 ft. by 18–25 ft.	Oval glossy green above and silvery beneath	Tropical-looking, white, in May; gray-green fruit	Give plenty of room. Flower petals edible
Ilex crenata JAPANESE HOLLY	Evergreen	☼ ◐ ● 2–9, 14–24	3–4 ft. by 4–5 ft.	Narrow, gray-green to dark green	Inconspicuous flowers, followed by black berries	Many varieties, most low and dense. Best in slightly acid soil
Ligustrum japonicum JAPANESE PRIVET, WAX-LEAF PRIVET	Evergreen	☼ ◐ ● ◖ 4–24	10–12 ft. by 5–6 ft.	Round to oval, 2–4 in. long, glossy dark green on top, white beneath	Tiny, white, fragrant spring flowers (some find fragrance objectionable)	Takes any amount of pruning, but flower production may suffer. Leaves and fruit cause gastric distress
Myrica californica PACIFIC WAX MYRTLE	Evergreen	☼ ○ 4–6, 14–17, 20–24	To 25 ft. by 20 ft.	Glossy, dark green, paler beneath; narrow, 2–4 in.	Flowers inconspicuous. Purplish waxy nutlets in fall	Makes very large informal hedge without pruning. Looks good year-round
Osmanthus heterophyllus HOLLY-LEAF OSMANTHUS	Evergreen	☼ ◐ ○ ◖ 3–10, 14–24	6–20 ft. by 6–20 ft.	Dark green, shiny, spine-edged, to 2½ in. long	Small, white, fragrant, followed by blue-back berrylike fruits	'Gulftide' and 'Ilicifolius' more upright; 'Purpureus' with purple new growth; 'Variegatus' smaller and denser, with leaves edged in creamy white
Photinia fraseri	Evergreen	☼ ◖ 4–24	10–15 ft. by 10–20 ft.	Glossy, dark green, 2–5 in. long, bright red in youth	White, in clusters, in early spring	Prune to keep in bounds. Aphids may attack. *P. f.* 'Indian Princess' is smaller and more compact (to 5–6 ft.)
Plumbago auriculata CAPE PLUMBAGO	Semi-evergreen	☼ ◐ ○ ◖ 8, 9, 12–24	6 ft. by 8–10 ft.	Fresh, light green, small	Light blue or white, blooms through much of the year	Needs well-drained soil and protection from desert sun. Combines well with other plants
Rhamnus frangula 'Columnaris' TALLHEDGE BUCKTHORN	Deciduous	☼ ◐ ◖ 1–7, 10–13	To 12–15 ft. by 4 ft.	Roundish, glossy, dark green, 1–3 in.	Small clusters inconspicuous; fruit red, turning to black	Plant 2½ ft. apart for uniform hedge that can be kept as low as 4 ft. Regular water in youth, moderate water once established
Thuja occidentalis 'Fastigiata' AMERICAN ARBORVITAE	Evergreen	☼ ◐ ◖ ● 2–9, 15–17, 21–24	To 25 ft. by 5 ft.	Scalelike, in flat sprays, very dense	None	Best with some shade and more water in hot areas. Set 4 ft. apart for dense hedge. Red spider mites only likely pest
Westringia fruticosa	Evergreen	☼ ◖ ● 8, 9, 14–24	3–6 ft. by 4–8 ft.	Needlelike leaves medium gray green above and white beneath	Small white flowers late winter; year-round in mild areas	Spreading, loose growth. Mixes well with other gray-leaves plants. Needs light, well-drained soil

☼ **Full sun;** ◐ **Part shade;** ● **Full shade;** ○ **Drought tolerant;** ◖ **Little water;** ● **Regular water;** ◖◖ **Ample water.**

To find your climate zone, see pages 14–21.

Ground Covers

One of the truly indispensible tricks for reducing garden maintenance is to plant areas of your property with ground covers—low-growing, often long-lived plants that provide various degrees of coverage. Whether you use them as verdant replacements for paving, borders, or lawns, the key is to select the appropriate ground cover plant for your needs; these pages will help you do that.

The easiest ground covers to maintain are those adapted to your region, and to the sunlight, soil and irrigation available. Some useful ground cover plants can be knee-high or taller, but from a distance they offer much of a lawn's uniform neatness in the areas where foot traffic is infrequent. The best plants for weed control grow densely and high enough (usually over a foot) to crowd out unwanted seedlings.

Resilient low-growing herbs such as chamomile or woolly thyme can take light foot traffic, and emit a pleasant fragrance when stepped on, but weeds can easily take root in these low-growers and can only be removed by occasional hand-pulling. Coarser ground covers or those with delicate foliage may be used in light traffic areas if you strategically place stepping stones where you occasionally walk. Refer to page 198 for specific planting instructions for ground covers.

Pick a plant. *A ground cover is not a type of plant, but one that is used in a certain way. Perennial gazania (above) flowers throughout the year. The low-growing herb chamomile (right) can replace a lawn. It won't tolerate much foot traffic but is deliciously fragrant. Many succulent plants, such as trailing ice plant* (Lampranthus), *form a dense, drought-tolerant ground cover.*

Creeping along. Liriope spicata, *or creeping lily turf, is slow-growing, but spreads widely to form an interesting lawn replacement that will smother out most weeds. The path laid between these grassy banks is simple cobblestones.*

GROUND COVERS WHERE YOU NEED THEM

For shade. Under trees or high decks, in narrow sideyards, or in other places where sunlight barely penetrates, proven performers include ajuga, sweet woodruff, redwood sorrel, fragrant *Sarcococca*, and baby's tears.

For sun. An expanse of heat-tolerant ground cover can add vibrancy to a sun-washed landscape. Drought-tolerant choices include Carmel creeper, Mexican daisy, sunrose, 'Flower Carpet' rose (see p. 93), lantana, African daisy, stonecrop, and ice plant *(Lampranthus*, see p. 114).

For fire protection. A 200-foot greenbelt or "reduced fuel zone" is recommended around the perimeter of properties in wildfire-prone areas. Plants that are suitable for this area include carpet bugle, snow-in-summer, bearberry cotoneaster, gazania, sedum, and star jasmine.

For traffic. No ground cover will tolerate football games as well as does turfgrass, but some can withstand light pummeling, especially if interspersed with stepping stones. Consider pussy toes *(Antennaria dioica)*, chamomile, thyme, blue star creeper, and baby's tears.

For slopes. Plants with dense, strong roots provide the most efficient, low-cost erosion control for slopes. Try Carmel creeper, bearberry cotoneaster, cape honeysuckle, periwinkle, or rosemary.

For fragrance. Some plants emit their fragrance only when stepped on; thyme and chamomile are among them. Others, such as roses, jasmine, rosemary, and *Sarcococca* release fragrance continually from their flowers or foliage.

EASY-CARE GROUND COVERS FOR WESTERN GARDENS

Botanical name COMMON NAME	Sun & Water/ Zones	Size & Appearance	Form & Comments
Ajuga reptans CARPET BUGLE	☼ ◑ ● All zones	3–6 in. by 1 ft. Dark green to bronzy, leaves to 4 in. wide; blue flowers on 6-in. spikes, spring to early summer	Spreads quickly by runners to form a dense, low, evergreen mat. Plant 12–18 in. apart. Remove old flower spikes. Needs good drainage
Antennaria dioica PUSSY TOES	☼ ○ ● All zones	1 in. by 6 in. Tiny, woolly, medium green leaves; pinkish white flowers, rising 3 in. above leaves in early summer	Low evergreen mat that spreads evenly. Good for dry, sunny spot in well-drained soil, or for filler around stepping stones
Arctostaphylos uva-ursi BEARBERRY, KINNIKINNICK	☼ ◑ ○ ● 1–9, 14–24	3–10 in. by 15 ft. Small round, glossy, leaves turn reddish in cold. Tiny white to pink urn-shaped flowers in early spring, followed by small red fruit	Creeping evergreen mat looks good all year. Plant in well-drained soil and mulch (see p. 188). Good on hillsides, paths, over walls. 'Massachusetts' and 'Point Reyes' are excellent. Related *A.* 'Emerald Carpet' (zones 6–9, 14–24) is up to 12 in., slightly mounding
Arctotheca calendula CAPE WEED	☼ ○ ● 8, 9, 13–24	1 ft. by 2 ft. Gray-green leaves are deeply divided, evergreen. Bright yellow daisies, year round but heaviest in spring	Space 1½–3 ft. apart. Spreads rapidly. Best for large areas, hillsides. Mow once per year
Arctotis acaulis AFRICAN DAISY	☼ ● 7–9, 14–24	6 in. by 2 ft. Woolly or rough, lobed leaves. Flowers 3-in.-wide, yellow with purplish centers	Spreading perennial resembles *Osteospermum*. Hybrids have many colors, but may self-sow and revert to orange
Artemisia caucasica SILVER SPREADER	☼ ○ ● All zones	6 in. by 2 ft. Silvery green aromatic leaves. Small yellow summer flowers	Low, spreading evergreen shrub, good for banks. Plant 1–2 ft. apart in well-drained soil. Cut back almost to ground any time to renew vigor. Divide in spring or fall (see p. 216)
Astilbe chinensis 'Pumila' FALSE SPIRAEA MEADOW SWEET	☼ ◑ ● ●● 2–7, 14–17; short lived in 8, 9, 18–24	8–12 in. by 12–18 in. Bright green leaves, sturdy, fernlike in shape. Lilac pink flower clusters 1 ft. tall in summer	Makes a low evergreen mat, to 4 in. deep, in full sun to part shade (zones 2–7, 14–17) or shade (zones 8, 9, 18–24). Best in moist, rich soil. Shear back after flowering. Apply a time-release all-purpose fertilizer in spring
Baccharis pilularis DWARF COYOTE BRUSH	☼ ○ ● 5–11, 14–24	8–24 in. by 6 ft. Small, toothed, bright green leaves; insignificant flowers	Dense, billowy evergreen mat. Shear in early spring before new growth begins (see p. 213), then feed with nitrogen-rich fertilizer. Choose male varieties 'Twin Peaks' or 'Pigeon Point', as females produce messy seeds. May get spider mites (see pp. 220–221)
Campanula poscharskyana SERBIAN BELLFLOWER	◑ ● 1–9, 14–24	1 ft. by 3–4 ft. Small, bright green, leaves. Small blue to lavender starlike flowers, spring to early summer	Vigorous, forms billowing mass. Evergreen in mild climates. Takes considerable sun near coast. Cut back hard every 2–3 years (see p. 216). Similar but more refined *C. portenschlagiana*, DALMATION BELLFLOWER, makes a 4–7-in. mounding mat, prefers more shade
Ceanothus griseus horizontalis CARMEL CREEPER	☼ ○ ● 1–9, 14–24	2 ft. by 5 ft. Glossy, oval, bright green leaves, to 2 in. long. Light blue flowers in 1-in. clusters in early spring	Low, spreading, evergreen shrub; needs good drainage. Water through first year only. In zones 1–3, 8, and 9, check with local nursery for best varieties. *C. g. h.* 'Yankee Point' is excellent
Cerastium tomentosum SNOW-IN-SUMMER	☼ ◑ ○ ● All zones	8 in. by 3 ft. Silvery gray, tiny leaves and white flowers covering plant in early summer	Plant 1 ft. apart in well-drained soil. Needs some shade in hot areas. Spreads vigorously, but may die out after a few years. Good in small areas, between stepping stones, on dry banks
Chamaemelum nobile CHAMOMILE	☼ ◑ ● All zones	3–12 in. by 3–12 in. Bright fresh green, finely cut, aromatic leaves. Small yellow buttons or daisies in summer	Soft, spreading, evergreen mass. Plant between stepping stones or 1 ft. apart for interesting small-scale lawn substitute. Mow every 2–3 months. 'Treneague', with no flowers, needs no mowing
Chlorophytum comosum SPIDER PLANT	◑ ● ● ● 15–17, 19–24	1 ft. by 1 ft. Arching, wide grassy blades to 3 ft. long. Tiny, white flower spikes	Makes uniform, soft, evergreen clumps, spreading by offshoots (plant them in pots for house plants). Plant 2 ft. apart in good soil for quick cover. 'Variegatum' and 'Vittatum' are both white striped
Correa pulchella AUSTRALIAN FUCHSIA	☼ ◑ ● 14–24	2 ft. by 8 ft. Small leaves are green above, gray beneath. Light pink, bell-shaped flowers suspended from branches Nov.–Apr.	Low, dense, spreading, evergreen shrub thrives in poor soil but must have good drainage. Good for rugged slopes but dislikes reflected heat. 'Orange Flame' (orange flowers), *C.* 'Dusky Bells' (deep red flowers), and *C.* 'Ivory Bells' (creamy white) available
Cotoneaster dammeri BEARBERRY COTONEASTER	☼ ○ ● All zones	3–12 in. by 10 ft. wide. Bright, glossy 1-in. oval leaves. Flowers small, white, in spring, followed by bright red fruit	Evergreen. Fast, low grower. Good for dry slopes. Prune awkward or dead branches all the way back. Similar *C.* 'Lowfast' spreads quickly to 15 ft. Both susceptible to fireblight disease (see p. 231)

☼ **Full sun;** ◑ **Part shade;** ● **Full shade;** ○ **Drought tolerant;** ● **Little water;** ● **Regular water;** ●● **Ample water.**   **To find your climate zone, see pages 14–21.**

Botanical name COMMON NAME	Sun & Water/ Zones	Size & Appearance	Form & Comments
Erigeron karvinskianus MEXICAN DAISY, SANTA BARBARA DAISY	☼ ☽ ○ ◐ 8, 9, 12–24	10–20 in. by 3 ft. Narrow, 1-in. leaves and daisylike flowers white to pink, year round	Vigorous but delicate-looking perennial. Use as filler between larger plants; let spill over a wall, container, or raised bed. Shear back when rangy (see p. 216)
Euonymus fortunei radicans COMMON WINTER CREEPER	☼ ☽ ◐ 4–9, 14–17	12 in. by 20 ft. Dark green, thick-textured leaves are 1 in. long	Tough, evergreen, vining shrub forms undulating mat on flat ground. Rootlets cling to vertical surfaces (will climb walls, rocks) or root in moist ground. Avoid overhead watering
Fragaria chiloensis WILD STRAWBERRY, SAND STRAWBERRY	☼ ☽ ◐ ◐ 4–24	6 in. by 15 in. Dark green, glossy leaves, with 3 lobes. White flowers like tiny roses, in spring, (rarely) followed by red fruit	Forms lush, low, evergreen mat. Takes sun at coast, some shade inland. Plant 1 ft. apart in slightly acid soil, mow annually, and feed with balanced fertilizer in late spring (see p. 189)
Galium odoratum SWEET WOODRUFF	● ◐ ◑ 1–6, 15–17	6 in. high by 12 in. Aromatic leaves on erect stems. Tiny white flowers, mainly in late spring and summer	Makes a solid evergreen carpet in rich, wet soil. Spreads rapidly and can become a pest. If it looks ragged, mow it in winter
Gazania	☼ ○ ◐ Annual; perennial in 8–24	14 in. by 18 in. Dark green to gray green leaves, often lobed. Flowers 4 in. wide on 6-in.-long stems, intermittently all year	Clumping types form low dense mounds; many hybrids available in yellow, orange, white, pink, and reddish purple. Trailing types spread rapidly by long stems, with yellow, white, orange, or bronze flowers. Feed both once in spring with a slow-release fertilizer
Geranium macrorrhizum CRANESBILL	☼ ☽ ◐ All zones	8 in. by 12 in. Nearly evergreen leaves are deeply divided, 4–8 in. wide; fragrant. Small magenta, pink, or white flowers are held above foliage in early summer	Dense, lush cover. Plant in well-drained soil 2 ft. apart in small bed or raised container—can overwhelm smaller plants. Deadhead (see p. 216)
Helianthemum nummularium SUNROSE	☼ ◐ All zones	8 in. by 3 ft. Glossy green to gray leaves to 1 in. long. Large numbers of small flowers, in clusters, Apr.–June in California and Arizona, May–July in Northwest, in reds, oranges, yellows, pinks, peach, salmon, and white	Small, spreading, evergreen shrub. Plant 2 ft. apart in well-drained soil in fall or early spring. Good near rocks. Shear after flowering (see p. 216). Many types available
Hypericum calycinum AARON'S BEARD, CREEPING ST. JOHNSWORT	☼ ☽ ◐ ◐ 2–24	To 1 ft. by 18 in. Leaves to 4 in. long, medium green in sun, yellow green in shade. Flowers bright yellow, 3 in. across	Vigorous informal spreader in any well-drained soil; will take over if not confined. Shear to ground in winter once every 2–3 years (see p. 216)
Juniperus JUNIPER	☼ ☽ ○ ◐ All zones	Varies by species. Needles or scales in wide range of colors from rich to dull green, blue, gray, olive, or variegated	Several species make excellent, dense ground covers. Two are *J. conferta*, SHORE JUNIPER (1 ft. by 8 ft.), and *J. chinensis procumbens*, JAPANESE GARDEN JUNIPER (3 ft. by 20 ft.)
Lamium maculatum DEAD NETTLE, SPOTTED NETTLE	● ◑ All zones	To 6 in. by 2–3 ft. Heart shaped, gray-green leaves have silvery markings. Flowers are white or pink, in clusters, May–Sept.	Vigorous perennial spreader for rich, moist soils. Space 6 in. apart for quick cover. Occasionally remove old, shabby growth. Best are 'Beacon Silver', 'Chequers' (pink flowers), and 'White Nancy' (white flowers)
Lantana montevidensis	☼ ○ ◐ 8–10, 12–22	1 ft. by 3 ft. Dark, small, textured leaves, often with red or purplish tinge, have strong fragrance when crushed. Rosy lilac flower clusters 1 in. across in Jan.–Aug., year round in frost-free areas	Evergreen freeform sprawler; may be annual in cold-winter climates. Pinch back monthly and prune hard each spring (see p. 216). A white-flowered form is available
Laurentia fluviatilis BLUE STAR CREEPER	☼ ☽ ◐ 4, 5, 8, 9, 14–24	2–3 in. by 6 in. Tiny, medium green leaves, very flat to ground. Pale blue, star-shaped flowers are sprinkled throughout plant in late spring and summer	Low and creeping, giving solid cover of small areas. Can take some foot traffic. Plant 6 in. apart for cover within a year
Liriope spicata CREEPING LILY TURF	☼ ☽ ◐ All zones	8 in. by 8 in., spreading. Deep green, grasslike leaves rise from center. Pale lilac to white flower spikes are held just above foliage	Forms evergreen clumps and spreads widely. Plant in sun near coast, partial shade inland, in good soil, and mow only if it looks shabby. 'Silver Dragon' has white-striped leaves. *Ophiopogon japonicus*, MONDO GRASS, is smaller, slower-growing, prefers more shade
Mazus reptans	☼ ☽ ◐ 1–7; evergreen in 14–24	2 in. by 4 in. Lance-shaped leaves to 1 in. long, bright green. Clusters of 2–5, purple to lavender flowers with white and yellow markings, in spring and early summer	Creeper for small-scale situations in moist, rich soil. Good between stepping stones
Myoporum parvifolium	☼ ◐ 8, 9, 12–16, 18–24	3 in. by 9 ft. Bright green, narrow leaves. White, ½-in. wide flowers in summer, followed by purple berries	Rapidly spreading, tough evergreen. Space 6 ft. apart in any but rocky soil for solid cover within 6 months. 'Putah Creek' slightly smaller

☼ **Full sun**; ☽ **Part shade**; ● **Full shade**; ○ **Drought tolerant**; ◐ **Little water**; ◐ **Regular water**; ◑ **Ample water.**   To find your climate zone, see pages 14–21.

Botanical name / COMMON NAME	Sun & Water / Zones	Size & Appearance	Form & Comments
Osteospermum fruticosum TRAILING AFRICAN DAISY, FREEWAY DAISY	☼ ◔ 8, 9, 12–24	6 in. by 2 ft. Leaves 1 in. long, medium to light green. Flowers purple to white, 2 in. wide, throughout the year but heaviest in Nov.–Mar.	Evergreen spreader best in open areas, excellent near seashore. Plant in well-drained soil 2 ft. apart for cover within a year. Mow or cut back hard in midsummer to encourage bushiness
Oxalis oregana REDWOOD SORREL OREGON OXALIS	◑ ● ◆ 4–9, 14–24	2–10 in. by 6 in. Velvety, medium green, cloverlike leaves to 4 in. wide. Small, pink or white flowers with lavender veins, in spring, sometimes fall	Lush carpet in moist, shady places. Looks good with ferns
Pachysandra terminalis JAPANESE SPURGE	◑ ● ◆◆ 1–10, 14–21	10 in. by 12 in. Dark green, thick, oval leaves in clusters. Small, fluffy, white flowers, in spring, followed by tiny white fruit	Dense low mat of attractive foliage. Plant in rich, acid soil. Good transition between lawn and shade-loving shrubs. 'Variegata' has white-edged leaves, 'Green Carpet' is lower-growing and more compact
Polygonum capitatum KNOTWEED	☼ ◑ ● ◔ ◆ 8, 9, 12–24	8 in. by 20 in. Small, dark green leaves, attractively marked with pink; small, pink, round-headed flowers held above leaves most of the year	Dense, vigorous, spreading carpet is better if confined or planted in a wild area
Ribes viburnifolium CATALINA PERFUME	☼ ◑ ○ 8, 9, 14–24	3 ft. by 12 ft. Round, leathery, dark green, 1 in. wide leaves are fragrant in rain or when crushed. Pink to purplish flowers Feb.–Apr.	Evergreen spreading low shrub. Takes full sun or half shade on coast, part shade inland. Plant in well-drained soil in fall. To keep low, cut out upright stems. May get spider mites near coast (see pp. 220–221)
Rosmarinus officinalis ROSEMARY	☼ ○ ◔ 4–24	2 ft. by 4–8 ft. Needlelike, aromatic leaves, glossy dark green above and grayish white beneath. Clusters of tiny lavender to blue to white flowers, in winter, spring, and sometimes in fall	Spreading evergreen shrubby herb. Plant 2 ft. apart for quick cover. Once established, needs no water, except in hottest areas. Choose variety with low, spreading habit, such as 'Collingwood Ingram', 'Huntington Blue' ('Huntington Carpet'), or 'Prostratus'
Rubus pentalobus BRAMBLE	☼ ◑ ◔ 4–6, 14–17	1 ft. by 1 ft. Small, round, dark green leaves, ruffled and crinkled, with occasional red or bronze fall color. Flowers small, white, simple, followed by edible berries	Evergreen spreader, evenly to 3 ft. per year. Plant in any soil with good drainage. 'Emerald Carpet' widely available
Sarcococca hookerana humilis	● ◔ 4–9, 14–24	1 ft. by 8 ft. Glossy, narrow oval, dark green leaves closely set on branches. Tiny, white flowers are hidden but fragrant in spring, followed by blue-black fruit	Forms a dark, fragrant evergreen carpet. Plant in rich soil in bright to deepest shade. May get scale (see pp. 220–221)
Sedum spurium STONECROP	☼ ◑ ○ ◔ All zones	2 in. by 6 in. Succulent roundish leaves, 1 in. across, dark bronzy green. Tiny pink flowers in summer	Uniform spreading mat for well-drained soil in sunny nooks, around stepping stones. 'Dragon's Blood' has bronzy leaves and rosy flowers
Soleirolia soleirolii BABY'S TEARS	◑ ● ◆ ◆◆ 4–24	1 in. high. Tiny, round, bright to medium green leaves	Aggressive creeper forms a lush mat. Can be invasive. Use with other shade and moisture lovers
Stachys byzantina LAMB'S EARS	☼ ◑ ◔ All zones	1 ft. by 3 ft. Soft, thick, woolly, white leaves lie close to the ground. Purple flower stalks in June–July	Good edging where its soft leaves can be touched. Damaged by frost and rain but recovers quickly. Cut back in spring, deadhead (see p. 216). 'Silver Carpet' has no flowers
Tecomaria capensis CAPE HONEYSUCKLE	☼ ◑ ◔ 12, 13, 16, 18–24	2 ft. by 15 ft. Dark green, shiny leaflets and brilliant orange to red, 2-in. flowers, Oct. through winter	Vining shrub—excellent for scrambling down hot, steep slopes. Prune out upright growth (see p. 213). Needs good drainage
Teucrium chamaedrys GERMANDER	☼ ○ ◔ All zones	1 ft. by 2 ft. Dark green, tiny, dense leaves. Small, red-purple or white flowers, in loose spikes in summer	Low, neat-looking evergreen mat needs twice-yearly shearing (see p. 216). Plant 2 ft. apart in any soil with excellent drainage
Thymus praecox arcticus (*T. serpyllum*) MOTHER-OF-THYME, CREEPING THYME	☼ ◑ ○ ◔ All zones	4 in. by 1 ft. Tiny, round, dark green, aromatic leaves. Small purplish or white flowers, June–Sept.	Plant 6 in. apart in well-drained soil. Good filler for small areas, as between pavers. Leaves can be used for seasoning. Attracts bees. *T. pseudolanuginosus*, WOOLLY THYME, similar, but with gray green, woolly leaves
Trachelospermum jasminoides STAR JASMINE	☼ ◑ ◔ 8–24	2 ft. by 5 ft. New leaves glossy, light green, darkening with maturity. White, sweetly-scented flowers in June–July (May–June in desert)	Evergreen vining shrub that eventually makes dense cover. Plant 2 ft. apart. Pinch tips to keep bushy, and cut out upright stems. Feed in spring, late summer with all-purpose fertilizer. May get scale, mealybugs, and red spider mites (see pp. 220–221)

☼ **Full sun;** ◑ **Part shade;** ● **Full shade;** ○ **Drought tolerant;** ◔ **Little water;** ◆ **Regular water;** ◆◆ **Ample water.**   **To find your climate zone, see pages 14–21.**

Turfgrasses

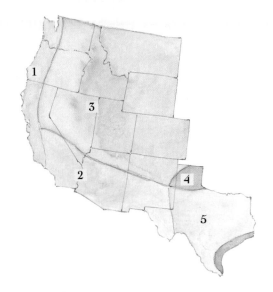

Traditional turfgrasses provide a perfect soft surface for children's play, sports activities, and simply lounging around. But not every garden needs a lawn. Although there's an attractive simplicity to maintaining a single crop plant such as lawn grass, weigh this against the amount of fertilizing, irrigating, mowing, weeding, and raking that the lawn requires. In fact, if the only person who ever walks on the lawn is the person who mows it, consider substituting a ground cover plant (see page 96) or an area of interesting paving.

Your climate plays a critical role in determining which grass species will be the easiest to care for (see map, right). Cool-season grasses are those that grow best between 60 and 75 degrees (generally spring and fall) and tolerate winter freezes—in hot weather they will grow slowly but remain green if well watered. Warm-season grasses prefer high temperatures and mild winters but turn brown during winter months. Although cool-season grasses such as bluegrass are well-adapted to parts of the country with abundant summer rainfall, they are not the best low-maintenance choice in arid areas. Information on specific grass types is given on page 103.

Recommendations for fertilizing lawns vary, but you can adjust the frequency of application according to how lush you wish your lawn to appear. See page 229 for more tips on keeping your lawn healthy.

Zone 1: West, Pacific Northwest
Winters are mild; summers cool. Rain is plentiful except during summer. Cool-season grasses are recommended.

Zone 2: Southwest
Summers are torrid, rainfall is scarce, and soils are dry. Warm-season grasses do best. Overseed (sow annual seed) with ryegrass for winter color.

Zone 3: Mountains, Plains
Climate is semi-arid, with a wide temperature range. Drought-tolerant natives, such as bluegrass are recommended; others need frequent irrigation.

Zone 4: Midcentral
Summers are warm and humid; year-round rainfall is abundant. Plant cool-season grasses where winters are mild; warm-season grasses elsewhere.

Zone 5: Central South
Climate is warm and humid most of the year; winters are mild. Rainfall is typically abundant, with occasional droughts. Warm-season grasses do best.

Note: *These zones do not correspond directly to either* USDA *zones or* Sunset Western Garden Book *zones.*

EASY LAWN CARE

Irrigation is critical, and it's best to install an automatic sprinkler (not drip irrigation) system before the lawn is planted. An alternative is the use of a hose-end sprinkler (see page 192). Planting a lawn is best accomplished by using sod—it's quick, easy to establish, and the turf suppresses weeds. Plugs are available for some native grasses such as buffalo grass, but the turf coverage is slower and weeds must be suppressed while the plugs 'fill in' (for planting instructions, see page 199). In either case, soil preparation is key. During the growing season, mowing keeps the lawn trim and healthy—and cuts down weeds before they set seed; mow when the grass is one third higher than the recommended height for your turf, leaving the clippings in place to add nitrogen to the soil. Seasonal chores such as de-thatching and aerating will also help keep the lawn healthy; the latter jobs may best be handled by a landscaping company with specialized equipment.

Lawn looks. Rugged native grasses create rough-looking, interesting lawns where smooth playing surfaces are not needed. The introduction of a few attractive 'weeds' such as English daisy can create a naturalistic lawnscape that children enjoy. And a green space designed to be seen but rarely stepped on need not be grass at all, but a ground cover or meadow (see p. 105).

Winter green. Overseed dormant warm-season grasses in winter with annual ryegrass or tall fescue. Simply cut the grass very short, add 1 lb. of seed for each 100 sq. ft. of lawn, and turn on the sprinklers. The annual grass will fade away in spring, when you begin mowing the perennial grass at recommended heights.

Think small. A well-designed small lawn can do the job of a larger expanse of grass, and takes less time to fertilize, irrigate, and mow. Studies have shown that 600 square feet of turf—about 20 by 30 feet—is sufficient for most family activities—but not for sports activities.

Roundabout. Use kidney shapes or curves to accommodate changes in grade, or undulate the lawn edges to avoid placing grass in the deep shade of trees.

Cutting edge. You'll mow even faster if you install mowing strips, also called mow bands, around the perimeter of your lawn. A ribbon of smooth concrete, antiqued brick, or decorative flat pavers, just wide enough to accomodate the wheels of your lawnmower, will allow you to cut to the very edge of the grass, eliminating hand-trimming and damage to flowers or ground covers that border your lawn.

Small is all. *A lawn doesn't have to be big to be the centerpiece of a garden. In this design, a bench placed at the edge of the grass offers a place to sit and watch children playing. The workspace, including a hose, is easily accessible, yet concealed by evergreens. A small mower can be wheeled from the storage cupboard along the pavers to the lawn. Any run-off from the slope will not adversely affect the turf, but the lawn may require a little less irrigation on that side.*

EASY-CARE TURFGRASSES FOR WESTERN GARDENS

COMMON NAME Botanical name	Sun & Water/ Zones	Mowing height	Description	Comments
COOL-SEASON GRASSES				
COLONIAL BENT GRASS *Agrostis tenuis*	☼ ❀❀ All zones	Mow to ¾ in.	Fine, deep green leaves	Somewhat fussy; Astoria and Highland strains are less so, but still require more work than other cool-season species noted below. Prefers well-drained, slightly acid soil. Dislikes hot, dry conditions
BLUEGRASS, KENTUCKY BLUEGRASS *Poa pratensis*	☼ ❀ ❀❀ 1–11, 14–17	Mow to 2 in.; higher in summer	Soft, narrow, blue-green leaves	Best in a sunny, well-draining soil, with frequent mowing and regular irrigation. Higher maintenance than many other turfgrasses
DWARF TALL FESCUE *Festuca elatior*	☼ ◖ All zones	Mow to 3 in.	Stiff, dark green leaves	In dry-summer climates, the sturdy and more drought-tolerant tall fescues have become the most popular choice for lawns, play areas, and sports turf. New hybrids of the dwarfed tall fescues, such as 'Bonsai' and 'Twilight' are slow growers, need less water and less frequent mowing
RED FESCUE *Festuca rubra*	☼ ◐ ❀ All zones	Mow to 1½–2 in.	Leaves fine, narrow, dark green	Pasture grass, usually blended with other turfgrasses. Creeping red fescue is shade tolerant. Unmowed, red fescues make attractive meadows; they also control erosion on slopes
PERENNIAL RYEGRASS *Lolium perenne*	☼ ❀ 1–6, 15–17	Mow to ½ in cool weather; to 3 in. in summer	Fine leaves, shiny green	Can be difficult to mow, as stems and flowers lie flat. Recommended varieties include 'Pennfine', 'Manhattan'
WARM-SEASON GRASSES				
BERMUDA GRASS *Cynodon dactylon*	☼ ◖ 8–10, 12–24	Mow to ½–1 in.	Winter dormant. Fine, deep green leaves	A fast-growing subtropical grass that spreads rapidly by surface and underground runners. Tolerates heat. De-thatch every 2 years. Hybrids such as 'Tifdwarf', 'Tifgreen', and 'Santa Ana' have the most vigor; can be invasive
ST. AUGUSTINE GRASS *Stenotaphrum secundatum*	☼ ◐ ❀ 12, 13, 18–24	Mow to 3 in.; 2 in. during cooler weather	Coarse-textured	Tough grass native to southeastern U.S. Spreads by surface runners. Turns brown under 55° F. Requires a power mower to cut its stiff blades
ZOYSIA *Zoysia japonica* hybrids	☼ ● ◖ 7–10, 12–24	Mow to ½–1 in.	Winter dormant. Dark green, prickly leaves	Spreads vigorously in warm, humid regions. Zoysia offered in newspaper advertisements by Eastern sources may not be adapted to Western climates
NATIVE AND PRAIRIE GRASSES				
BLUE GRAMA *Bouteloua gracilis*	☼ ◖ 1–3, 7–11, 14–24	Mow to 1½ in.	Bluish green, fine leaves	Very pretty, bunching pasture grass to 20 in. high, with dark red to purple flower spikes in summer. Use as meadow grass or mow to make a lawn in alkaline soils. Native to mountain and plains regions; will stay green through winter in zones 1–3
BUFFALO GRASS *Buchloe dactyloides*	☼ ◖ 1–3, 10–11	Mow to 2–4 in.	Stiff, bright or dark green leaves	Promising hybrids of this midwest native make a dense, attractive turf that takes foot traffic. Spreads rapidly by surface runners once established. If left unmowed, forms irregular surface rather than smooth turf
CRESTED WHEATGRASS *Agropyron cristatum*	☼ ◖ 1–3, 10	Mow to 2 in.	Fine green leaves	A bunching grass native to mountain regions, adapted to dry summers. Irrigate by soaking to a soil depth of 18–20 in. every 4 weeks. Western wheatgrass, *A. smithii*, will slowly form a sod and tolerates extreme temperatures

☼ Full sun; ◐ Part shade; ● Full shade; ○ Drought tolerant; ◖ Little water; ❀ Regular water; ❀❀ Ample water.

To find your climate zone, see pages 14–21.

left to right St. Augustine, dwarf fescue, ryegrass, 'Santa Ana' Bermuda, 'El Toro' zoysia

Ornamental Grasses

Once found mostly in prairies or native landscapes, elegant selections of ornamental grasses and grasslike plants are now firmly established in Western gardens. Adaptable, graceful, and often drought-tolerant, they suit borders, containers, meadows, and pondsides. Use taller grassy plants to make a hedge or screen; plant the smaller types in groups among flower beds to get the benefit of their airy textures and leaf colors—which range from bright red bloodgrass to pitch black mondo grass or powder blue fescue. Many sprout feathery seed heads that glitter in sun and wave with breezes.

Many ornamental grasses are long-lived and are rarely bothered by pests—even voracious deer avoid them. Occasional "finger-combing" removes the dead leaves of less sharp-edged types (such as blue fescue); others need nothing more than a once-a-year haircut in early spring (see page 217).

The problem with many grasses is that they grow *too* well. Those that spread by runners, such as some bamboos, can be hard to keep in bounds. Clumping grasses, such as fescue, remain where they're planted; but choose species that won't self-seed. Jubata grass *(Cortaderia jubata)* is a weedy pest in much of Coastal California; *Pennisetum setaceum* is also considered by many in Southern California to be a weed. The Guide on pages 107–108 will help guide your selection; ask your local Cooperative Extension for recent recommendations.

Foils for foliage. Hybrid New Zealand flax comes in reds, greens, yellows, and variegated forms. Here, a burgundy form blends beautifully with sea holly (Eryngium amethystinum) *and Mexican feather grass (above). Pennisetum setaceum 'Rubrum' (right) is a favorite with its burgundy foliage and pink feathery seed flowers.*

GRASSES IN THE GARDEN

Waving from the window. You don't need a prairie to enjoy the waving, rustling plumes of ornamental grasses. Use shallow-rooted Mexican feather grass *(Stipa tenuissima)* or quaking grass *(Briza media)* in containers and even window boxes.

Thin strip. For a contemporary or Asian look, plant a narrow, somewhat shady sidewalk border with tufts of black mondo grass. A sunny strip, bordered on both sides by concrete, is the perfect spot for a rugged runner such as ribbon grass *(Phalaris arundinacea* 'Picta') or Japanese blood grass *(Imperata cylindrica* 'Rubra').

Mix n' match. Dwarf purple fountain grass *(Pennisetum setaceum* 'Eaton Canyon') pairs well in borders with airy plants such as pink *Gaura lindheimeri* or penstemons. Upright grasses, such as eulalia grass *(Miscanthus sinensis)* or spike-leafed New Zealand flax *(Phormium tenax)* look distinctive when planted in formal urns, singly, or surrounded by *Helichrysum* or ivy geraniums.

Wet spot. A variegated form of *Acorus gramineus*, matched with ferns and surrounded with baby's tears, can brighten up even the soggiest area; its ginger-citrus scent adds to the charm.

MEADOWS AND NATURAL LAWNS

A low-maintenance approach for a natural-looking landscape is a meadow of native or well-adapted grasses, allowed to grow freely rather than groomed like a traditional lawn. For a meadow that requires a little more effort, tall annual and perennial flowers (such as cosmos or purple coneflowers) can be added to the mix.

Most important is to choose plants that are not invasive—especially if a meadow forms just part of your overall landscape, or if your property borders others with traditional lawns. Blown by winds or carried by birds, grass seeds can quickly become pest plants in surrounding areas.

Despite its wild appearance, a meadow requires the same preparation as a turf lawn, though its upkeep will require less effort. First rid the ground of weeds by applying a herbicide. After digging in organic matter, plant your chosen grasses and wildflowers by plugs or seeding (see page 199). It's best to do this in mid autumn or late winter when seasonal rain can help get your meadow plants established.

Though even native grasses appreciate supplemental watering in the first summer, you may not need to irrigate your meadow again. In fall, let the grasses and flowers ripen their seedheads to bring textures (and invite birds) to this part of the garden. Mow old grass and spread fertilizer once a year, in the early spring before new growth emerges.

Here are some grass choices for meadow plantings. All may not be available in your local nursery; see pages 232–233 for other vendors.

Evergreen grasses for no-mow meadows

Briza media
PERENNIAL QUAKING GRASS

Carex tumulicola
BERKELEY SEDGE

Festuca amethystina
FESCUE

Sesleria autumnalis
AUTUMN MOOR GRASS

Sesleria heuffleriana
MEADOW MOOR GRASS

Meadow grasses to walk on

Buchloe dactyloides
BUFFALO GRASS (*dormant in winter*)

Carex pansa
CALIFORNIA MEADOW SEDGE

Carex texensis
CATLIN SEDGE

Accent grasses for sunny meadows

Miscanthus sinensis (varieties)
EULALIA *or* JAPANESE SILVER GRASS

Miscanthus transmorrisonensis
EVERGREEN MISCANTHUS

Muhlenbergia rigens
DEER GRASS

Pennisetum setaceum 'Rubrum'
RED FOUNTAIN GRASS

Stipa gigantea
GIANT FEATHER GRASS

Stipa tenuissima
MEXICAN FEATHER GRASS

New kind of lawn. *Buffalo grass (top) forms a clumping, naturalistic lawn that can tolerate foot traffic and needs little water. It can be mown or left to grow in clumps. A mixture of grasses and perennials (bottom) includes daisy-flowered Rudbeckia. A simple mown strip serves as a pathway.*

Glorious grasses. *Clockwise from top: Bold clumps of maiden grass and bronzy sedges accent a flagstone pathway. Burgundy New Zealand flax complements steely-blue fescues, with Meyers asparagus* (Asparagus densiflorus 'Myers') *in the foreground. Japanese silver grass in three varieties provides bold upright form and sensuous movement in the breeze. Sturdy* Pennisetum setaceum *tolerates heat, sun, and drought, but will reseed enthusiastically in mild climates.*

EASY-CARE ORNAMENTAL GRASSES FOR WESTERN GARDENS

Botanical Name COMMON NAME	Sun & Water/ Zones	Size	Leaves & Flowers	Comments
Acorus gramineus JAPANESE SWEET FLAG	◑ ◕ All zones	12–18 in. by 10 in.	Evergreen leaves to ¼ in. wide; glossy, rich green, in upright fans; fragrant when crushed. Flowers inconspicuous	Sturdy, slow-spreading perennial. 'Ogon' has arching, golden-yellow leaves; 'Variegatus' has white-edged leaves; 'Pusillus' is green dwarf, 3–4 in. tall. All are good in containers
Anthoxanthum odoratum SWEET VERNAL GRASS	☼ ◑ ● 3–24	8 in. by 12 in.	Evergreen leaves to ½ in. wide. Soft, medium green mounding clumps; fragrant when brushed. Showy, slender flower heads on upright stalks in late spring	Perennial. Excellent for meadow plantings. Occasional mowing keeps fresh-looking. Needs light shade in hot, dry areas
Briza media PERENNIAL QUAKING GRASS	◑ ● 2–24	12–18 in. by 10–15 in.	Evergreen leaves to ½ in. wide, soft and medium green, in upright clumps. Flowers are small, heart-shaped puffs in loose clusters on tall stalks; become pale golden brown	Sturdy perennial for accents, edging, or mass planting. Flowers excellent for cutting and drying. *B. maxima* is annual for all zones, full sun
Calamagrostis acutifolia FEATHER REED GRASS	☼ ● 2–24	2–4 ft. by 2½ feet.	Semi-evergreen leaves to ½ in. wide; glossy and medium green, arching from upright clumps. Large, feathery flower heads, greenish purple becoming golden brown, on upright 3–6 ft. stalks	Perennial. *C. arundinacea* 'Karl Foerster' is similar to more widely available *C. acutifolia* 'Stricta', except former has more plentiful, denser flowerstalks
Carex morrowii VARIEGATED JAPANESE SEDGE	◑ ◕ 1–9, 14–24	1–2 ft. by 2 ft.	Evergreen leaves to ½ in. wide; lustrous green with golden yellow lengthwise stripes, in rounded, weeping clumps. Flowers inconspicuous	Colorful perennial for edging and accents. 'Old Gold' ('Evergold' or 'Aureovariegata') has stripes in centers of leaves; 'Goldband' ('Kaganishiki') is smaller, with colored leaf margins
Carex pendula GIANT WOOD SEDGE	◑ ● ◕ 3–24	3–4 ft. by 3–5 ft.	Evergreen leaves to ¾ in. wide; dark green and strongly arching, in dense clumps. Flowers tiny and brown, in showy hanging strands on arching stalks	Slow-growing perennial for bold accents or mass planting. Handsome near ponds and streams
Chasmanthium latifolium SEA OATS	☼ ◑ ● All zones	2–5 ft. by 2 ft.	Deciduous leaves to ¾ in. wide and 6 in. long; soft, on stiff stems in upright clumps. Flowers large and showy, in flattened clusters; light green becoming copper brown	Highly decorative perennial for borders and accents. Flowers good in dried arrangements. Partial shade in hot-summer areas
Cyperus papyrus PAPYRUS	☼ ◑ ● ◕ 16, 17, 23, 24	6–10 ft. by 2 ft.	Tall, graceful, dark green stems topped by 1½-ft. wispy tufts	Grows well in rich, constantly moist soil. Protect from hot, dry winds. Good in containers
Deschampsia caespitosa HAIR GRASS	☼ ◑ ● All zones	1–3 ft. by 1–3 ft.	Semi-evergreen leaves to ½ in. wide; dark green, in dense upright clumps. Flowers tiny and abundant, in airy sprays on tall, slender, arching stalks	Perennial. 'Goldstaub' and 'Goldschleier' have golden yellow flowers; 'Bronze Veil' ('Bronzeschleier') has bronzy yellow flowers; 'Fairy's Joke' ('Vivipara') has tiny plantlets on arching stalks
Festuca amethystina FESCUE	☼ ◑ ● All zones	8–12 in. by 10–12 in.	Leaves evergreen and fine-textured; soft and bluish green, in dense, slightly weeping clumps. Narrow, feathery flower heads on slender stalks; bronzy green becoming tan	Perennial. 'Superba' has pale blue green foliage and pink flowers; 'April Gruen' has bluish, then olive, foliage; blue green flowers. Both require good drainage. *F. ovina* 'Glauca', BLUE FESCUE, is similar
Festuca californica CALIFORNIA FESCUE	☼ ◑ ◔ 7–10, 12–24	3 ft. by 3 ft.	Evergreen leaves to ½ in. wide; medium green to silver blue, in arching clumps. Airy flower sprays, pale green becoming tan, on long, arching stalks in spring	Excellent perennial for dry shade under oaks. Requires good drainage. 'Berkeley Blue' and 'Salmon Creek' have attractive blue foliage tinged burgundy
Hakonechloa macra 'Aureola' JAPANESE FOREST GRASS	◑ ● ● All zones	1½ ft., spreading	Deciduous. Slender, graceful, golden, weeping leaves	Prefers bright shade and regular water. Looks like a miniature bamboo. Needs rich, well-drained soil. Good in containers
Helictotrichon sempervirens BLUE OAT GRASS	☼ ● All zones	3 ft. by 3 ft.	Evergreen leaves to ½ in. wide; silver blue, in slightly arching, rounded clumps. Flowers infrequent	Reliable and dramatic perennial. Somewhat slow to mature. Groom periodically for best appearance. Requires good drainage
Imperata cylindrica 'Rubra' ('Red Baron') JAPANESE BLOOD GRASS	☼ ◑ ● 4–24	12–18 in. by 6–12 in.	Deciduous leaves to ½ in. wide; soft, bright green flushed with scarlet from tip downward; erect, in slowly spreading colonies	One of the showiest perennial grasses. Red color increases as leaves mature. Seen to best advantage backlit by early morning or late afternoon sunlight

☼ Full sun; ◑ Part shade; ● Full shade; ○ Drought tolerant; ◔ Little water; ● Regular water; ◕ Ample water.

To find your climate zone, see pages 14–21.

Botanical Name COMMON NAME	Sun & Water/ Zones	Size	Leaves & Flowers	Comments
Juncus 'Carmen's Japanese' CARMEN'S JAPANESE RUSH	☼ ◐ ● ●● 8–24	2½ ft. by 3 ft.	Evergreen leaves, fine-textured and cylindrical; dark green, in arching clumps. Tiny, golden flower clusters at ends of long stalks become seeds	Sturdy, fast-growing perennial. Highly adaptable; especially effective near ponds and streams
Leymus (Elymus) condensatus 'Canyon Prince' CANYON PRINCE WILD RYE	☼ ○ ◔ 7–10, 12–24	3–6 ft. by 2½ to 3 ft.	Evergreen leaves to 1 in. wide; powder blue, smooth and leathery, in upright, slightly arching, slowly spreading clumps. Flowers are showy, powder blue, wheatlike heads on tall stalks; mature to tan	Striking, well-behaved perennial. Dramatic color accent or background subject. Effective in containers
Luzula sylvatica SYLVAN WOODRUSH	◐ ● ● 2–24	8–12 in. by 12–18 in.	Evergreen leaves to ¾ in. wide; bright green, soft and glossy; arching in clumping rosettes. Flowers yellow green to brown, in clusters on tall slender stalks	Woodland perennial effective as ground cover among ferns and other shade lovers. Needs good drainage. 'Marginata' has leaves edged with cream
Milium effusum 'Aureum' BOWLES' GOLDEN GRASS	◐ ●● All zones	1½ ft. by 1 ft.	Arching, greenish-gold evergreen leaves. Flowers 12–18 in. above foliage in early summer	Bright accent for partly shady areas. Attractive clumps good in woodland gardens. Needs constant moisture
Miscanthus sinensis EULALIA GRASS	☼ ◐ ● ●● All zones	6 ft. by 3 ft.	Deciduous leaves to ¾ in. wide and 2½ ft. long; bright green, on upright stalks; clumping. Flowers are large and showy in feathery plumes on tall stalks; silver, tan or reddish purple	Popular perennial. 'Variegatus' has white-striped leaves, 'Gracillimus', MAIDEN GRASS, has narrow leaves and red flowers; 'Yaku Jima' has narrow leaves, grows 3-4 ft. tall; 'Zebrinus' has leaves banded with yellow
Miscanthus transmorrisonensis EVERGREEN SILVER GRASS	☼ ◐ ● 5–24	3 ft. by 4–5 ft.	Evergreen leaves to ½ in. wide, 2–3 ft. long; glossy green, on arching stems; clumping. Slender plumes, reddish becoming tan and fluffy, on arching stalks	Elegant perennial. Graceful compact form useful for accents, groupings, and large-scale ground cover. Flowers appear year-round
Muhlenbergia rigens DEER GRASS	☼ ◐ ○ 7–24	3 ft. by 3 ft.	Evergreen leaves to ½ in. wide; grey green becoming tan; long lasting	Sturdy perennial, upright in youth, mounding when mature. Tolerant of most soils, conditions
Panicum virgatum SWITCH GRASS	☼ ◐ ◔ ●● 1–11, 14–21	3 to ft. by 2 ft.	Deciduous leaves to ½ in. wide; gray green or silver blue in tight, upright clumps. Airy flower sprays, pink fading to sliver, white or tan, on upright stalks	Tolerant perennial. 'Haense Herms' has grey green leaves that turn red-orange in fall; 'Heavy Metal' is silver blue, bright yellow in fall
Pennisetum alopecuroides 'Moudry' BLACK-FLOWERED FOUNTAIN GRASS	☼ ● 3–24	2 ft. by 2-3 ft.	Deciduous leaves to ¾ in. wide; glossy rich green, dropping, in dense clumps. Showy brown black plumes appear in late summer or border plantings	Foliage turns yellow-orange then tan in fall. Flowers can be cut while immature for dried arrangements
Pennisetum setaceum 'Rubrum' ('Cupreum') PURPLE FOUNTAIN GRASS	☼ ◐ ○ ◔ 8–24	4 ft. by 4 ft.	Evergreen leaves to ½ in. wide; glossy red-purple and arching in mounded clumps. Showy pinkish purple plumes on long, arching stalks	Tender perennial grown as annual in colder climates. Rapid-growing in warm soil and full sun. Does not set seed, as does *P. setaceum*. Needs good drainage
Phalaris arundinacea RIBBON GRASS	☼ ◐ ● ●● 1–10, 14–24	2–3 ft. by 3 ft.	Semi-evergreen leaves to 1 in. wide, 6 in. long; bright green, striped white, pink or cream; drooping in spreading mounds. Soft white spikes on tall stalks, turning tan	Fast-growing perennial. 'Picta' has white stripes; 'Mervyn Feesey' ('Feesey's Form') has pink and white center stripes; 'Dwarf Garters' ('Wood's Dwarf') is compact, striped white and lavender
Sesleria autumnalis AUTUMN MOOR GRASS	☼ ● 3–24	12–18 in. by 15 in.	Evergreen leaves to ¼ in. wide; yellow green in upright, slightly arching clumps. Slender flowerheads on tall stalks, green maturing to brown; long lasting	Sturdy perennial. Useful as border, mass, or ground cover planting. Delicate-looking flower spikes resemble miniature cattails
Stipa gigantea GIANT FEATHER GRASS	☼ ◔ ● 4–9, 14–24	2 ft. by 2 ft.	Evergreen leaves to ⅛ in. wide; gray green, arching in dense clumps. Oatlike, golden yellow flowers in large airy heads on 3–6 ft. stalks	Spectacular giant perennial. Needs little water once established. Provide good drainage. Showy flowers are long lasting, good in dried arrangements; sets little seed
Stipa tenuissima MEXICAN FEATHER GRASS	☼ ● 4–24	1–2 ft. by 2 ft.	Semi-evergreen leaves are fine textured; silky, lime green drying to tan, in dense mounding clumps. Flowers delicate, pale green becoming golden	Vigorous but short-lived perennial. Cut back hard (during warm weather) to renew growth. Requires good drainage. Can self-sow on moist soils

☼ Full sun; ◐ Part shade; ● Full shade; ○ Drought tolerant; ◔ Little water; ● Regular water; ●● Ample water.

To find your climate zone, see pages 14–21.

THE ORNAMENTAL GARDEN

Grass Medley

An island of weaving panicles, this all-grass arrangement shows what can be done with a single plant group that's as diverse as ornamental grasses. Silvery fescues form a front-of-the-border transition to surrounding paving or gravel; bright red Japanese blood grass punctuates the greens and golds of its more muted cousins. For further emphasis, place a rusted metal sculpture or a terracotta birdbath in the center.

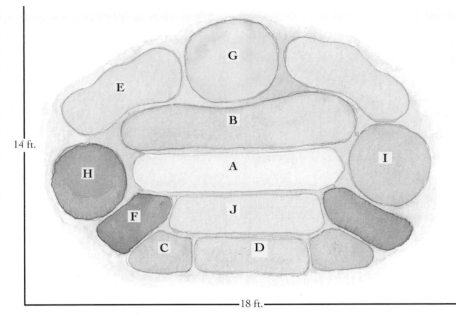

14 ft.

18 ft.

Festuca amethystina
FESCUE

Pennisetum alopecuroides 'Moudry'
BLACK-FLOWERING PENNISETUM

Stipa tenuissima
MEXICAN FEATHER GRASS

THE PLANTS

A. *Briza media* (5)
PERENNIAL QUAKING GRASS

B. *Calamagrostis arundinacea* 'Karl Foerster' (5)
FOERSTER'S FEATHER REED GRASS

C. *Festuca amethystina* (13)
FESCUE

D. *Festuca cinerea* 'Blausilber' (11)
BLUE-SILVER FESCUE

E. *Helictotrichon sempervirens* (5)
BLUE OAT GRASS

F. *Imperata cylindrica* 'Rubra' (13)
JAPANESE BLOOD GRASS

G. *Miscanthus sinensis* 'Gracillimus' (1)
MAIDEN GRASS

H. *Miscanthus sinensis* 'Yaku Jima' (1)
JAPANESE SILVER GRASS

I. *Pennisetum alopecuroides* 'Moudry' (1)
BLACK-FLOWERING PENNISETUM

J. *Stipa tenuissima* (13)
MEXICAN FEATHER GRASS

Ferns

O
ften overlooked in the nursery, ferns make ideal plants for shady, low-maintenance gardens. Naturalize them in quiet woodland gardens, beside streams, or beneath a grouping of trees. Use them as fillers in the shady flower bed, or mass them as ground covers where grass refuses to grow.

Ferns can look at home in formal settings, set into geometric beds bordered with emerald green boxwood, or providing a feathery backdrop to drifts of white impatiens. A damp, shady side-yard along the north side of your house can be an ideal place for a fern garden.

Although native western forms can take summer droughts in stride, even these tough and resilient species will look lusher if you give them regular summer water. Set up a drip irrigation system or hide a soaker hose beneath a mulch of wood chips (see page 192).

Routine maintenance for ferns is simple: trim off dead or injured fronds once a year (see page 217), and fertilize the plants occasionally with a diluted liquid fertilizer. The ferns listed on the facing pages harbor few pests; even snails and slugs usually do not chew them.

Shady splendor. *The emerging golden fiddleheads of young ferns bring an unusual color to the spring garden (above, left). Dramatic tree ferns (Dicksonia) can be used as accent plants in entryways, or underplanted themselves with shade-loving clivia. This one (above, right) is at a mature height. Chartreuse mother fern (Asplenium bulbiferum) is underplanted here with white impatiens (left); it draws the eye even in deep shade.*

EASY-CARE FERNS FOR WESTERN GARDENS

Botanical name COMMON NAME	Sun & Water/ Zones	Height/ Spread	Form and Foliage	Comments
Adiantum aleuticum (formerly *A. pedatum*) FIVE-FINGER FERN	☼ ● 💧💧 1–9, 14–21	1–2½ ft. by 1–2½ ft.	Rich green fronds fork in fingerlike pattern on slender stems	Watch for snails and slugs (see pp. 220–221). Delicate, airy look
Asparagus densiflorus 'Myers' MYERS ASPARAGUS	☼ ◐ 💧 💧 12–24	2 ft. by 2–3 ft.	Many stiff, upright stems densely covered with needlelike leaves	Not a true fern, but excellent for combining with shade, container plants. *A. d.* 'Sprengeri', SPRENGER ASPARAGUS, has arching, drooping stems; tolerates full shade or sun, poor soil
Asplenium bulbiferum MOTHER FERN	● 💧💧 15–17, 20–24	To 4 ft. by 4 ft.	Light green, lacy fronds emerge symmetrically to form graceful clump	Watch for snails and slugs (see pp. 220–221). Tiny plantlets appear along fronds and can be removed and planted
Athyrium filix-femina LADY FERN	● 💧💧 1–9, 14–24	To 4 ft. by 4 ft., spreading	Billowing clusters of lacy fronds arise from a short trunk	Remove brown fronds in spring (see p. 217). Vigorous yet graceful
Athyrium nipponicum 'Pictum' JAPANESE PAINTED FERN	● 💧💧 1–9, 14–24	1½ ft. by 1½ ft.	Makes a tight clump of fronds. Leaflets purple at base, then lavender, then gray green at tips	Same culture as for *A. filix-femina*. One of the most colorful ferns
Blechnum spicant DEER FERN	● 💧 1–9, 14–17	1–3 ft. by 1–3 ft.	Narrow, dark green, lance-shaped fronds arise in vase shape	Evergreen and tough—looks good all year. New fronds often reddish or rich brown
Cyathea cooperi AUSTRALIAN TREE FERN	☼ ◐ 💧 15–24	To 20 ft. by 12. ft.	Upright with broad bright green fronds to 6 ft.	Dramatic. Hardy to 20° F. Hairs on leafstalks can irritate skin
Dicksonia antarctica TASMANIAN TREE FERN	◐ ● 💧 8, 9, 14–17, 19–24	To 15 ft. by 12 ft.	Many 3–6 ft., delicate-looking evergreen fronds emerge from thick, reddish-brown trunk	Best out of wind. Takes full sun in Zones 17 and 24. Hardiest tree fern, slow growing. Easily transplanted
Dryopteris erythrosora AUTUMN FERN	◐ ● 💧💧 4–9, 14–24	1½–2 ft. by 2 ft., spreading	Broad triangular fronds emerge copper-colored in spring, then turn deep green	Good for seasonal color
Matteuccia struthiopteris OSTRICH FERN	◐ ● 💧 💧💧 1–10, 14–24	2–6 ft. by 2–4 ft., spreading	Rich green fronds fan out at top, taper gradually to narrow base	Takes more sun along coast. Tolerates extreme cold. Dormant in winter
Nephrolepis cordifolia SOUTHERN SWORD FERN	◐ ● 💧 💧 8, 9, 12–24	2–3 ft. by 1–2 ft., spreading	Narrow, bright green, 2–3 ft. fronds stand erect	Needs less water than most ferns—very tough and adaptable. Use as filler or ground cover; can be invasive. Watch for slugs and snails (see pp. 220–221)
Osmunda regalis ROYAL FERN	● 💧💧 All zones, but best in 4–6	To 5 ft. by 3 ft.	Big, deep green, coarse-textured fronds, pink in youth, stand upright to form vase shape	Leaflets resemble rich brown flower clusters. Dormant in winter
Pellaea rotundifolia ROUNDLEAF or BUTTON FERN	◐ 💧 14–17, 19–24	To 1 ft. by 1 ft.	Small, nearly round, dark glossy green leaflets on spreading fronds	Best in rich soil, filtered shade. Charming small fern with darker, richer color than most
Polystichum munitum SWORD FERN	● 💧 💧 4–9, 14–24	2–4 ft. by 2–4 ft.	Deep green fronds emerge symmetrically from central base	Best in rich soil. Needs little water once established. Remove dead or tattered fronds. Easy to grow, this western native blends well with other plants
Polystichum setiferum SOFT SHIELD FERN	● 💧 4–9, 14–24	2–3 ft. by 3–4 ft.	Dark green fronds lower and more spreading than *P. munitum*	Many varieties, sometimes called "English ferns," are available from specialists. Good among rocks. Combines well in planting beds. *P. polyblepharum*, TASSEL FERN, is similar but taller and more upright, darker green
Rumohra adiantiformis LEATHERLEAF FERN	☼ ◐ 💧 14–17, 19–24	To 3 ft. by 3 ft., spreading	Deep, glossy green, triangular fronds	Takes more sun and less water than most ferns. Tough, leathery fronds often used in floral arrangements. Spreads slowly. In areas with high salt content in water, leaf edges may brown
Woodwardia fimbriata GIANT CHAIN FERN	◐ ● 💧💧 4–9, 14–24	To 9 ft. by 6 ft., usually less	Rather coarse, bright green fronds stand upright and spread from central base	Imposing, dramatic, strong-growing plant, good near water, under trees

☼: Full sun; ◐ Part shade; ● Full shade; ○ Drought tolerant; 💧 Little water; 💧 Regular water; 💧💧 Ample water.

To find your climate zone, see pages 14–21.

Succulents

Many Westerners identify cacti and succulents with desert gardens. But these sturdy, drought-tolerant plants can easily be used in combinations with other garden plants to add exotic appeal to entranceways, patios, flower borders, terraced slopes, and containers.

The most appealing features of succulents are their color range—from golden barrel cactus to almost-black aeoniums—their interesting sculptural shapes, and their surprisingly showy flowers. Many multiply easily; and new plants are easily broken off the parent plant and re-rooted.

When planted in a suitable site, succulents rarely need to be pruned or checked for pests. Nearly all can survive weeks without water, but most look better if watered regularly during the spring and summer. To remove dust and city soot, simply hose down your plants now and then. A few species, such as the popular *Sedum telephium* 'Autumn Joy' will be quite at home in an irrigated flower bed. The range of succulents available for garden culture varies widely from region to region; see the Guide on page 114.

Aloe, aloe. With its coral flowers and many species, aloes make striking, no-fuss garden plants. At top, an aloe and red-flowered Linum *are surrounded by a gravel mulch. An informal blending of textures (above) includes aloe and* Echeveria. *The powder-blue hen-and-chicks (*Echeveria imbricata*) makes an ideal front-of-border edging (left).*

What is a Succulent?

A succulent is any plant that stores water in juicy leaves, stems, or roots, enabling it to withstand periodic drought. Most succulents are native to desert or semi-arid lands, including South America and southern Africa. Many of those are frost-tender, but other species come from colder climates, such as cobweb houseleek (Sempervivum arachnoideum), *native to Europe. Succulent plants may be planted directly in the ground or in containers—arrange them in a strawberry pot for an easy, low-care display. This border planting of succulents includes dramatic agaves.*

What is a Cactus?

Cacti are succulent plants native only to the Western Hemisphere, their range covering climate extremes from the New England coastline to Death Valley. Generally leafless, cacti have stems modified into thick-skinned cylinders, pads, or jointed stems that store water during periods of drought. Most species have sharp spines to protect plants against browsing animals, and a great many offer large, colorful flowers. The golden barrel and saguaro cactus shown here are well suited to dry landscapes featuring other heat-lovers such as tall whiplike ocotillo (Fouquieria splendens) *and red bougainvillea.*

A FEW SPINY TIPS

Drainage. Succulents and cactus will not survive without loose, well-draining soil that resembles the soil of their native habitats. Slopes, rock walls, terraces, and sandy or rocky soils make the best planting sites.

Plant partners. Although there's great variety in form and color, mixing a few species usually looks better than a mass of single plants. An exception is the striking look of several golden barrel cactus.

Irrigation. Group drought-tolerant, desert species together in areas you prefer not to irrigate; for many of these plants, winter rains provide all the irrigation they need.

Safety. Use heavy rubber gloves or long-handled tweezers to weed or work around spiny plants. Even the tiny prickles of innocuous-looking prickly pear cactus can irritate the skin for hours and are frustratingly difficult to extract.

Weeds. To cut down weeding chores, set plants into holes cut through a layer of a permeable landscape fabric (see p.198). Cover the fabric with sand, soil, or crushed stones.

Security. Use prickly cacti as barrier plants to keep intruders away from fences or low windows.

Containers. Try smoother-leaved succulents, such as jade plant, kalanchoe or sedums, in window boxes or pots.

EASY-CARE SUCCULENTS FOR WESTERN GARDENS

Botanical name COMMON NAME	Sun & Water/ Zones	Size & Appearance	Comments
Aeonium arboreum	☼ ◐ ◌ 15–17, 20–24	Branching stems to 3 ft. tall; 6–8 in. rosettes of green or maroon fleshy leaves. Yellow flowers in clusters	Decorative and sculptural, good for containers. Best with some shade in hottest climates. *A. a* 'Zwartkop', BLACK AEONIUM, has nearly black leaves. *A. decorum*, bushy, compact, rounded to 1 ft., with red-tinted leaves and pink flowers. *A. urbicum*, flattened, "dinner plate" rosettes of narrow green leaves in a loose arrangement
Agave attenuata	☼ ◐ ◌ ◌◌ 20–24	Makes a 5-ft. clump of soft, green, fleshy leaves. Greenish yellow flowers on long spikes	Will not thrive in excessive cold or heat
Aloe	☼ ◐ ◌ 8, 9, 12–24	Clumps to 2–3 ft.; flowers orange, pink, or coral. Thick, gray-green, spiny-edged leaves	Handsome, vigorous plant for dry places; recommended species include *A. aristata*, TORCH PLANT; *A. saponaria; A. striata*, CORAL ALOE; *A. variegata*. May be a skin irritant
Carnegiea gigantea SAGUARO, GIANT CACTUS	☼ ○ 12, 13, 18–21	Columnar and branching, with prominent parallel ridges; slow-growing to 50 ft.	White May blossoms are state flower of Arizona. Edible fruit. Plant nursery stock only
Cephalocereus senilis OLD MAN CACTUS	☼ ○ ◌ 21–24	Slender, columnar cactus, slow growing to 40 ft. Covered with grayish white hairs	Good container plant; older, night-blooming specimens striking in desert gardens
Cotyledon undulata	◐ ○ ◌ 17, 23, 24	Rounded to 1½–2 ft. with fleshy leaves with powdery bloom. Drooping, orange flowers in spring	No overhead water
Crassula argentea JADE PLANT	☼ ◐ ○ 8, 9, 12–24	Height and width to 8–9 ft. Fleshy, dark green, 2-in. leaf pads. Pink, star-shaped flowers in clusters, winter to early spring	Well-known houseplant that makes a sturdy, branching landscape shrub. *C. falcata*, PROPELLER PLANT, shrubby to 4 ft., with fleshy, gray-green, sickle-shaped leaves and dense clusters of scarlet flowers in late summer
Dudleya brittonii CLIFF LETTUCE	☼ ◌ 12, 13, 16, 17, 21–24	Matures to trunks 1–2 ft. high. Leaves leathery, 1½ ft., in rosettes, covered with a chalky bloom	Needs bright light and shelter from rain, hail, and frost. Best in a sheltered atrium or container
Echeveria elegans HEN AND CHICKS	☼ ◐ ◌ 8, 9, 12–24	Ground-hugging rosettes spread easily to 4 ft. Leaves gray green, pointed, to 4 in. Nodding low stalks hold pink-and-yellow blooms	Easy creeper for rock gardens, dry spots. Hybrids have leaves tinted gray, burgundy, or pearly blue. *E. agavoides* has rosettes to 8 in. across and stiff, fleshy, bright green leaves, sometimes reddish at sharp tips; red-and-yellow flowers. *E. imbricata* has spineless, gray-green rosettes of fleshy leaves and clusters of bell-shaped, orange-red flowers
Echinocactus grusonii GOLDEN BARREL CACTUS	☼ ◌ 12–24	Ball-shaped to 4 ft. high and 2½ ft. around with stiff, yellow spines. Yellow flowers in late spring	Nice when casually grouped or in contemporary arrangements
Kalanchoe	☼ ◐ ● ◌ 17, 21–24	Fleshy glossy or woolly leaves. Clusters of bell-shaped flowers erect or drooping	Many species and hybrids; often grown as houseplants
Lampranthus spectabilis TRAILING ICE PLANT	☼ ○ ◌ 14–24	Sprawling to 2 ft. wide, with fleshy, gray-green leaves. Dramatic pink, red, or purple flowers in spring	Tolerates salt, smog, and general neglect. Good cover for streetsides, seaside gardens, or dry banks. *Drosanthemum floribundum*, ROSEA ICE PLANT, is similar
Opuntia ficus-indica PRICKLY PEAR CACTUS	☼ ○ ◌ 8, 9, 12–24	Treelike, branching growth to 15 ft.; dull green, flat leaf pads with clusters of sharp bristles. Shiny, yellow, 4-in. flowers in spring. Tasty, spiny red fruit in winter	Prune (with gloves) by snapping off pads at joints. *O. bigelovii*, TEDDY BEAR CHOLLA, takes full sun and little water in Zones 11–24. To 8 ft., with branching, cyclindrical stems armed with sharp shiny spines
Sedum acre GOLDMOSS SEDUM	☼ ◐ ◌ All zones	2–5 in. tall, quickly trailing or creeping with tiny, pale green, rounded leaves. Yellow flowers in spring	Good for dry walls or between stepping-stones. *S. telephium* 'Autumn Joy' forms a rounded mound to 2 ft. and has fleshy, pale leaves and coppery rose, flat-topped flower clusters in fall. *S. spectabile* has similar habit and softer, rose-colored flowers
Sedum rubrotinctum PORK AND BEANS	☼ ◐ ◌ 8, 9, 12, 14–24	Has sprawling, 6–8 in. stems. Leaves like jelly beans, fleshy, bronze or green with reddish tints. Small, reddish yellow flowers	*S. spathulifolium* (all zones) tolerates more shade, has trailing 2-ft. stems, blue-purple leaves, and light yellow flowers in late spring. 'Cape Blanco' and 'Purpureum' have purple leaves
Sempervivum tectorum HEN AND CHICKENS	☼ ◌ All zones	Gray-green leaves, tipped reddish brown, in flattened rosettes. Dull red flower stems to 2 ft. in late summer	Easy to grow as edging or rock garden plant, even in the coldest climates

☼ **Full sun**; ◐ **Part shade**; ● **Full shade**; ○ **Drought tolerant**; ◌ **Little water**; ● **Regular water**; ●● **Ample water.**   **To find your climate zone, see pages 14–21.**

Succulents on Display

An entire bed of succulents needn't look monochromatic, as this colorful selection shows. Silver and grey aeoniums, kalanchoe, and *Aloe striata* contrast with the many greens, while brilliant *Crassula falcata* and nearly-black *Aeonium arboreum* 'Zwartkop' provide dramatic contrasts. A few well-placed boulders create the effect of a rock garden. One caveat—these plants don't need much water, but the soil must be well-drained or they'll suffer from root rot.

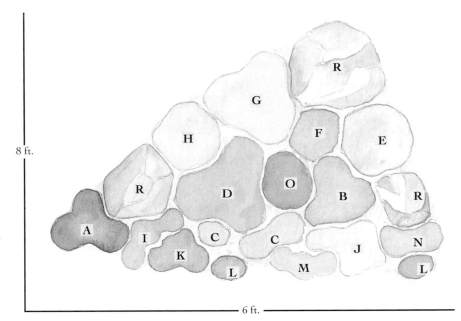

8 ft.

6 ft.

Aeonium arboreum 'Zwartkop'
BLACK AEONIUM

Sedum spathulifolium 'Cape Blanco'
STONECROP

Echeveria

THE PLANTS

A. *Aeonium arboreum* 'Zwartkop' (3)
   BLACK AEONIUM

B. *Aeonium decorum* (3)

C. *Aeonium urbicum* (3)

D. *Aloe aristata* (3)
   TORCH PLANT

E. *Aloe striata* (1)
   CORAL ALOE

F. *Cotyledon undulata* (1)
   SILVER-CROWN

G. *Crassula falcata* (3)
   PROPELLER PLANT

H. *Dudleya brittonii* (1)
   CLIFF LETTUCE

I. *Echeveria imbricata* (3)
   HEN AND CHICKS

J. *Echeveria secunda* 'Glauca' (5)
   HEN AND CHICKS

K. *Kalanchoe blossfeldiana* (3)

L. *Sedum album* (3)
   STONECROP

M. *Sedum rubrotinctum* (3)
   PORK AND BEANS

N. *Sedum spathulifolium* 'Cape Blanco' (5)
   STONECROP

O. *Senecio mandraliscae* (1)

R. *Rock*

Flower Gardens

I t's virtually impossible to imagine a garden without flowers. For most of us, in fact, herbaceous and woody perennials, annual flowers, and bulbs are the heart of the garden—its color, fragrance, and beauty. For many, flowers have associations of familiar places, smells, even memories of childhood or special occasions.

The best flowering plants bloom for weeks or months—some even produce blossoms on and off year-round. A low-maintenance flowering plant doesn't succumb easily to insects or diseases, nor does it require a great deal of fertilizer to stay healthy or stakes to stay upright. It won't get too big too quickly, but will grow steadily to its mature size.

All flowers have their preferences—some for sun, others for shade. Woodland plants require rich soil; desert plants prefer a perfectly drained situation. Make sure you know the conditions in your garden (see pages 10–11). Read about different flowers' needs before you select them for your garden; if you choose properly, you'll be able to put them in the ground without extra amendments or fertilizers. Give them the minimum of care and you'll be rewarded with reliable growth and the luscious blooms for which every gardener hopes.

In the plans that follow, specific varieties may not be available in your local nursery. Ask for something similar.

Spring shades. Flowers offer the best opportunity to play with colors in the garden. Choose species that complement each other, such as orange California poppy and blue love-in-a-mist, or work with subtly matched shades. To get ideas, find plants you like at the nursery and walk around, holding different plants against each other. Take samples home and see how they look at different times of the day.

BLOOMING EASY

Pick and choose. The cardinal rule for easy care is to select plants that suit your conditions—primarily sun, soil, and year-round temperatures. Plants that struggle against inappropriate conditions will be more susceptible to diseases and pests, and will always require additional pampering

Think ahead. Decide how much work you are willing to do *before* you select your plants. Some perennials need to be lifted and divided every few years (see p. 216); some annuals reseed prolifically. The charts on the following pages list such special characteristics; if you are unwilling to do the type of work required by that plant, choose another.

Birds of a feather. Group plants by their soil and water needs, so you can tailor irrigation, soil preparation, and fertilizing chores to suit.

Ask around. In addition to the plants recommended in this book, look for All-America Selections (AAS), which have been rated for their ability to grow well in a wide variety of climates. Your local nursery or garden center, your neighbors, and your County Cooperative Extension Service can also give you valuable advice on flowering plants that thrive in your area.

Go for the show. Plant colorful flowers where you'll see them most often. If your front walkway is rarely used, plant a ground cover there and put your blossoms in raised planters near the patio, in a border or island bed that can be viewed from those sections of the garden that are most often used. For perimeter plantings and front yard, create color interest with well-chosen ground covers, flowering trees, and blooming shrubs.

Keep it simple. The massed effect of a single plant, such as bearded iris or daylilies, can be a dramatic statement. By keeping the design concept simple, you lessen the work required.

Mix it up. Combine flowering perennials and annuals with easy-care succulents (see pp. 112–115), ornamental grasses (see pp. 104–109), and foliage plants (see p. 118). Many of the photos in this book show such combinations to stunning effect.

Have a plan. The flower plans on pp. 124–127 were designed for low-maintenance. Use them as blueprints, or adapt them to your own situation.

Go vegetarian. If you already have a vegetable garden, consider making room there for annual flowers, for show and for cutting.

ANNUALS

Their presence may be transient, but annuals provide quick and showy color, fragrance, and form for the garden. Some are considered warm-season, blooming through summer; in mild climates, cool-season annuals provide a winter show. Annuals can be seen as the disposable members of the garden— if they fail to please, simply pull them up and toss them in the compost. Some annuals are easily sown from seed, but local nurseries always have a supply of six-packs with seasonal favorites (like the pansies shown here). Use annuals in containers, in raised beds, or to fill in blank spaces in perennial borders. Some annuals tend to drop seeds that emerge the following season. Unless you want the same plants in the same place each year, you'll have to deadhead before they set seed or weed out the emerging seedlings.

PERENNIALS

Long-lived bloomers that come back year after year, perennials are the garden's floral workhorses—even if the plant's foliage dies down in winter, its crown and root system will survive to send up new growth the following year. (Strictly speaking, bulbs are also perennial, such as the freesias shown with California poppies at right). Some perennials are evergreen; they may flower once a year, but retain their foliage year-round. Most of these plants are available in nursery containers or through mail order as plugs or even bare-root. In some perennials, the crown becomes too big for the plant to flower well and must be 'divided' every few years. For instructions on this and other care, including deadheading or shearing for better bloom, see page 216. Keep in mind that some plants considered perennial in mild climates don't survive cold winters and are treated as annuals in such regions.

Dependable, durable. *Yarrow and lavender are among the finest perennials for low-maintenance gardens. See pp. 121–123 for more choices.*

Fancy Foliage

These annuals and perennials are showy and easy to grow in various garden conditions, with only one thing missing: showy flowers. All have special leaves—large and colorful, unusual in shape, or fragrant—and many can replace blooming plants in your color scheme, making a year-round contribution rather than a brief display. Consider a single *Artemisia* 'Powis Castle' as a silvery white background for a bed of colorful flowers. Plant a stand of cast-iron plant in a pitch-dark corner where less rugged plants struggle. A big pot filled with horsetail makes a dramatic accent; a small pot overflowing with *Oxalis purpurea* makes a subtler statement. Piggy-back plant is perfect for children's gardens; they love to touch the soft leaves, and miniature plantlets can be plucked and planted for easy-care house plants.

Foliage foils. Many gray-leafed foliage plants make excellent partners for more brightly-colored perennials, such as 'Moonshine' *yarrow (above).* 'Sundowner' *New Zealand flax is surrounded in a terracotta container (right) by red-flowered* 'Eternity' *kalanchoe. The kalanchoe could be replaced in winter with flowering cabbage for a different look.*

Alocasia
ELEPHANT'S EAR

Artemisia

Arum italicum
ITALIAN ARUM

Asparagus densiflorus 'Myers'
MYERS ASPARAGUS
and A.d. 'Sprengeri'
SPRENGER ASPARAGUS

Aspidistra elatior
CAST-IRON PLANT

Cabbage, flowering

Centaurea cineraria, gymnocarpa
DUSTY MILLER

Coleus hybridus
COLEUS

Equisetum hyemale
HORSETAIL *(in containers only)*

Eryngium amethystinum
SEA HOLLY

Helichrysum petiolare
LICORICE PLANT

Hosta
PLANTAIN LILY

Houttuynia cordata 'Chameleon'

Oxalis purpurea

Pelargonium crispum, P. graveolens, P. tomentosum
SCENTED GERANIUMS

Phormium tenax
NEW ZEALAND FLAX

Pulmonaria saccharata
BETHLEHEM SAGE

Rhoeo spathacea
MOSES-IN-THE-CRADLE

Santolina chamaecyparissus
LAVENDER COTTON

Senecio cineraria
DUSTY MILLER

Tanacetum densum amanii

Tiarella cordifolia
FOAMFLOWER

Tolmiea menziesii
PIGGY-BACK PLANT

Tradescantia fluminensis
WANDERING JEW

Botanical name COMMON NAME	Sun & Water	Height, Spread & Form	Appearance	Care & Comments
Ageratum houstonianum FLOSS FLOWER	☼ ◐ ●	4–12 in. by 4–12 in.; low and mounding	Soft green, hairy, heart-shaped. Dense clusters of tiny balls of fluff in pale to deep lavender blue, pink, or white	Plant in spring 6–8 in. apart for summer and fall bloom (or plant in late summer in mild-winter areas for fall color). Where summers are hot, best in filtered shade. Dwarf lavender varieties commonly available, blend well with other plants
Begonia semperflorens BEDDING BEGONIA, WAX BEGONIA	◐ ● ●●	6–12 in. by 6–10 in.; small compact mound	Leaves shiny green, red, bronze, or variegated. Flowers small, roundish, waxy; white, pink, or red	Set out plants in spring (any time in mild climates) in moist soil. Filtered shade is best; dark-leaved kinds take more sun. Bloom is almost continuous. May get whitefly (see pp. 220–221)
Calendula officinalis CALENDULA, POT MARIGOLD	☼ ●	1–2 ft. by 1–2 ft.; upright, branching	Long, narrow, somewhat sticky leaves. Flowers bright orange, yellow, apricot, or cream; daisy-shaped, 2–4 in. across	In colder areas, plant in spring for bloom through midsummer; in mild-winter areas, plant in late-summer or early-fall. Well-drained soil is best. Deadhead (see p. 216) or cut fresh blooms for long-lasting bouquets
Catharanthus roseus MADAGASCAR PERIWINKLE	☼ ◐ ●	6 in.–2 ft. by 6 in.–2 ft.; bushy and upright or lower and spreading	Glossy, bright green, fleshy leaves are 1–3 in. long. Flowers white through mauve pink, often with a darker center, to 1 in. wide	Plant in late spring for long display of color. Very tolerant of high temperatures, humidity. Self-sows
Centaurea cyanus CORNFLOWER, BACHELOR'S BUTTON	☼ ●	1–2 ft. by 1–2 ft.; upright, somewhat branching	Gray-green, narrow leaves to 3 in. long. Blooms compact, arranged in heads of blue, pink, rose, wine red, and white	Sow seed in early spring in cold-winter areas, late summer or fall where winters are mild. Work a handful of lime into soil before planting. Deadhead (see p. 216). Good cut flowers
Cerinthe major purpurescens	☼ ●	2 ft. by 1 ft.; arching stems	White-spotted 2-in. leaves and numerous purple bracts. Flowers long, blue	Showy foliage and flowers. Good in containers. Can be grown easily from seed
Chrysanthemum frutescens MARGUERITE, PARIS DAISY	☼ ●	4 ft. by 4 ft.; mounding. Perfect for containers	Bright green leaves, divided into segments. Flowers are white, yellow, or pink daisies, 1 to 2 in. across	Choose compact plants with small leaves. Plant in spring for summer-long bloom, encouraged by pinching or light shearing once a month (see p. 216). Several varieties available
Clarkia amoena FAREWELL-TO-SPRING, GODETIA	☼ ●	1–3 ft. by 1–3 ft.; low and spreading or upright and bushy	Narrow leaves, to 2 in. long. Upright buds open into cup-shaped pink or lavender flowers	Dwarf Gem is low, spreading; Tall Upright grows to 3 ft. Sow in sandy soil in fall in mild-winter areas, in spring elsewhere, for spring bloom. Not at its best in hottest regions
Consolida ambigua LARKSPUR	☼ ●	1–2 ft. by 1–f ft.; upright and elegant	Deep green, fernlike leaves. Long, spikes of star-shaped flowers in blue, violet, pink, or white	Sow seeds in fall. Best massed, or as edging. All parts are poisonous
Cosmos bipinnatus	☼ ●	3–8 ft. by 3–4 ft.; upright, open, and branching	Bright green, delicate foliage, much divided. Daisylike flowers, in white, pink, purple, or crimson, with yellow centers	Plant in spring to summer for bloom through fall. Avoid fertilizer. Self-sows freely. Good for masses of color or as an airy filler among shrubs, bulbs
Eschscholzia californica CALIFORNIA POPPY	☼ ○ ●	8–24 in. by 8–24 in.; mounding	Fernlike, blue-green foliage. Single silky blooms, 2 in. wide, in colors from pale yellow to deep orange, opening in sunlight	Spread seed by hand in fall rains on cultivated soil for summer-long color. Best suited for informal areas, sunny hillsides, casual dry gardens. Self-sows readily
Gaillardia pulchella	☼ ●	2 ft. by 2 ft.; low and clumping	Soft, hairy, narrow leaves. Daisylike flowers, to 2 in. across, in warm tones of red, yellow, and bronze, often striped, held 2 ft. above foliage	Sow seed in warm soil after frosts, or set out nursery plants for bloom into autumn. Heat-lover. Good cut flowers
Helianthus annuus COMMON SUNFLOWER	☼ ● ●●	2–10 ft. by 1–3 ft.; tall and upright	Hairy, coarse leaves. Familiar flowers with dark center surrounded by small yellow to orange petals, up to 10 in. across	Fast growers. Sow seeds in spring. Easy to grow, but large size and strong color can dominate small garden. Great for children's gardens
Impatiens wallerana BUSY LIZZIE	◐ ● ●	6 in.–2 ft. by 6 in.–2 ft.; low and mounding	Oval, dark green leaves, semi-glossy on succulent stems. Circular, 5-petaled flowers, to 2 in. across, in white and bright shades of orange, red, pink, and violet all summer	Takes more sun near coast, but not hot afternoon rays. If plant looks shabby, cut back to 6 in.; it will bound back. *I. oliveri*, POOR MAN'S RHODODENDRON, is giant relative. Grows to 8 ft.–10 ft. with pale pink flowers
Limonium sinuatum SEA LAVENDER	☼ ○ ●	To 2 ft. by 2 ft.; sprawling rosette	Leathery, deeply lobed leaves, to 6 in. Flowers have tiny white centers surrounded by showy papery envelope in blue, lavender, or rose	Sow seed in early to mid-spring in well-drained soil. Good cut flowers. Often self-sows

☼ Full sun; ◐ Part shade; ● Full shade; ○ Drought tolerant; ◌ Little water; ● Regular water; ●● Ample water.

To find your climate zone, see pages 14–21.

Botanical name COMMON NAME	Sun & Water	Height, Spread & Form	Appearance	Care & Comments
Lobelia erinus	☼ ◐ ●	4–6 in. by 4–6 in.; compact and round or somewhat trailing, depending on variety	Tiny, narrow leaves, bright green to bronze, densely covering stems. Flowers are light blue to violet, pink, reddish purple, or white, small, from early summer to frost	Needs good soil. Good for edging or spilling over a wall or container edge. Can bloom year round in mild climates. All parts are poisonous
Lobularia maritima SWEET ALYSSUM	☼ ●	1 ft. by 1 ft.; low and mounding	Narrow, 1-in.-long leaves. Tiny, white, honey-scented flowers, in crowded clusters	Plant in spring for dependable filler, edging, or bulb cover. Shear back one month after blooming starts to keep compact and encourage bloom (see p. 216). Spreads easily
Nicotiana alata	☼ ◐ ●	1–3 ft. by 1–2 ft.; upright	Large, soft, oval, sticky leaves. Small fragrant trumpet-shaped flowers atop slender stems, in white, pink, red, and lime green; some kinds open only at night or on cloudy days	Sow seed in spring in good soil for summer bloom, under windows, so scent can waft inside. *N. a.* 'Grandiflora' is especially fragrant. Similar *N. sylvestris*, 5 ft. tall, has white flowers, leaves to 20 in. long, and intense fragrance
Nigella damascena LOVE-IN-A-MIST	☼ ◐ ●	1–2 ft. by 2–3 ft.; branching, spreading	Threadlike, light green leaves. Blue, white, rose flowers, 1 in. across, followed by very papery seedpods	Sow seed in good soil in early spring; plants come quickly into bloom and dry during summer. Branches with seedpods are excellent for dried bouquets. 'Miss Jekyll' (blue) and 'Persian Jewels' (mixed) are recommended
Papaver nudicale ICELAND POPPY	☼ ○ ◓	1–2 ft. by 6 in.	Large flowers in wide color range atop thin stems	Plant in well-drained soil. Deadhead frequently (see p. 216)
Petunia hybrida COMMON GARDEN PETUNIA	☼ ●	1–2 ft. by 2–3 ft. sprawling	Broad, thick, sticky leaves. Funnel-shaped flowers in broad color range, 2–4 in. wide	Plant in good soil and fertilize monthly. Pinch back frequently. May get pests (see pp. 220–225)
Rudbeckia hirta GLORIOSA DAISY, BLACK-EYED SUSAN	☼ ◓	3–4 ft. by 2–3 ft.; upright, mounding	Rough, hairy, medium green leaves. Daisylike flowers, 2–4 in. across, with orange-yellow rays and black-purple center	Sow seed in early spring for summer bloom. Gloriosa Daisy has large flowers in yellow, orange, or mahogany. 'Pinwheel' has mahogany-and-gold flowers. 'Marmalade' (2 ft.) and 'Goldilocks' (10 in.) are good for edging, ground cover
Scabiosa atropurpurea PINCUSHION FLOWER, MOURNING BRIDE	☼ ◓	2–3 ft. by 2–3 ft.; upright, billowing mound	Coarsely toothed leaves. Wiry stems hold clusters of 3-in. pinchushions in shades of mauve, pink, maroon, salmon, and white	Plant in fall for Dec.–Apr. bloom in warm winter areas; early spring for summer bloom elsewhere. Good filler, cut flower
Tagetes erecta AMERICAN or AFRICAN MARIGOLD	☼ ●	1–3 ft. by 1–3 ft.; stiffly upright, branching	Fernlike leaves, usually strongly scented; flowers are palest yellow through gold to orange and brown-maroon, with many petals packed into a 3–4 in. ball; blooms through summer if deadheaded (see p. 216)	Easy from seed sown in early spring. Avoid overhead watering of taller kinds. Most types have double flowers, from dwarf whites to 3-ft. brilliant orange. *T. patula*, FRENCH MARIGOLD, 18 in. tall, includes many strains. Triploid hybrids, 10–14 in., are most vigorous
Thunbergia alata BLACK-EYED SUSAN VINE	☼ ◐ ●	To 6 ft.; twining vine	Rigid, heart-shaped, dark green leaves. Orange, yellow, or white trumpets, 1–2 in. wide, with purple black throat	Plant seeds in early spring, after frost danger. Good for fence or trellis, or for spilling from a window box. *T. gregorii*, ORANGE CLOCK VINE, to 6 ft., somewhat sturdier, with orange flowers
Tropaeolum majus GARDEN NASTURTIUM	☼ ◐ ●	To 6 ft.; twining vine	Bright green, round leaves, 2–7 in. across on long twining stalks. Broad, long-spurred, 2½-in. trumpets in maroon, red brown, orange, red, yellow, or white	Quick climber to scramble up a fence, down a hillside, or over a wall. Young leaves, flowers, and seedpods are edible. Mounding forms available. Naturalizes along coast. Easy to grow, but will reseed prolifically
Verbena hybrida GARDEN VERBENA	☼ ◓	6–12 in. by 1–3 ft.; low and spreading	Oblong, 2–4 in., bright green or gray-green leaves. Flowers in flat clusters, 2–3 in. wide, in white, pink, red, purple, blue, and combinations	Plant in well-drained soil for fast cover alongside sunny path, in crevices of rock wall, or with other heat-loving plants. May get mildew; give no overhead sprinkling
Viola tricolor JOHNNY-JUMP-UP	☼ ◐ ●	6–12 in. by 6–12 in.; tufted, spreading mound	Small leaves and flowers charmingly upright, in purple and yellow, as well as other color mixes and white; winter and spring	Plant in rich soil. Perfect filler for pots. Self-sows prolifically. *V. wittrockiana*, PANSY, available in many colors. Deadhead to prolong bloom (see p. 216); look for F1 and F2 hybrids
Zinnia elegans	☼ ○ ●	1–3 ft. by 1–3 ft. upright and bushy	Flowers to 6 in. across, packed with tiny petals in white, pink, salmon, rose, red, yellow, orange, lavender, or green. Oblong leaves to 5 in.	Plant in well-drained soil in late spring to early summer. Better in open spaces; will mildew in moist areas. Many strains including dwarf plants and various flower sizes

☼ **Full sun;** ◐ **Part shade;** ● **Full shade;** ○ **Drought tolerant;** ◓ **Little water;** ● **Regular water;** ●● **Ample water.**   **To find your climate zone, see pages 14–21.**

120   THE ORNAMENTAL GARDEN

EASY-CARE PERENNIALS FOR WESTERN GARDENS

Botanical name COMMON NAME	Sun & Water/ Zones	Size & Form	Appearance	Care & Comments
Achillea filipendulina FERNLEAF YARROW	☼ ○ ◕ All zones	5 ft. by 2 ft.; dense clumps	Evergreen foliage is fernlike; flat flower clusters, to 6 in. wide, held high in shades of yellow, summer through early fall	Plant in well-drained soil. Deadhead, and divide clumps every 3–4 years (see p. 216). 'Coronation Gold', to 3 ft., has large, gold flowers. *A.* 'Moonshine', 2 ft. tall, has gray-green foliage and pale yellow flowers
Aconitum napellus GARDEN MONKSHOOD	● ◕◕ 1–9, 14–21	To 5 ft.; upright leafy foliage	Large, dark green leaves; flowers are blue or violet, in spikes, late summer to fall	Great for vivid color in shady. Dies down completely in winter. All parts are extremely poisonous
Agapanthus orientalis LILY-OF-THE-NILE	☼ ◐ ◕ 7–9, 12–24	3–5 ft. by 2–3 ft.; dense, fountainlike clump	Arching evergreen straplike leaves to 2 ft. long. Clusters of up to 100 tiny blue or white flowers held atop stems 4–5 ft. tall	Flowers profusely summer to fall. Divide every 5–6 years. Excellent in containers. *A.* 'Peter Pan' is a good dwarf variety. *A.* 'Storm Cloud' has intensely blue flowers
Alchemilla mollis LADY'S-MANTLE	☼ ◐ ● ◕ 2–9, 14–24	2 ft. by 2 ft.; low, billowing mound	Rounded, soft gray-green, to 6 in. Tiny, chartreuse flowers, early summer	Small-scale ground cover or edging. After rain or watering, sparkling beads of water remain at center of leaves
Anigozanthos flavidus KANGAROO PAW	☼ ◕ ◕ 12, 13, 15–24	4–6 ft. by 2 ft.; upright clump	Dark green, leathery, sword-shaped evergreen leaves to 3 ft.; woolly, flowers resemble kangaroo paws, in red, purple, green, or yellow, on stems to 6 ft. long	Needs well-drained, sandy soil. May get snails and slugs (see pp. 220–221). Flowers attract hummingbirds. Cut spent flower spikes to ground for spring to fall bloom. Best are hybrids 'Harmony Yellow', 'Red Cross', 'Regal Claw'
Aquilegia COLUMBINE	☼ ◐ ◕ All zones	2–3 ft. by 1½ ft.; erect and branching	Fresh green, fernlike foliage. Nodding flowers, to 3 in. across, in pastels, bicolors, and white, spring into summer	Well-drained soil. May get leaf miners (see pp. 220–221). Music series, 18–24 in., has long spurs, intense hues and soft pastels. McKana Giants, to 2½ ft., have two-toned flowers in different color combinations
Armeria maritima COMMON THRIFT	☼ ◕ All zones	1 ft. by 1 ft.; tight, low, spreading mound	Grasslike, rich green leaves. Profuse small white or pink flower clusters held upright, nearly year-round near coast	Evergreen mounds spread slowly. Needs excellent drainage—set among rocks, in containers, low walls. Divide when center of clump begins to die out (see p. 216)
Astilbe arendsii FALSE SPIRAEA, MEADOW SWEET	☼ ◐ ◕◕ 2–7, 14–17	1–4 ft. by 2 ft.; dense, low mound	Medium green, stiff evergreen leaves, usually toothed. White, pink, or red plumes on 1–3 ft. stems, through summer	Cut back after flowering. Divide every 4–5 years (see p. 216)
Aurinia saxatilis BASKET-OF-GOLD	☼ ◐ ◕ All zones	8–12 in. by 8–12 in.; tight, spreading clump	Gray-green, hairy leaves, 2–5 in. long. Tiny, golden yellow, fragrant flowers, held above foliage, spring and early summer	Better in gravelly, well-drained soil. After flowering, shear back lightly (see p. 216). Spreads quickly and reseeds. Perfect for tumbling over low rock walls or lining sunny pathways
Bergenia crassifolia WINTER-BLOOMING BERGENIA	☼ ◐ ◕ 1–9, 12–24	20 in. by 20 in.; low and spreading	Glossy, dark green, fan-shaped, leaves are evergreen, to 8 in. across, 12 in. long. Dense clusters of inch-wide rose, lilac, or purple flowers on red stems, Jan.–Feb.	Takes sun near coast. Cut back yearly to keep dense and low (see p. 217). Spreads slowly; divide when it fails to flower (see p. 216). May get snails and slugs (see pp. 220–221). *B. cordifolia*, HEARTLEAF BERGENIA, has larger leaves, rose flowers
Centranthus ruber JUPITER'S BEARD, RED VALERIAN	☼ ● ◕ 7–9, 12–24	To 3 ft. by 2 ft.; shrubby, upright, open	Gray-green to bluish green fleshy foliage to 4 in. long. Large flower clusters in white or rose to deep pink, late spring	Best for fringe areas of garden, rough slopes, streetside. Self-sows prolifically, but easy to weed out. Deadhead or shear back to keep compact and prolong bloom (see p. 216)
Cimicifuga racemosa BLACK SNAKEROOT	◐ ◕ 1–7, 17	Large clumps with 7 ft. flower spikes	Shiny, dark green leaves, to 3 in. long, deeply toothed. Slender stems hold spikes of tiny white flowers in late summer	Good with large ferns in rich moist soil. Can take more sun if given plenty of water. Clumps can remain undisturbed for years
Clivia miniata	● ◕ 12–17, 19–24	1–2 ft. by 2 ft.; stately, permanent, evergreen clumps	Dark green, straplike leaves. Clusters of bright orange or red flowers, up to 3 in.; early spring	Best when left undisturbed. Excellent in containers; will survive for years with regular feeding. May get slugs and snails (see pp. 220–221). Solomone Hybrids have pale to deep yellow flowers
Coreopsis verticillata THREADLEAF COREOPIS	☼ ◕ 14–24	1–3 ft. by 1–2 ft.; bushy and mounding	Threadlike, dark green foliage. Bright yellow daisies, 2 in. across, profuse summer through fall	Prefers well-drained soil. Shear or deadhead flowers for continued bloom (see p. 216). 'Moonbeam' has pale yellow flowers. *C. grandiflora* is 1–2 ft. high with bright yellow flower. Self sows
Dianthus plumarius COTTAGE PINK	☼ ◐ ◕ All zones	6 in.–1 ft. by 8 in.; loose, low mound	Gray-green foliage. Fragrant, fringed flowers, pink, or white, June–Oct.	Plant in light, fast-draining, rich soil. Deadhead (see p. 216), or cut fresh blooms for bouquets
Dicentra spectabilis COMMON BLEEDING HEART	● ◕ 1–9, 14–24	2–3 ft. by 2–3 ft.; vase-shaped mound	Fernlike, soft green foliage. Rose pink, pendulous, heart-shaped blooms, to 1 in. long, on arching stems	Plant with other shade lovers in rich, well-drained soil. Flowers in late spring, then dies back by midsummer. *D. s.* 'Alba' is an excellent pure white form

☼ Full sun; ◐ Part shade; ● Full shade; ○ Drought tolerant; ◔ Little water; ◕ Regular water; ◕◕ Ample water.

To find your climate zone, see pages 14–21.

Botanical name COMMON NAME	Sun & Water/ Zones	Size & Form	Appearance	Care & Comments
Dietes vegeta FORTNIGHT LILY, AFRICAN IRIS	☼ ◑ ● 8, 9, 12–24	4 ft. by 3 ft.; large evergreen clump	Stiff narrow leaves, to 4 ft. long. Stalks hold 3-in. white flowers with purple and gold in center; blooms at 2-week interval	Divide overgrown clumps every 4–5 years (see p. 216). Deadhead blossoms to prevent reseeding, but leave flower stalks in place
Echinacea purpurea PURPLE CONEFLOWER	☼ ● All zones	4–5 ft. by 2 ft.; stiffly upright, spreading at top	Dark green leaves are coarse and hairy. Daisylike flowers, up to 5 in. across, with white or purple petals, in late summer	Best at back of garden for naturalistic look. Excellent for cutting. Attracts butterflies. May get mildew (see pp. 230–231). 'Bright Star' and 'Crimson Star' are good purple forms. 'White Swan' is pure white
Echinops exaltatus (*Echinops ritro*) GLOBE THISTLE	☼ ● All zones	3–4 ft. by 2 ft.; narrow and upright	Thistlelike, gray-green leaves, to 8 in. long. Tiny, steel blue flowers, in round heads up to 2 in., midsummer to fall	Interesting contrast with other flowers. Cut blooms for drying. Look for 'Taplow Blue' or 'Veitch's Blue'
Erysimum 'Bowles Mauve' WALLFLOWER	☼ ◑ ● 4–6, 14–17, 22, 23	3 ft. by 6 ft.; erect, spreading evergreen dome	Long, narrow, gray-green leaves. Mauve flowers, in 18-in. spikes, held well above foliage; can be year-round	Prolific bloomer. May decline after several years. Blends well with other plants
Euphorbia characias wulfenii	☼ ● 4–24	4 ft. by 4 ft. dome-shaped evergreen bush	Narrow, blue-green leaves, crowded on stems. Large chartreuse flower clusters, early spring	When stalks turn yellow, cut at the base. *E. epithymoides* forms a dense mound, to 1½ ft., with bright yellow flowers in spring and good fall color. Cut nearly to ground in winter (see p. 217)
Francoa ramosa MAIDEN'S WREATH	◑ ● 4, 5, 8, 9, 12–24	3 ft. by 2 ft.; evergreen clumps	Large, green leaves wavy at edges. Tiny pure white to pale pink flowers held on high stems; long summer bloom	Elegant form. Divide every few years (see p. 216)
Gaura lindheimeri	☼ ○ ● All zones	3 ft. by 3 ft.; upright and open	Bright green leaves. 1-in. white flowers, summer through fall	Deadhead (see p. 216). Cut back to 8 in. midseason to encourage fuller growth. 'Siskiyou Pink' has pink blooms
Geranium 'Johnson's Blue' CRANESBILL	☼ ◑ ● 3–9, 14–24	1–2 ft. by 1–2 ft.; sprawling mound	Delicate, 2–8 in. wide violet flowers, open and round, profuse from spring to fall	*G. sanguineum* (all zones) has smaller leaves; flowers deep purple to crimson, May–Aug. Forms clumps
Helleborus orientalis LENTEN ROSE	◑ ● ●● All zones	1 ft. by 1 ft.; low evergreen clump	Large, dark green, star-shaped leaves and white, greenish, purple, or rose flowers, often with spots in Mar.–May	Add a handful of lime to bed when planting. *H. niger*, CHRISTMAS ROSE (1–7, 14–17), similar, earlier blooming, with larger, greenish white flowers
Hemerocallis hybrids DAYLILY	☼ ◑ ● All zones	1–6 ft. by 2–3 ft.; grasslike clump	Long, narrow leaves. Open trumpets, to 8 in. across, in yellows, oranges, reds, lavenders, and combinations	Size and bloom time varies according to variety; some are evergreen, some deciduous. Divide every 5–6 years (see p. 216). 'Stella d'Oro' is an excellent yellow repeat bloomer
Heuchera sanguinea CORAL BELLS	☼ ◑ ● All zones	1 ft. by 1 ft.; tufted evergreen mound	Round to heart-shaped leaves are fuzzy, medium green, 1–2 in. across. Tiny coral, white, or red bells along wiry stems to 2 ft. high, midspring into summer	Best in rich, well-drained soil. *H.* 'Palace Purple', with tiny white flowers, has maplelike purplish leaves to 4 in.
Iberis sempervirens EVERGREEN CANDYTUFT	☼ ● All zones	To 1 ft. by 1½ ft.; spreading low mound	Narrow, shiny, dark green leaves; flattened flower clusters of purest white, early spring to June	After blooming stops, cut plant down to 4 in. tall. Several varieties available in different sizes. 'Snowflake' has broader leaves, larger flowers, longer bloom
Iris BEARDED IRIS	☼ ◑ ● All zones	2–4 ft. by 1–2 ft.; open clumps	Sword-like, gray-green leaves. Fragrant flowers, with 'beards' in all colors	Wonderful low-maintenance plant, but prefers well-drained soil; divide every 3–4 years for best bloom (see p. 216)
Iris sibirica SIBERIAN IRIS	☼ ● 1–10, 14–23	To 4 ft. by 1 ft.; upright, spreading, grassy clump	Slender, grasslike leaves are bright green. Flowers 3 in. across, white, purple, blue, pink, or light yellow	Water deeply during dry spells. *I. douglasiana* (4–24), an evergreen Western native, likes acid soils in full sun or light shade; has flowers from purple through blue to yellow, cream, and white
Kniphofia uvaria RED-HOT POKER, TORCH-LILY, POKER PLANT	☼ ◑ ○ ● 1–9, 14–24	3–4 ft. by 3 ft.; dense evergreen grassy clump	Arching, grasslike leaves and small, tubular flowers that form a poker-shaped cluster, in orange red, yellow, coral, and cream, spring through summer.	Groom by combing out dead foliage, flowers (see p. 217). Flowers held high above foliage; make good cut flowers. Cut old leaves to base in fall. 'Royal Standard' has profuse red and yellow midsummer flowers

☼ **Full sun;** ◑ **Part shade;** ● **Full shade;** ○ **Drought tolerant;** ● **Little water;** ● **Regular water;** ●● **Ample water.**

To find your climate zone, see pages 14–21.

THE ORNAMENTAL GARDEN

Botanical name COMMON NAME	Sun & Water/ Zones	Size & Form	Appearance	Care & Comments
Lavandula angustifolia ENGLISH LAVENDER	☼ ◐ ◌ ● / 4–24	3–4 ft. by 3–4 ft.; mounding, shrubby	Gray, narrow 2-in. leaves. Flowers lavender, fragrant, in spikes held above foliage, July-Aug.	Indispensible plant for low maintenance gardens; likes poor soil. Shear after bloom (see p. 216–217). 'Hidcote' is a dwarf form. *L. dentata*, FRENCH LAVENDER (8, 9, 12–24), is similar, slightly more spreading, with compact flower heads, toothed leaves; long bloom. *L. stoechas*, SPANISH LAVENDER (4–24), has dark, pineapple-shaped flowers in early summer
Lavatera thuringiaca TREE MALLOW	☼ ● ● / 8, 9, 14–24	6 ft. by 5 ft.; open and shrubby	Large, maplelike, gray-green leaves. Purplish pink 3-in. flowers	Blooms most of the year. Shear back twice yearly to keep dense. 'Barnsley' is an excellent variety with light pink flowers
Limonium perezii SEA LAVENDER	☼ ◌ ● / 13, 15–17, 20–24	3 ft. by 2 ft.; tough, floppy, evergreen clump	Leathery, gray-green leaves, to 1 ft. long. Purple flowers with tiny white center, on stalks up to 3 ft. long	Plant in well-drained, sandy soil that is not too rich. Summer-long bloom. Good cut flowers. Perfect beach plant. *L. latifolium* (1–10, 14–24) is slightly smaller, with lavender blue flowers
Linum perenne PERENNIAL BLUE FLAX	☼ ● / All zones	2 ft. by 18 in.; erect, wispy	Long stems with small, narrow leaves. Light blue flowers, May–Sept.	Self-sows freely. *L. p. lewisii*, western native flax, is similar but sturdier
Nepeta faassenii CATMINT	☼ ● / All zones	2 ft. by 1 ft.; billowy mounds	Soft, gray leaves, to 1 in. long. Flowers lavender blue, in loose spikes	Plant in well-drained soil in a place where it can spread. Shear in early summer after bloom (see p. 216). Attractive to cats
Oenothera missourensis EVENING PRIMROSE	☼ ◌ / All zones	9 in.–2 ft. by 1 ft.; low, sprawling mat	Soft, velvety foliage, to 5 in.; lemon yellow flowers to 5 in. across	Plant in sandy, well-drained soil. Blooms through summer. *O. tetragona*, SUNDROPS, grows to 2 ft., with smaller yellow flowers
Pelargonium hortorum COMMON GERANIUM, GARDEN GERANIUM	☼ ● ● / 8–9, 12–24	3 ft. by 2 ft.; shrubby, upright, branching	Round, velvety leaves, usually with concentric colored markings. Flowers clustered at the end of long stems, many colors, spring through fall	Pinch growing tips and deadhead (see p. 216). Among best strains are Diamond and Elite. *P. domesticum*, LADY WASHINGTON PELARGONIUM, similar, but with wavy leaf margins. *P. peltatum*, IVY GERANIUM, trailing to 3 ft., with succulent leaves
Penstemon heterophyllus purdyi BEARD TONGUE	☼ ◌ ● / 6–24	1–2 ft. by 2 ft.; upright, shrubby, somewhat spreading	Narrow, pointed leaves to 3 in. long. Clusters of rosy lavender to deep blue trumpetlike flowers, Apr.–July	Good for slopes and very dry spots. Many hybrids available. *P. barbatus* (all zones), to 3 ft., sprawling, with red flowers; *P. strictus* 'Bandera', ROCKY MOUNTAIN PENSTEMON (1–3, 10–13), 2 ft. tall, with purple flowers. Must have excellent drainage
Perovskia atriplicifolia RUSSIAN SAGE	☼ ◌ / All zones	3–4 ft. by 2–3 ft.; upright, open	Gray-green, toothed, small leaves. Tiny, lavender blue flowers held in long spikes	Needs well-drained soil. Looks like a plume of lavender smoke. Blooms most of summer if deadheaded (see p. 216). Cut to ground in winter
Polygonatum odoratum SOLOMON'S SEAL	● ●● / 1–7, 15–17	To 3 ft. by 1 ft.; upright clump	Oval, pointed, bright green leaves, 4–6 in. Small, pure white flowers, hanging like drops from arching stems	Plant in moist, woodland-type soils. Flowers appear in spring. Plant dies down in winter, spreads slowly. *P. o.* 'Variegatum' has beautiful foliage edged in creamy white
Rudbeckia fulgida 'Goldsturm'	☼ ● / All zones	To 3 ft. by 2 ft.; upright mound	Dark green, narrowly oval, to 6 in. long. Bright orange daisies with dark centers	Prolific bloom in summer. Spreads slowly; divide clumps every 3–4 years (see p. 216). Good cut flowers
Salvia superba	◐ ● / All zones	1–3 ft by 1 ft.; upright, multibranched	Rough, gray-green, narrow leaves. Violet blue flowers with reddish bracts crowded onto erect spikes, spring through summer	*S. clevelandii* (10–24) forms 3-ft. mound of fragrant foliage; lavender flowers in summer. *S. elegans*, PINEAPPLE SAGE (8–24), grows to 2–3 ft. and has light green leaves; red flowers in autumn. *S. leucantha*, MEXICAN BUSH SAGE (10–24), to 4 ft., with arching stems, grayish foliage, and velvety flower spikes; cut to ground each winter. Deadhead (see p. 216)
Scabiosa caucasica PERENNIAL PINCUSHION FLOWER	☼ ● / All zones	2 ft. by 2 ft.; rosette, with long flowering stems	Long-stalked leaves and blue, lavender, and white flowers, in clusters to 3 in. across	Blooms over long period, from midsummer to winter. Long-lasting cut flowers. Deadheading encourages flowers (see p. 216). Fama strain has light blue, large-petaled flowers on long stems
Tulbaghia violacea SOCIETY GARLIC	☼ ● / 13–24	2 ft. by 1 ft.; grassy clump	Bluish green narrow leaves. Rosy lavender clusters on 1–2 ft. stems	All parts have strong garlic or onion odor; good for seasoning. Variegated types available
Verbena bonariensis	☼ ● ◌ / 8–24	To 6 ft. by 6 in.; upright and wispy	Basal leaves coarse and toothed. Fragrant purple flower spikes held on very long, practically leafless stems 3–6 ft. tall	Does poorly in wet conditions. Blooms summer through early fall. Self-seeds freely. Good with silver leafed plants
Veronica SPEEDWELL	☼ ● ● / All zones	10–18 in. by 10–18 in.	Medium to apple green foliage. Tall spikes of tiny white, rose, pink, or blue flowers	Plant in well-drained soil that is not too rich. Blooms midsummer. 'Sunny Border Blue' is 1 ft. tall, with rich violet blue flowers over a long period

☼ Full sun; ◐ Part shade; ● Full shade; ◌ Drought tolerant; ● Little water; ● Regular water; ●● Ample water.   To find your climate zone, see pages 14–21.

Quiet Annuals

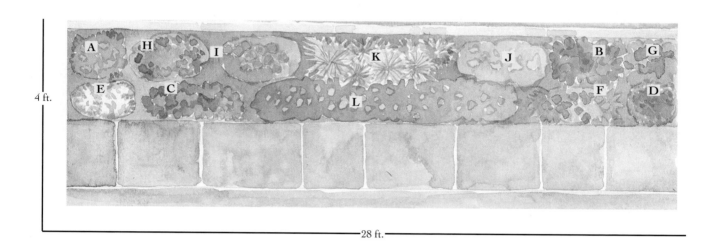

Annuals are often used to make an electric statement of color in the garden, but many are available in subtler shades that combine beautifully with each other and with whites and grays. This narrow border, composed mostly of annuals, brings a muted palette of salmon, soft blue, peach, and gray tones to an area between a sidewalk and street. Mexican feather grass and well-spaced perennials visually weave the border together.

Senecio cineraria
DUSTY MILLER

Lobelia erinus 'Cambridge Blue'

THE PLANTS

A. *Centaurea cyanus* 'Florence' (5)
CORNFLOWER

B. *Limonium sinuatum* 'Pastel Shades' (5)
SEA LAVENDER

C. *Limonium sinuatum* 'Sunset Shades' (7)
SEA LAVENDER

D. *Lobelia erinus* 'Cambridge Blue' (7)

E. *Lobularia maritima* (12)
SWEET ALYSSUM

F. *Nicotiana alata* (salmon) (5)

G. *Pelargonium hortorum* 'Maverick Light' (5)
COMMON GERANIUM

H. *Salvia farinacea* 'Strata' (6)
MEALY-CUP SAGE

I. *Scabiosa atropurpurea* (salmon) (8)
PINCUSHION FLOWER

J. *Senecio cineraria* (5)
DUSTY MILLER

K. *Stipa tenuissima* (9)
MEXICAN FEATHER GRASS

L. *Verbena hybrida* 'Peaches n' Cream' (24)
GARDEN VERBENA

Waterwise Wonder

The traditional English border goes West with this mix of sun-loving Mediterranean and native perennials. These tough, drought-tolerant plants require little irrigation to keep them blooming all summer long; several, including the tree mallow and Santa Barbara daisy, bloom through the year. To see what this plan looks like freshly-planted, turn to page 196.

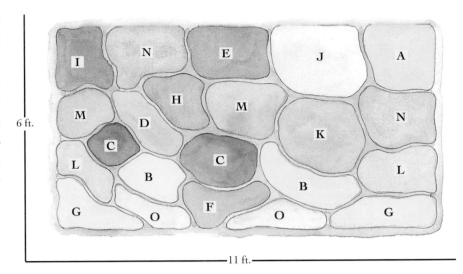

Erigeron karvinskianus
SANTA BARBARA DAISY

Lavandula angustifolia
ENGLISH LAVENDER

Stachys byzantina 'Silver Carpet'
LAMB'S EARS

THE PLANTS

A. *Achillea filipendulina* (2)
FERNLEAF YARROW

B. *Achillea* 'Moonshine' (7)
YARROW

C. *Asclepias tuberosa* (7)
BUTTERFLY WEED

D. *Coreopsis verticillata* 'Moonbeam' (2)

E. *Echinacea purpurea* 'Bright Star' (1)
PURPLE CONEFLOWER

F. *Erigeron karvinskianus* (4)
SANTA BARBARA DAISY

G. *Euphorbia epithymoides* (12)
CUSHION SPURGE

H. *Geranium endressii* 'Wargrave Pink' (1)
CRANESBILL

I. *Lavandula angustifolia* (5)
ENGLISH LAVENDER

J. *Lavatera thuringiaca* 'Barnsley' (2)
TREE MALLOW

K. *Nepeta faassenii* (4)
CATMINT

L. *Pennisetum alopecuroides* (7)
FOUNTAIN GRASS

M. *Penstemon gloxinioides* (5) 'Apple Blossom'
BORDER PENSTEMON

N. *Perovskia* 'Blue Spire' (6)
RUSSIAN SAGE

O. *Stachys byzantina* 'Silver Carpet' (5)
LAMB'S EARS

White at Night

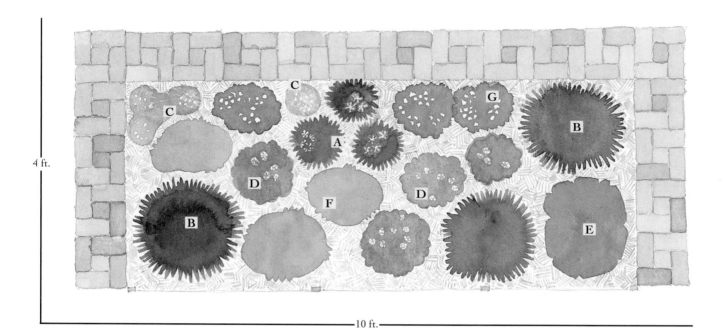

4 ft.

10 ft.

A white garden conveys elegance and composure, while bringing surrounding colors into harmony. This one contains readily available plants that are sun- and drought-tolerant; the whole bed requires just a weekly watering with the hose or drip system. Three fortnight lilies anchor the scene with their dark, evergreen leaves, and the centers of their mostly white flowers add the only hints of color: pale gold and purple.

Dietes bicolor
FORTNIGHT LILY

Verbena hybrida
GARDEN VERBENA

THE PLANTS

A. *Agapanthus* 'Dwarf White' (3)
LILY-OF-THE-NILE

B. *Dietes bicolor* (3)
FORTNIGHT LILY

C. *Lobularia maritima* (4)
SWEET ALYSSUM

D. *Pelargonium hortorum*
'Snowmass' (4)
COMMON GERANIUM

E. *Salvia greggii* (white) (1)
AUTUMN SAGE

F. *Scabiosa caucasica*
'Miss Willmott' (3)
PERENNIAL PINCUSHION
FLOWER

G. *Verbena hybrida* (white) (3)
GARDEN VERBENA

Summer Blues

This grouping of silvers and blues can form an element in an arrangement of raised beds or stand alone as an island border. All the plants need full sun and will tolerate some aridity. A tall butterfly bush is placed in the center; along with the lavender, it provides fragrance and attracts beneficial bees and other insects. Lower growing tanacetum and artemisia punctuate opposite corners with evergreen gray foliage and yellow buttonlike flowers. After the bearded irises have bloomed, white and blue annual lobelia can be used to fill in around them.

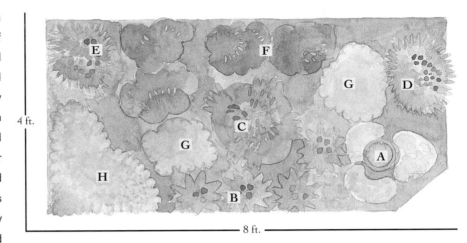

4 ft.

8 ft.

Bearded iris

Linum perenne
PERENNIAL BLUE FLAX

Tanacetum densum amanii

THE PLANTS

A. *Artemisia stellerana* 'Silver Brocade' (3)
BEACH WORMWOOD

B. *Bearded iris* (6)

C. *Buddleia davidii* 'Lochinch' (1)
BUTTERFLY BUSH

D. *Lavandula intermedia* 'Alba' (1)
LAVENDER

E. *Lavandula intermedia* 'Provence' (1)
LAVENDER

F. *Linum perenne* (4)
PERENNIAL BLUE FLAX

G. *Salvia chamaedryoides* (1)
SAGE

H. *Tanacetum densum amanii* (3)

Bulbs

One of the most dramatic and simple low-maintenance landscaping schemes is to plant an expanse of bulbs across a slope or meadow. Year after year the springtime reward is great swaths of color that are pest free, dependable, and require little care. Daffodils are Mediterranean natives and are well-adapted to dry summers. Even a small, oval-shaped grouping of a single bulb type is striking; and bulbs mix easily in borders with other plants.

There are some things you can do to make an easy plant even easier. Some bulbs are unpalatable to gophers (daffodils among them), but for those that aren't, plant in wire baskets (see page 223). A dramatic show of bulbs requires hundreds of plants; the job of planting can be made easier with an electric bulb auger. In naturalized settings, grassy cover disguises bulb foliage, which must not be cut until it has yellowed. Another way to camouflage wilting bulb foliage is to oversow planted bulbs with short-lived flowering annuals, such as Iceland poppies.

A decline in flower quality may signal overcrowding. Dig up dormant bulbs and divide them, then replant.

There are several types of bulbs. In this book, some bulblike plants (such as iris, daylily, and agapanthus) are listed with the Perennials (see pages 121–123).

A mass of bulbs. Daffodil (top) and crocus (bottom) both naturalize well over slopes and meadows. Although planting an expanse of bulbs may seem like a lot of work, the reward is years of trouble-free flowers in spring. And bulbs such as daffodils cost just pennies apiece.

THE ORNAMENTAL GARDEN

EASY-CARE BULBS FOR WESTERN GARDENS

Botanical name COMMON NAME	Sun & Water/ Zones	Height & Appearance	Comments
Allium ORNAMENTAL ALLIUM	☀ ◑ ● ◌ / All zones	6 in. to 5 ft. depending on species. Flowers usually ball-shaped from 1–10 in., may be white, yellow, pink, red, blue, or lavender	Plant in fall. Easy naturalizers include *A. moly* (10 in. tall, yellow flowers in June); *A. neopolitanum* (1 ft. tall, white flowers in spring); and *A. sphaerocephalum* (2 ft. tall, reddish-purple flowers, May–June)
Amaryllis belladonna BELLADONNA LILY, NAKED LADY	☀ ○ / 4–24	2–3 ft. Strap-shaped leaves form fountainlike clumps; dies back in early summer. Flowers lilylike; medium rose pink with paler or darker markings, midsummer	Plant in late summer. Ideal for southern zones with no summer rain; mix among drought-tolerant, low-growing perennials, annuals, or ground covers. 'Hathor' has white flowers. Bulbs are poisonous
Arum italicum ITALIAN ARUM	☀ ◑ ● ◌ / 4–24	1 ft. Attractive, arrow-shaped leaves emerge in fall and persist all winter. Flowers in spring, followed by striking clusters of red fruit	Tolerates shade, but flowers and fruits best in partial sun. *A. italicum* 'Pictum' (or 'Marmoratum') has marbled leaves
Babiana BABOON FLOWER	☀ ◑ ◌ ◌ / 4–24	6–12 in. Six-petaled flowers in shades of red, cream, blue, white, and lavender, blooming in mid- to late spring	Plant in fall. Hybrids of *B. stricta* come in a variety of colors; *B. rubrocyanea* red, royal blue. Bulbs require no summer watering, as they are dormant. Naturalizes in warm and well-drained soil
Chionodoxa GLORY-OF-THE-SNOW	◑ ◌ ● / 1–7, 14–20	6 in. Flowers small, six petaled, star shaped, ranging from shades of blue to violet, pink, and white, early spring	Plant in fall; naturalizes easily. In hot, dry summers grows best in partial shade. Excellent under spring-flowering shrubs
Crocosmia crocosmiiflora MONTBRETIA	☀ ◑ ○ / 5–24	3–4 ft., clumping. Stiff sword-shaped leaves and long stems, with yellow, orange, cream, red flowers in summer	Plant corms in spring in well-drained rich soil. Water first year only. Good for naturalizing on slopes or in fringe areas
Crocus	☀ ◑ ◌ ● / All zones	3–6 in. Flowers cup shaped; white, cream, yellow, orange, violet to deep purple, many with stripes or streaks of a contrasting color; spring or fall	Plant in fall. Appreciates winter chill. Easiest species include *C. goulimyi* (fall blooming, good for southern zones), *C. tomasinianus* (naturalizes freely), and *C. chrysanthus* varieties
Freesia	☀ ◑ ◌ ● / 8, 9, 12–24	12–18 in. Fragrant trumpets held like candelabras on long stems in white, yellow, orange, pink, red, purple, and blue	Plant in fall. Good cut flowers; colorful edgers in a border. Self-sows and naturalizes easily. Needs no summer water
Galanthus elwesii, G. nivalis SNOWDROP	☀ ◑ ● / 1–9, 14–17	6–18 in. Pendent white flowers in late winter and early spring	Appreciates winter chill—happy even in the coldest climates. Plant in drifts in fall; bulbs naturalize freely. *G. nivalis* bulb is poisonous
Gladiolus tristis	☀ ● / All zones	1½ ft. Tiny creamy flowers in spring	Plant corms Oct.–Nov. Fragrant, good in containers and for cut flowers. Naturalizes easily
Ipheion uniflorum SPRING STAR FLOWER	☀ ◑ ◌ ● / 4–24	8 in. Flowers star shaped, pale to deep blue. Leaves flat, bluish green	Plant in fall in any soil. Leaves smell like onions when crushed. Use as edging, ground cover; will persist for years
Ixia maculata hybrids AFRICAN CORN LILY	☀ ○ ◌ / 7–9, 12–24	16–24 in. Flowers six petaled, in clusters, dark centered red, yellow, cream, pink or orange, blooming in mid-to late spring	Plant in fall; naturalizes well. Thrives in dry summers, but needs water during growth and bloom
Muscari GRAPE HYACINTH	☀ ◑ ○ ◌ / All zones	4–18 in. In early spring, short spikes in shades of blue, purple, or white appear in clumps of grassy leaves	Plant in fall. Extremely easy to grow; naturalizes freely. Divide when crowded
Narcissus DAFFODIL	☀ ◑ ○ ◌ / All zones	3–18 in., depending on species. Flowers orange, yellow, cream, or white; many bi-color, a few bordered or shaded with pink or red, blooming in early to late spring	Plant in fall; many naturalize freely but need winter cold to survive more than one season
Schizostylis coccinea CRIMSON FLAG	☀ ◑ ● ●● / 5–9, 14–24	1½ ft. tall. Narrow evergreen leaves. Spikes to 2 ft. with 2-in. crimson flowers, Oct.–Nov.	Plant in spring with generous amount of peat moss or other organic matter. Water generously until flowering stops, then sparingly until new growth appears in spring
Watsonia	☀ ◌ / 4–9, 12–24	3½–6 ft. Fragrant, tubular flowers are on upright spikes, in shades of pink, rosy red, or white; blooms in late spring or summer (depending on species)	Plant in fall. A good back-of-the-border plant; flowers are fragrant and long lasting when cut. *W. beatris* is evergreen; *W. pyramidata* is deciduous
Zantedeschia aethiopica COMMON CALLA	☀ ◑ ● ●● / 5, 6, 8, 9, 14–24	1–4 ft. Large, arrow-shaped leaves. Flowers cornucopia shaped, white or cream	Plant in fall; foliage is evergreen or semi-evergreen and tolerates a range of soils and garden conditions, including damp areas (but can be invasive). Good container plants

☀ Full sun; ◑ Part shade; ● Full shade; ○ Drought tolerant; ◌ Little water; ● Regular water; ●● Ample water.   **To find your climate zone, see pages 14–21.**

Spring into Action

A group of perennials and shrubs is transformed in spring by waves of bloom from a selection of bulbs that were planted the previous fall. From the towering *Watsonia* to the diminutive grape hyacinth, each bulb makes its statement, then fades back into the well-planned cover of chrysanthemum, sweet alyssum, and catmint. A simple stone edging and a clipped rosemary hedge make permanent borders for the changing scene within.

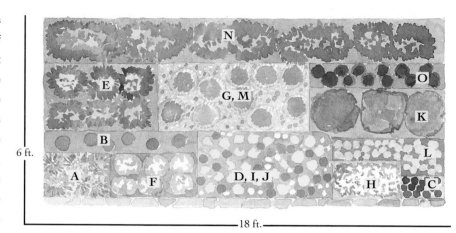

Agapanthus 'Peter Pan'
LILY-OF-THE-NILE

Euphorbia characias wulfenii

Nandina domestica 'Nana'
HEAVENLY BAMBOO

THE PLANTS

A. *Agapanthus* 'Peter Pan' (6)
   LILY-OF-THE-NILE

B. *Allium schubertii* (6)
   ORNAMENTAL ALLIUM

C. *Babiana stricta* (12)
   BABOON FLOWER

D. *Chrysanthemum multicaule* (24)

E. *Euphorbia characias wulfenii* (6)

F. *Iberis sempervirens* (6)
   EVERGREEN CANDYTUFT

G. *Iris (Dutch)* 'Symphony' (50)

H. *Lobularia maritima* (12)
   SWEET ALYSSUM

I. *Muscari botryoides* 'Album' (25)
   GRAPE HYACINTH

J. *Muscari tubergenianum* (25)
   GRAPE HYACINTH

K. *Nandina domestica* 'Nana' (3)
   HEAVENLY BAMBOO

L. *Narcissus*
   (Jonquilla Hybrid) (30)
   DAFFODIL

M. *Nepeta faassenii* (10)
   CATMINT

N. *Rosmarinus officinalis*
   'Tuscan Blue' (10)
   ROSEMARY

O. *Watsonia beatricis* 'Scarlet' (12)

Cover Up

A mix of bulbs and annuals was planted by scattering bulbs inside lines (drawn with powdered lime directly on the soil), planting them at their appropriate depths, then mixing seeds of annuals into the top layer of soil. Most of the bulbs emerge through the foliage and flowers of the annuals, though the taller ornamental allium and the daffodil give solid lines of massed bloom. Although the number of plants seems large, most of these bulbs cost just pennies apiece—a bargain for such an impressive show each spring.

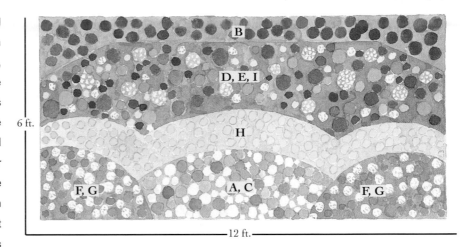

Lobularia maritima
SWEET ALYSSUM

Nigella damascena
LOVE-IN-A-MIST

Ixia maculata
AFRICAN CORN LILY

THE PLANTS

A. *Allium neapolitanum* 'Cowanii' (50)
ORNAMENTAL ALLIUM

B. *Allium sphaerocephalum* (100)
DRUMSTICKS

C. *Centaurea cyanus* 'Polka Dot' (48)
CORNFLOWER

D. *Eschscholzia californica* mix (24)
CALIFORNIA POPPY

E. *Ixia maculata* (100)
AFRICAN CORN LILY

F. *Lobularia maritima* (32)
SWEET ALYSSUM

G. *Muscari armeniacum* (40)
GRAPE HYACINTH

H. *Narcissus* 'Dutch Master' (100)
DAFFODIL

I. *Nigella damascena* (24)
LOVE-IN-A-MIST

Water-loving Plants

ater gardening has become extraordinarily popular, and with good reason. The presence of water adds a calming, cooling effect to even the busiest city patio or the hottest Southwestern courtyard. The requirements for designing and constructing water features are discussed on pages 70–73. But the amount of work your feature calls for increases with the complexity of its contents, including the type and number of plants and animals. Most catalogs and suppliers refer to three types of water plants: floaters, whose roots dangle in the water; oxygenating plants, which grow submerged beneath the surface; and marginal plants for the shallower areas around the pond's circumference. Whether or not fish are added to the pond, these plants work together to maintain the pond's essential balance of oxygen and other gases; when this balance is disturbed the result is algae, weeds, and stagnant water.

Bubble, bubble. Water hyacinths (Eichhornia crassipes) *can be plopped in the pond and—even if chewed by raccoons—will quickly multipy. Duckweed is considered an unwelcome addition to most ponds as it chokes other plants and blocks sunlight, but just skim off the excess with a wooden board. This bubbling mask keeps the water moving.*

MORE WATER, LESS WORK

If you inherit an established, well-functioning water garden, you may be able to maintain it with a once-yearly clean up and regular feeding for the pond's inhabitants (if the pond is subject to winter freezing, more work is required to keep fish healthy in winter). But if you are starting from scratch, the best way to keep down the work of a water feature is to keep it simple. Rather than fussy water lilies, put some colored glass balls or floating candles in the water. Install a fountain, or place some artwork in or around the pond. Instead of submerging plants in special pots, place a few floaters on the surface. And take advantage of the moisture-loving marginal or bog plants listed on the facing page to surround the water feature with color. If you want to make an impact with plants in the pond, try a single water lily (hardy types can overwinter in the pond).

BOGGED DOWN

A perpetually damp spot of ground may indicate an underground spring nearby or another cause of poor drainage. Such constantly wet soils lack the oxygen that most garden plant roots need to function. You might try to correct this drainage problem by re-grading or installing drains (see p. 63), but a simpler solution is to let nature dictate. Simply use the space to showcase thirsty plants that would be unhappy elsewhere. Left in containers at the edge of a pond or planted in the ground, these plants can thrive where most others would quickly succumb to oxygen starvation or fungal diseases. A selection is listed at right; ask at your local nursery for others that grow well in your area.

So sweet. Sweet flag (Acorus gramineus) *comes in variegated forms that spread freely to brighten up a shady, damp spot. It's one of the easiest plants to divide and replant. Baby's tears* (Soleirolia soleirolii) *also spreads with ease around flagstones and other plants. Mix both these plants with shade-loving ferns for a completely trouble-free shade garden.*

SOME LIKE IT WET

Plants with an asterisk can grow with their roots submerged in water.

Low-growing plants

Astilbe chinensis 'Pumila'

Corydalis

Galium odoratum
SWEET WOODRUFF

Houttuynia cordata *

Lamium maculatum
DEAD NETTLE

Mentha spicata
SPEARMINT

Soleirolia soleirolii
BABY'S TEARS

Flowering plants

Aconitum napellus
GARDEN MONKSHOOD

Caltha palustris
MARSH MARIGOLD*

Chives

Cimicifuga racemosa
BLACK SNAKEROOT

Iris ensata
JAPANESE IRIS*

Iris pseudacorus
YELLOW FLAG*

Ligularia

Lobelia cardinalis
CARDINAL FLOWER*

Zantedeschia aethiopica
COMMON CALLA*

Foliage plants

Acorus gramineus
SWEET FLAG

Arundo donax
GIANT REED

Bamboo
MANY SPECIES

Carex
SEDGE*

Chasmanthium latifolium
SEA OATS

Cyperus papyrus
PAPYRUS*

Equisetum hyemale (containers only)
HORSETAIL

Ferns (many, see p. 110)

Juncus
RUSH*

Liriope spicata
CREEPING LILY TURF

Miscanthus sinensis
EULALIA GRASS

Trees & Shrubs

Acer rubrum
SCARLET MAPLE

Aesculus parviflora
BOTTLEBRUSH BUCKEYE

Betula nigra
RIVER BIRCH

Cercidiphyllum japonicum
KATSURA TREE

Clethra alnifolia
SUMMERSWEET

Cornus stolonifera
REDTWIG DOGWOOD

Lindera
SPICEBUSH

Sabal palmetto, S. minor
CABBAGE PALM;
DWARF PALMETTO

Salix
WILLOW, MANY SPECIES

Taxodium
CYPRESS, SEVERAL SPECIES*

5

The Edible Garden

O ne of life's greatest culinary pleasures and the edible gardener's greatest reward is the taste of home-grown produce. But for the busy gardener, edible plants may seem to be more trouble than they are worth. Many vegetables are fussy about soil, sun, and water. Pests love them. And we demand a greater level of perfection from our edible plants than from flowers, for instance, where a few slugs or chewed leaves don't make much difference.

But this doesn't mean you have to forego home produce. As always, it's important to decide just how much time and expertise you have to spare, then choose accordingly. And even if you decide against growing lettuce or tomatoes, herbs are among the most trouble-free plants in any garden.

If you raise edibles, you must be diligent in your use of pesticides, herbicides, and disease-controls. Consult "The Healthy Garden", starting on page 218, for advice on preventing and controlling problems.

Edible Plants

ost vegetables require excellent soil conditions, regular fertilizing, and diligent watering. Because they are grown for size and flavor, the plants need not just to survive, but to thrive. And although some vegetables—the ones listed here—are relatively trouble-free, many of the favorites are thirsty, hungry, and prone to pests, diseases, and cultural problems. Before you decide to plant a vegetable patch, ask yourself how much you'll really use the edibles you plan to grow. Then make your choices from those crops that require little care.

It's important to grow vegetables during the appropriate season. Cool-season crops won't grow unless soil temperatures are cool, in early spring and late fall. Warm-season crops are not only frost-tender but will not thrive unless the soil is well warmed.

If you decide to grow only one or two types of vegetables, don't be afraid to mix them in with ornamental plants and culinary herbs—a few such "edible landscaping" schemes are given on the following pages.

Most fruit trees require a regular program of spraying and pruning. Citrus are an exception, but in frost-prone areas plant them in containers and protect over the winter. For advice on preventing pests and diseases, see "The Healthy Garden" starting on page 218.

Raise them up, eat them up. *Raised beds and containers provide one critical ingredient for edible plants: good soil. The drawback? You must ensure that they receive adequate irrigation and feeding. See pp. 148 and 189, and the irrigation section starting on p. 191 for more information.* ***Top, left*** *Swiss chard and cabbage in colorful containers.* ***Top, right*** 'Meyer' *lemon in a perfect pot.* ***Above*** *Raised beds can take on any shape; these are filled with leafy vegetables that are at the right height for harvesting.*

Cover up. A thick layer of mulch (see p. 188) will keep down weeds, retain moisture, and even discourage some soft-bodied crawling pests. Be careful to keep it an inch or two away from stems, however, to prevent rot.

Jump start. Although many plants, such as arugula, can easily be grown from seed, your vegetables will have a better chance of maturing if you plant seedlings from nursery containers such as six-packs. One slug can make short work of a tiny seedling.

Repeat performers. Among the best candidates for the vegetable bed are perennials that don't need replanting each year; see the Guide below.

Garden hogs. Plants such as pumpkin and zucchini can grow very large in a small amount of time. Avoid these rampant growers.

"Cut-and-come again." Look for crops such as broccoli and lettuce that obligingly resprout after trimming for a second harvest.

Can't live without you. If there is a particular vegetable you really can't live without, then concentrate your efforts. Suppose garden-fresh tomatoes are a treat you can't find in your local supermarket. It won't be that much trouble to fill a raised bed with good soil and plant it with a few 'Early Girl' tomatoes.

Read the label. Like annuals, the All-America Selection (AAS) plants have been selected for their ability to perform well in many different areas. Look for these, and for plants labeled as resistant to disease. Tomatoes, for instance, are labeled V, F, N, or T for resistance to certain diseases.

Keep it cool. An advantage to cool-season crops is that winter rains will provide much of the irrigation the plants need.

Cover crops. So-called green manures help improve the quality of your soil, fix nitrogen in it, and provide coverage for bare winter beds. Simply sow seeds of clover, mustard, or vetches, allow them to grow until spring, then cut them down and turn them into the soil.

Experiment. Don't be afraid to try something new. Many western nurseries stock a variety of cool-season leafy vegetables called "Asian greens" or "Asian vegetables," which include mustard, bok choy, broccoli, and cabbage. Many gardeners have found these easy to grow and tasty in stir-fries or as vegetable side dishes.

EASY-CARE EDIBLE PLANTS FOR WESTERN GARDENS

	COMMON NAME	Sun & Water/ Zones	Description	Comments & Recommended Varieties
COOL-SEASON EDIBLES	ARUGULA, ROQUETTE	☼ ● All zones	To 3 ft. Dark green, peppery-tasting leaves, 1–4 in. long; delicate white flowers on long stems	Easy; sow seed in succession for a constant supply in spring and fall. Pick leaves when small. If left to flower, reseeds readily. Recommended: Italian arugula (*Arugula selvatica*)
	BEET	☼ ●● All zones	Edible, ribbed, 1-ft. leaves with purplish or metallic sheen. Red, round roots are best harvested when 1–3 in. across	Recommended: 'Detroit Dark Red', 'Chiogga', 'Lutz'
	BROCCOLI	☼ ● All zones	Central stalk to 4 ft. bearing green or purple edible flower buds; leaves crinkled, coarse	Harvest flower buds before flowers open. BROCCOLI RABE is an Italian relative with stronger flavor; leaves and buds are edible
	FAVA BEAN (BROAD BEAN, HORSE BEAN)	☼ ● All zones	Thick, veined leaves on upright stems to 2–4 ft.; occasionally need support. Long pods contain 4–8 lima-type beans but may be eaten like string beans when young	Not a true bean but a type of vetch, rarely bothered by pests. White, pealike flowers have sweet fragrance at night. Recommended: 'Aquadulce'
	GARLIC	☼ ● All zones	Long, thin leaves in tufts to 2 ft. tall, edible underground bulbs	In all but coldest regions (zones 1–2), plant cloves in fall for following summer harvest; garlic is mature when tops begin to brown. Best in rich, moist, well-drained soil. Cut off any flower stalks for best bulb development. Recommended: 'Gilroy CA Late', 'German Red Rocambole'
	LEAF LETTUCE	☼ ◑ ● 1–7, 10, 11 (spring crop); 8, 9, 12–24 (fall/winter crop)	1 ft. wide and high. Decorative, frilly, curled, soft green leaves, some tinted red or yellow, in loose rosettes	Easier than head lettuces, loose-leaf lettuces will resprout when cut for harvest during their growing season. Need moisture, cool temperatures. Protect from snails (see p. 222). Recommended: 'Red Oakleaf', 'Black Seeded Simpson', 'Merveille des Quatre Saisons'

☼ Full sun; ◑ Part shade; ● Full shade; ○ Drought tolerant; ◔ Little water; ● Regular water; ●● Ample water.   To find your climate zone, see pages 14–21.

COMMON NAME	Sun & Water/ Zones	Description	Comments & Recommended Varieties
MUSTARD	☼ ● All zones	Upright green or reddish leaves, 6–12 in. tall, many varieties available	Plant in early spring or late summer. Fast and easy to grow; ready to eat in 35–60 days
SPINACH	☼ ●● All zones	Thick, dark green, wrinkled or savoyed leaves grow to 1 ft.; flat-leaved types available	Slow growing; takes some frost. Resprouts when cut. Recommended: 'Melody', 'Bloomsdale Long Standing', 'Tyee'
AMARANTH	☼ ◗ ● All zones	Crinkled leaves on stems 1–4 ft. high; colored varieties available	Hot-weather spinach substitute with edible leaves and stems. Recommended: 'Tampala', 'Mirah'
OKRA	☼ ● All zones	Tropical annual to 5 ft.; palmate leaves 1 ft. across; hibiscus-like flowers followed by edible seedpods, 3–8 in. long	Needs warm weather for best harvest, pods are best when small, 1 to 4 in. long; harvest every other day for a continuous supply. Best in colder regions with cool nights. Recommended: 'Perkins Spineless', 'Dwarf Green Long Pod'; 'Clemson Spineless' is an All-America Selection
ONION	☼ ● All zones	Pale green, hollow leaves in tufts; attractive ball-shaped flowers	Young roots may be harvested for scallions (green onions) or left to mature into globes that can be stored over winter. White, yellow, and red types available. Best well weeded and well watered. Plant from "sets"; use different spot each year to minimize diseases and pests. Recommended: 'Walla Walla Sweets', 'First Edition'
SNAP BEAN (STRING BEAN, GREEN BEAN)	☼ ● All zones	Climbing types to 10–12 ft; bush types to 2–4 ft. Heart-shaped green leaves. White or pinkish flowers	Fast-maturing, annuals with tender, fleshy fruit pods in green, light yellow, or purple. Bush types need less support. May get aphids and whiteflies (see pp. 220–221). Recommended: 'Blue Lake', 'Royalty'. Scarlet runner beans are showy, with bright green leaves and red, pink, white, or red flowers followed by dark green pods. Best harvested when young
SORREL	☼ ◗ ● All zones	Perennial, 12–36 in. tall, fleshy lance-like leaves forming a rosette	Best in a nitrogen-rich, moist soil. Very easy; cut off flower stalks to ensure leaf production. Two widely available species: French sorrel (*Rumex scutatus*) and the larger-leaved garden sorrel (*R. acetosa*)
SPROUTS	☼ ◗ ● All zones	Appearance varies depending on type; most are 1–2 in. long, with 2 small leaves and a single white root	Seed sprouts need only some water and a container to thrive. Radish, alfalfa, mung beans, lentils, and broccoli seeds can be purchased at health food stores. Rinse and strain the seeds; place in a clear glass jar, keep in a bright but not sunny spot. Rinse the sprouts daily and harvest promptly when green leaves appear
SWISS CHARD	☼ ● All zones	Leafy plant to 1½ ft. tall with prominent stems and ribs	Easy from seed or nursery packs. New leaves grow up in center; harvest older leaves from outside plant. Rarely bolts. 'Rhubarb' has vivid red stalks; good as ornamental
TOMATO	☼ ○ ● All zones	Sprawling or climbing to 4–6 ft., depending on variety. Leathery dull green leaves are poisonous. Starry yellow flowers. Fruits red, pink, orange, yellow, purplish, green or pale white, depending on variety	Demands warm soils and good sunshine. Plant in a different spot each year to minimize diseases and pests. Recommended: 'Early Girl Improved', 'Better Boy', 'Big Beef', 'Celebrity', 'Dona', and cherry types 'Sweet 100' and 'Santa'
TOMATILLO	☼ ◗ ● All zones	Annual with bushy, sprawling growth to 4 ft.; fruit about 2 in. wide surrounded by a papery husk, resembling a cherry tomato	When picked green, tomatillos are used in Mexican cooking for salsas and other dishes. Culture similar to tomatoes; needs warmth to produce well. Recommended: 'Toma Verde'
ASPARAGUS	☼ ●● All zones	Feathery, ferny deep green leaves turn reddish in fall. Flowers insignificant, followed by inedible red berries on female plants. Stalks to 6 ft.	Dependable crop that needs 2–3 years to get established. Harvest stalks as they emerge from ground in early spring. Plant as crowns in rich soil. Recommended: 'UC 57'
CITRUS	☼ ● Zones 8, 9, 12–24; or indoors	Variable appearance according to species; most have glossy, deep green leaves, fragrant flowers, and attractive fruit. Standard trees grow to 20–30 ft. tall and wide; dwarf varieties range from 4 to 15 ft.	Can be subject to a variety of insect pests and a few fungus ailments. Some can be grown in containers and brought indoors for the winter. Choose oranges, lemons, limes, tangerines, and many others based on your local climate; check with your County Extension Service for recommendations
JERUSALEM ARTICHOKE (SUNCHOKE)	☼ ● ●● All zones	Narrow stalks to 6–8-ft. Drooping oval leaves, 6–8 in. long; 3–4 in. bright yellow "sunflowers" in late summer	Native American sunflower relative has edible tubers, harvested from late fall to early spring. Tolerates most soils, eager to spread where soils are damp. Plant as tubers. Recommended: 'Fuseau'

Row groups (left margin labels):
- WARM-SEASON EDIBLES (MUSTARD through TOMATILLO)
- "PERENNIAL" EDIBLES (ASPARAGUS through JERUSALEM ARTICHOKE)

☼ **Full sun;** ◗ **Part shade;** ● **Full shade;** ○ **Drought tolerant;** ◔ **Little water;** ● **Regular water;** ●● **Ample water.**   **To find your climate zone, see pages 14–21.**

Ornamental Edibles

There's no need for vegetables and ornamentals to live on opposite sides of the garden; for visual and culinary interest, plant the two together. This sunny, colorful corner beside a curving pathway can be watered by drip irrigation tubes or a soaker hose that winds through the bed. Edibles are placed near the path to make harvesting easier; taller ornamentals are planted toward the back. Scarlet runner beans race to the top of 10-foot bamboo poles, forming a teepee of colorful flowers and tasty young pods.

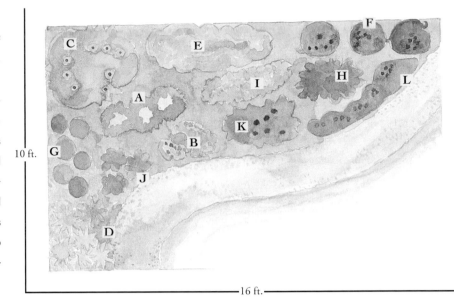

10 ft.

16 ft.

Achillea 'Moonshine'
YARROW

Salvia leucantha
MEXICAN BUSH SAGE

Tomato 'Sweet 100'

THE PLANTS

A. *Achillea* 'Moonshine' (3)
   YARROW

B. *Geranium sanguineum* (3)
   CRANESBILL

C. *Helianthus annuus* (6)
   COMMON SUNFLOWER

D. *Hemerocallis* (6)
   DAYLILY

E. *Salvia leucantha* (2)
   MEXICAN BUSH SAGE

F. *Scarlet runner bean* (3)

G. *Sorrel* (6)

H. *Swiss chard* (6)

I. *Tagetes erecta* (6)
   AMERICAN MARIGOLD

J. *Tomatillo* (3)

K. *Tomato* 'Sweet 100' (3)

L. *Viola tricolor* (12)
   JOHNNY-JUMP-UP

An Easy Potager

True potagers are often boxed in with low hedges that require clipping and shaping. Let this mix of summer perennials, annuals, herbs, and easy-to-grow vegetables spill out over a brick pathway for a carefree look, or raise up the whole arrangement in a timber-framed bed. Long-lived Swiss chard and amaranth will last through the warm months—unlike leafy spinach and lettuce, summer sun won't make them bolt. Aphids may appear on your edibles. Use non-toxic methods to keep them at bay (see pages 220–225).

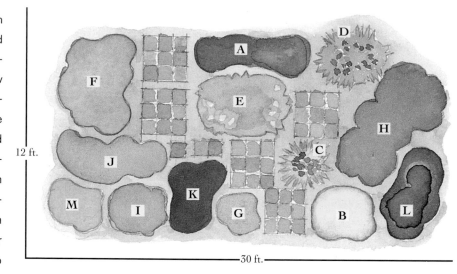

Swiss chard

Tropaeolum majus
GARDEN NASTURTIUM

Calendula officinalis
POT MARIGOLD

THE PLANTS

A. *Amaranth* (6)

B. *Calendula officinalis* (6)
POT MARIGOLD

C. CHIVES (3)
Allium schoenoprasum

D. *Dianthus plumarius* (8)
COTTAGE PINK

E. *Dwarf citrus* 'Meyer' lemon (1)

F. *Jerusalem artichoke* (8)

G. LEMON THYME (3)
Thymus citriodorus

H. LEMON-SCENTED GERANIUM (6)
Pelargonium crispum

I. ROSEMARY (3)
Rosmarinus officinalis

J. SAGE (12)
Salvia officinalis

K. SWEET BASIL (6)
Ocimum basilicum 'Dark Opal'

L. *Swiss chard* (4)

M. *Tropaeolum majus* (3)
GARDEN NASTURTIUM

Space-saving Square

This square plot, only 10 by 10 feet, produces plenty of produce over a long period without too much work. The cool-season vegetables (lettuce, beets, garlic, fava beans, and spinach) are ready for harvesting at about the time the warm-season ones (cherry tomatoes and scarlet runner beans) are being planted. In fact, a tomato and bean plot could do double duty by first being planted with onions, harvested early in the season as scallions.

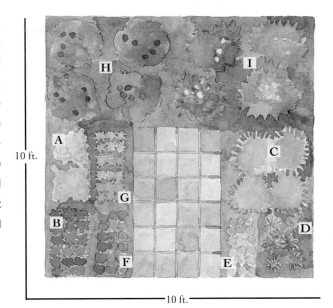

Garlic

Asparagus

Leaf lettuce 'Black Seeded Simpson'

THE PLANTS

A. *Asparagus* (6)

B. *Beets* (12)

C. *Fava beans* (4)

D. *Garlic* (6)

E. *Leaf lettuce* 'Black Seeded Simpson' (12)

F. *Leaf lettuce* 'Red Oakleaf' (12)

G. *Spinach* (16)

H. *Tomato* 'Sweet 100' *(on stakes)* (4)

I. *Scarlet runner beans* (4)

Herbs

ost of the culinary herbs we enjoy in our gardens (and kitchens) are tough Mediterranean perennials, ideally suited to the dryer regions of the West. Others are quick-growing annuals that have been reliable standbys in home gardens since medieval times.

The Mediterranean types include rosemary, thyme, lavender, sage, and oregano, all of which grow into slightly woody, evergreen plants. Once established, these perennials need little summer water, absolutely no fertilizer, and no grooming beyond a trimming to get fragrant leaves for the stewpot. In fact, too much water or fertilizer causes floppy, weak growth, and dilutes the essential oils that give herbs their distinctive fragrance and flavors. As a bonus, these oils deter insect and animal pests, including slugs and deer.

Annual herbs, such as basil, dill, and cilantro, have softer leaves and require more protection from slugs and insects. (see page 222). Larger plants from nursery containers can outgrow predators; small seedlings are more vulnerable.

With a few exceptions (such as mints) herbs demand full sun and fast-draining soil. Long windowboxes or patio pots may be enough for a small herb collection. Raised beds, a bit of sloping ground around a terrace, or planters built into a retaining wall can give you room for a grouping of different lavenders or oregano. If space is limited, integrate perennial herbs into a mixed flower border.

One plant, many places. The plants we call "herbs" can fit almost anywhere in the garden. **Top** A raised bed provides well-draining soil for sages and ornamental oregano. **Bottom, left** Rosemary, lavender cotton, and lavender serve as shrubby ground cover. **Bottom, right** Variegated sage and thyme make an appearance in a container with yarrow and a small yellow rose.

EASY-CARE HERBS FOR WESTERN GARDENS

COMMON NAME / Botanical Name	Sun & Water/ Zones	Description	Uses & Comments
BORAGE / *Borago officinalis*	☼ ◐ ● ◖ ◕ / All zones	1–3 ft. by 1–3 ft.. Bristly gray-green leaves and showy flowers, like blue stars, that face down	Good in herb or ornamental garden; will reseed. Leaves and flowers edible, good in summer drinks
CHIVES / *Allium schoenoprasum*	☼ ◐ ◖ ◕◕ / All zones	Grasslike spears grow in perennial clumps from bulbs; round purple flowers on top of thin stems, to 2 ft.	Delicate onionlike flavor. Use as garnish or in salads, cream cheese, cottage cheese, egg dishes, gravies, and soup
CILANTRO (CORIANDER) / *Coriandrum sativum*	☼ ◕ / All zones	Bright green, fernlike leaves to 15 in.; flat clusters of tiny, pinkish white flowers	Young leaves used in salads, soups, poultry recipes, and variety of Mexican and Asian dishes. Crushed seeds used for seasoning sausage, beans, stews, cookies, wines. Self-sowing annual
FENNEL, COMMON / *Foeniculum vulgare*	☼ ○ / All zones	Yellow-green, finely cut leaves; flat clusters of yellow flower stalks grow to 5 ft.	Use seeds to season bread; leaves as garnish for salads and fish. Grown as annual; will reseed to point of weediness
FRENCH TARRAGON / *Artemisia dracunculus*	☼ ◖ ○ / All zones	Shiny, dark green, narrow leaves; woody stems to 2 ft. Spreads slowly by creeping rhizomes; dies to ground in winter. Flowers are greenish white in branched clusters	Use fresh or dried leaves to season salads, eggs and cheese dishes, fish. Good in containers
LAVENDER / *Lavandula* species	☼ ◖ / All zones	Gray-green foliage to 4 ft.; purple or lavender flowers on 2-ft. spikes	All used for perfume and sachets, in biscuits and desserts, and as ornamental perennial in flower gardens (see p. 123)
LAVENDER COTTON / *Santolina chamaecyparissus*	☼ ○ ◖ / All zones	Shrubby evergreen herb to 2 ft. high; woody stems densely covered with grayish hairs. Yellow butttonlike flowers in summer	Fragrant leaves used for decorating, crafts, as moth deterrent and in place of thyme in cooking. *S. rosmarinifolius* has deep green leaves, chartreuse flowers
LEMON VERBENA / *Aloysia triphylla*	☼ ◕ / 9, 10, 12–24	Leggy, gangly deciduous perennial to 6 ft. with narrow 3-in.-long leaves. Small whitish flowers in summer	Use lemon-scented leaves in teas and iced drinks, with apple jelly. Use as fragrant plant in garden; pinch to reduce legginess (see p. 217)
MINT, PEPPERMINT, and SPEARMINT / *Mentha* species	☼ ◐ ◕ / All zones	Dark green, strongly scented leaves. To 1 ft. high; with extensive spread. Small purple flowers in 1–3-in. spikes	Peppermint leaves good for flavoring tea. Spearmint is preferred for cooking; use leaves with lamb, in cold drinks, as garnish, and in apple jelly. Spreads rapidly; grow in pot or within barrier
OREGANO / *Origanum vulgare*	☼ ◕ / All zones	Shrubby perennial to 3 ft. with slightly fuzzy, pungent leaves; purplish pink blossoms	Especially popular in Italian and Spanish dishes. Pinch to keep from flowering. *O. v.* 'Aureum' has yellow leaves, pink flowers
PARSLEY / *Petroselinum crispum*	☼ ◐ ◕ / All zones	Tufted, finely cut, dark green leaves; grows to 1 ft.	Use the leaves fresh or dried as seasoning, fresh as garnish. Biennial that will die out after 2 years
ROSEMARY / *Rosmarinus officinalis*	☼ ○ ◖ / 4–24	To 6 ft., depending on species. Narrow leaves. Small clusters of light lavender blue, ¼-in. flowers	Pinch tender tips for seasoning. As ornamental perennial, has many uses in low-maintenance garden (see p. 100)
SAGE, COMMON / *Salvia officinalis*	☼ ◖ / All zones	An attractive, shrubby perennial to 2 ft. by 3 ft., with round, grayish leaves and a covering of feltlike, white hairs. Rarely flowers	Use in stuffing for meat and poultry, sausage flavoring, herb vinegar, herb butter. 'Berggarten' is best culinary variety
SWEET BASIL / *Ocimum basilicum*	☼ ◕ / All zones	To 2 ft., with green, shiny 2-in.-long leaves and spikes of white flowers	Use fresh or dry to give pleasant, sweet, mild flavor to tomatoes, cheese, fish, poultry, salads; basis of pesto sauce. Pinch flowers as they form to prevent seeding (see p. 217). Protect from slugs and snails (see p. 222). 'Dark Opal' has bronze leaves
SWEET BAY / *Laurus nobilis*	☼ ◐ ◖ ◕ / 5–9, 12–24	12–40 ft. (grown as shrub or tree). Leaves leathery, aromatic, 2-4 in. long, dark green; clusters of small, yellow flowers, followed by 1-in.-long, black or dark purple berries	Add leaves to soups, stews, and other dishes that simmer for a long period of time. Perfect in containers
SWEET MARJORAM / *Origanum majorana*	☼ ◖ / All zones (annual), 4–24 (perennial)	Tiny, oval, gray-green leaves; spikes of white flowers in loose clusters at the top of plant. To 2 ft.	Use for seasoning meats, salads, vinegar, casserole dishes
THYME, COMMON / *Thymus vulgaris*	☼ ◐ ◖ / All zones	Shrubby perennial to 12 in., with narrow to oval, ¼-in.-long, fragrant, gray-green leaves. Tiny lilac flowers	Seasoning for fish, shellfish, poultry stuffing, soups, vegetables, and vegetable juices. Good container plant
WINTER SAVORY / *Satureja montana*	☼ ◖ / All zones	Low and spreading, to 15 in. Stiff 1-in.-long leaves, with tiny white to lilac flowers	Use leaves fresh or dried to season meats, fish, soups, egg dishes, and vegetables; add to vinegar salad dressing. Needs sandy soil

☼ **Full sun;** ◐ **Part shade;** ● **Full shade;** ○ **Drought tolerant;** ◖ **Little water;** ◕ **Regular water;** ◕◕ **Ample water.**

To find your climate zone, see pages 14–21.

Compact Herb Garden

Find a small nook just outside the kitchen door and plant this assortment of culinary treats. These plants are especially easy to grow–they actually look and taste better without extra water or fertilizer–and their fragrance and beauty are added attractions beyond their culinary value. The rose 'Sunsprite' provides blooms to serve as cheerful embellishments for the table. A single terracotta pot placed near the chives would add a Mediterranean touch to the scene.

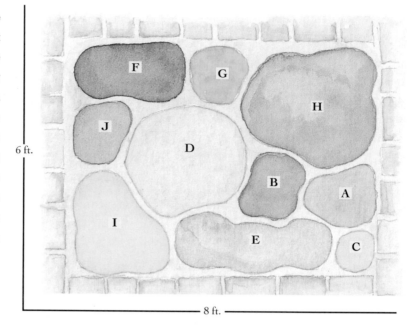

6 ft.

8 ft.

Nepeta faassenii
CATMINT

GOLDEN MARJORAM
Origanum vulgare 'Aureum'

LAVENDER COTTON
Santolina chamaecyparissus 'Nana'

THE PLANTS

A. CHIVES (3)
Allium schoenoprasum

B. FRENCH TARRAGON (4)
Artemisia dracunculus

C. GOLDEN MARJORAM (3)
Origanum vulgare 'Aureum'

D. LAVENDER COTTON (3)
Santolina chamaecyparissus 'Nana'

E. *Nepeta faassenii* (3)
CATMINT

F. OREGANO (2)
Origanum vulgare

G. *Rosa* 'Sunsprite' (1)
ROSE

H. ROSEMARY (3)
Rosmarinus officinalis
'Collingwood Ingram'

I. SAGE (3)
Salvia officinalis 'Icterina'

J. SWEET MARJORAM (1)
Origanum vulgare

An Herbal Walkway

Hand-painted tiles and containers of clipped dwarfed boxwood lend an air of formality to this charming herb-lined seating area, as do the diamond shapes fashioned from bricks set on edge in a sand bed. Woolly thyme exudes fragrance underfoot, and snippets of sage, lavender, and savory can be collected as you pass from the bench to the kitchen. A fruitless olive would be an ideal accent placed behind the bench.

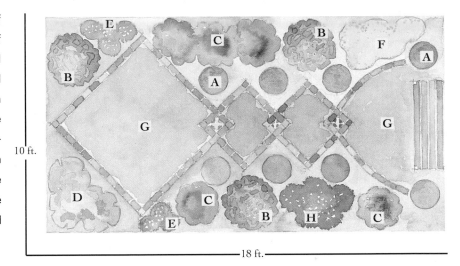

10 ft.

18 ft.

Buxus sempervirens 'Suffruticosa'
TRUE DWARF BOXWOOD

THYME, WOOLLY
Thymus pseudolanuginosis

FRENCH LAVENDER
Lavandula dentata

THE PLANTS

A. *Buxus sempervirens*
'Suffruticosa' (8)
TRUE DWARF BOXWOOD

B. FRENCH LAVENDER (3)
Lavandula dentata

C. SAGE (3)
Salvia officinalis 'Purpurascens'

D. SAGE (3)
Salvia officinalis 'Tricolor'

E. THYME, COMMON (6)
Thymus vulgaris

F. THYME, LEMON (5)
Thymus citriodorus

G. THYME, WOOLLY (48)
Thymus pseudolanuginosis

H. WINTER SAVORY (5)
Satureja montana

6
The Decorative Garden

The garden is no place for limits on your imagination. There's no need to merely imitate a classic English border or reproduce a French formal garden. Instead, contemporary western garden designers often employ decorative elements in the place of plants, and the low-maintenance gardener can benefit greatly from their innovations. What, after all, could be easier than an elegant urn set among ornamental grasses? Why fuss over a clipped hedge when a line of old bowling balls fills the space perfectly and makes a creative statement as well? Rather than hauling in heavy equipment to renovate poor soil, why not plant in easy-care containers? Or, if you've tried unsuccessfully to screen a plain concrete wall with plants, perhaps you should just give up and paint it pink! The following pages offer a sampling of ideas ranging from classical to whimsical. Use them as sparks for your own artistic expression.

Above *Mix container and flower forms for interest. Here, an ornamental oregano and kalanchoe have textures and colors that are just different enough—but don't conflict—in their stone pots.*

Above, right *Large containers can add emphasis, height, and color to a mixed border or even a raised bed. This impressive urn is filled with geraniums and lobelia, but would look just fine if left empty, too.*

Right *Clay chimney pots with a patina of age lend old-world charm to this kitchen garden.*

Left Ornamental grasses make wonderful container subjects, either singly or in groupings. Miscanthus sinensis 'Purparescens', shown here in October, illustrates why it is commonly known as flame grass.

Below A mass of one type of plant can be more striking than combinations — and it's certainly simple to design. Primroses are lined up in this impressive container 'table.' These flowers are finicky in areas other than the Northwest, but equally suitable plants could be substituted in warmer zones.

Right *Plastered, painted walls adorned with equally colorful containers are echoed with a simple, symmetrical plant arrangement of* Sedum *'Autumn Joy' and blue oat grass* (Helictotrichon sempervirens).

Below *A fanciful mural transforms these concrete walls into a lush, tropical scene. Potted plants blend into the scene.*

Below, right *A small porch or even a houseboat can be turned into a riot of color by harmonizing brightly painted surfaces with potted plants such as geraniums and lobelia.*

Below, left A half-circle pool connects to a water channel that cuts between two walls. A stone ball adds to the geometry, as do structural plants such as the ocotillo at left.

Below Containers and cut flowers don't need to be restricted to indoor settings; they can sit anywhere—even on a stained concrete bench in the garden. Outdoor dining tables are another favorite spot for flower arrangements.

Clockwise from opposite page *Find room for art in the garden by turning a practical object into a decorative element. This playful gate of painted sticks enlivens an arched opening in a plain wall. Glass beads or polished stones can form a sculptural 'mulch' for lavender cotton and low-growing grasses. A colorful mosaic compass is set into a flagstone pathway. An unused chair finds itself firmly seated in a grassy meadow with a clay pot for a companion.*

Left A child's sandbox can take on any shape. Standing stones transform this one but allow plenty of room for play. Place a sandbox or play area in partial shade to protect children from the sun, but avoid sites under trees that shed excessive litter.

Right Find room in the garden to display your own artwork or crafts. This miniature clay village was handmade by the garden's owner and arranged on a rocky outcrop with an assortment of succulents within a boxwood edging.

Left A resilient cactus has survived a humorous face-carving and 'haircut;' the plant continues to grow, surrounded by licorice plant (Helichrysum petiolare) and geraniums.

Right Oversized, theatrical pieces of sculpture require a garden of suitable proportions. You might expect to find a classical sculpture in a woodland glade, but instead a large frog sits on a bed of wood chips, guarding a fork in the path.

7

Plans for Low Maintenance

Whether you're installing a new garden or modifying an existing one, the most important step comes before the first spade of dirt is turned, and that is the development of a plan. Even if you never commit a formal drawing to paper, it's important to have an overall sense of your garden's layout and the type of plants you'd like to have in it. Many homeowners approach the development of their garden in stages; deciding which elements they would like—and can afford—to install first. This allows flexibility, too, in the evolution of the design. On the following pages are plans that demonstrate a variety of regional and decorative styles. Use these to get ideas, and adapt them to your own garden. Don't be afraid to mix and match elements from several different plans but remember that the most successful designs have a unity of materials rather than a jumble of disconnected ideas.

For a family with children in preschool, grade school, and high school, low maintenance is a high priority in the garden—and everywhere else. This backyard in California's Napa Valley demonstrates how plants and hardscape combine to create a flexible yet attractive backdrop for family life.

A play area for toddlers, set off by a low germander hedge, is located near the house, where a parent can keep a watchful eye on the sandbox, even from indoors. Douglas fir chips, soft underfoot, are spread thickly as mulch in unplanted areas. Flagstone is used as paving for two patios and as facing for a low concrete bench; in the less formal patio, further from the house, fragrant woolly thyme creeps among the stones. This area could easily be transformed into a vegetable or herb garden when the children outgrow the space.

Screened from view by a dense hop bush is a garden shed, where tools and chemicals can be safely locked away. A composter tucked behind the shed is concealed by shrubbery. For adults who can't keep up with the youngsters, a comfortable wooden bench offers a resting spot within view of the house. The gentle curves of a wide concrete path can be easily traversed on a tricycle or skateboard.

The wooden play structure (metal structures can become too hot in the sun) rests on a concrete base buried beneath an 8-inch layer of sand (to cushion falls). Rugged rockroses, 3–4 feet tall, separate this area from the lawn and give it a feeling of privacy, yet don't hide it completely from the house. Spreading loquat trees will soon grow enough to provide shade and prevent sunburns. As the children grow, this part of the yard could be transformed into a flower garden or pool area—or the lawn could be expanded into it.

Centrally located and visible from all parts of the yard is a compact Bermuda-grass lawn. Flagstone stepping stones are set at ground level to allow the lawn mower to pass over them, and brick mowing strips surround a smaller turf area below the driveway, making edging unnecessary.

An automated irrigation system delivers water to three different stations, or "zones." Drought- tolerant plants (such as manzanita, smoke tree, and daylily) are watered by low-delivery drip lines. The lawns are watered by pop-up sprinkler heads, and shade-loving, finer-textured plants (such as Japanese maple, heavenly bamboo, and sword fern) receive extra irrigation from a soaker hose.

THE PLANTS

A. *Acer palmatum* 'Dissectum' (3)
LACELEAF JAPANESE MAPLE

B. *Arctostaphylos* 'Emerald Carpet'(24)
MANZANITA

C. BERMUDA GRASS
Cynodon dactylon 'Santa Ana'

D. *Cistus* 'Doris Hibberson' (9)
ROCKROSE

E. *Coleonema pulchrum* (3)
PINK BREATH OF HEAVEN

F. *Cotinus coggygria* 'Royal Purple' (1)
SMOKE TREE

G. *Dodonaea viscosa* 'Purpurea' (4)
HOP BUSH

H. *Erigeron karvinskianus* (4)
MEXICAN DAISY

I. *Eriobotrya deflexa* (2)
BRONZE LOQUAT

J. *Hardenbergia violacea* 'Happy Wanderer' (1)

K. *Hemerocallis hybrids* (8)
DAYLILY

L. *Jasminum polyanthum* (1)
JASMINE

M. *Nandina domestica* (8)
HEAVENLY BAMBOO

N. *Pittosporum tobira* 'Wheeler's Dwarf' (6)
TOBIRA

O. *Polystichum munitum* (12)
SWORD FERN

P. *Prunus laurocerasus* 'Zabeliana' (15)
ZABEL LAUREL

Q. *Prunus serrulata* 'Amanogawa' (1)
JAPANESE FLOWERING CHERRY

R. *Ribes sanguineum glutinosum* 'Claremont' (1)
PINK WINTER CURRANT

S. *Teucrium chamaedrys* (20)
GERMANDER

T. *Thymus praecox arcticus* (24)
MOTHER-OF-THYME

U. *Viburnum davidii* (5)

V. *Westringia fruticosa* (15)

CARING FOR YOUR GARDEN

"The surest way to avoid problems in permanent land-scapes is to plant the right plant in the right place. Once plants are well established, with their growing conditions met, preventive maintenance is the next most critical fac-tor in keeping them healthy."

Sunset Western Garden Problem Solver

8

Installing Your Garden

When installing your garden, it is crucial to think before you act. After you've decided on the plants you want, it's time to bring your design to life, following an orderly sequence of clearing the site, building hardscape, improving the soil, installing an irrigation system, and—finally—the most important step: planting. Follow these steps to make the process simpler—and to create a garden that will be manageable for years to come.

Proper installation of the plants themselves really does mean the difference between sustained, healthy growth and a sickly struggle to survive. In these pages, you'll find recommendations for a basic collection of garden tools, as well as equipment for those with disabilities or other special needs. You'll read about soil improvement, time-saving irrigation systems, the role of mulch in an easy-care regime, and how to feed your plants for consistent good health.

15 Essential Tools

Although there are tools designed to speed just about every gardening chore imaginable, buy yours one at a time—as you need them—and always invest in quality over quantity. In the long run, it's far less expensive to buy one durable, dependable, high-quality tool than many low-cost (and inferior) replacements. Maintain and store your tools properly (see page 184), and they'll last for years, even if temporarily forgotten in a planting bed or left out in the rain.

How do you tell if a tool is worthy? Look for blades made from a single piece of forged steel (stamped, sheet-metal blades or blades welded from several pieces are likely to break, bend, and rust). The connection between handle and blade should be stout, and the handle should fit comfortably in your hand. For workhorse tools such as spades and shovels, straight-grained ash or molded fiberglass handles are most durable. Other hardwoods or plastics are fine for rakes, cultivators, and hand tools because they're subject to less stress. Before buying a tool, pantomime it in use; it shouldn't be too heavy and the handle should suit your height—some tools have handles that adjust to the user's preference with the press of a button

Hand trowels are invaluable for digging small holes. Blade width varies from narrow to wide; a 3-in. blade works well for all-around gardening.

This weeder can reach deep taproots (such as those ever-present dandelions). Three-tined cultivators scratch out weed seedlings and loosen soil.

Cotton gloves are inexpensive, comfortable, and washable—but not durable. Leather or latex-coated cotton feel just as good and last much longer. Gloves with gauntlets will protect your forearms from insects, poison oak, and scratches. A hat is essential in sunny climates; make sure it has a wide brim.

To reduce trips to the faucet, choose the largest watering can you can carry full. It should be balanced, for easy pouring with one hand. Metal cans should have a hot-dipped galvanized finish.

Bulb planters lift out plugs of soil, leaving behind a hole just the right size for a bulb. Some have calibrated blades so you can gauge depth.

Hand pruners can slice through woody stems up to ½ in. thick. Bypass pruners (left) are best because they slice the plant fibers rather than crush them, the way anvil pruners do.

INSTALLING YOUR GARDEN

Spading fork breaks up the soil before planting or amending, and lets you cultivate around plants without severing their roots. In heavy soil, a fork's thin tines slip through the soil more easily than a shovel blade.

Digging spade is a garden mainstay. Use it to prepare soil for planting, to dig straight-sided planting holes, to divide clumps of plants, and to edge around garden beds. Wear sturdy boots when digging in the garden.

Shovel has dished blades and pointed or rounded tips. It's not as practical as a spade for preparing soil, but is excellent for digging planting holes and scooping up soil or amendments to fill raised beds.

Scuffle hoe has a move-able blade that lets it skim just below the soil surface to dislodge or slice off weeds under the soil line, often killing them outright. Other hoes call for a chopping motion that can be tiring for the user.

Use bamboo and metal (above) lawn rakes to pile up mounds of leaves and debris. Steel garden rake breaks up soil clods and catches stones, roots, and weeds between its tines—invaluable when preparing soil for planting.

Wheelbarrows come in all shapes and sizes. For heavy loads, two-wheeled carts typically offer more stability than traditional wheelbarrows.

Hedge shears work like giant scissors and are a must if you have hedges to trim. The longer the handles, the greater your reach; keep blades clean and sharp.

Tip bags don't—thanks to a broad, flat base. Because the mouth of the bag is held open with a plastic hoop rim, you can use both hands to stuff the bag full.

Electric mulching mower grinds up grass blades, eliminating tedious raking, bagging, and disposal of clippings. To cut maintenance time further, some manufacturers sell fertilizer spreaders that attach to the mower (see p. 189)

Edger (also called lawn knife) has a flat blade in the shape of a half moon. It slices through turfgrass in 8-in. swaths, making short, neat work of slicing turf when planting, or of cutting an edge on even large lawns.

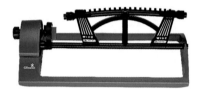

Good-quality hoses are lightweight and resist kinking (see p. 195), but don't leave them lying in the sun for extended periods. Sprinkler may be oscillating (moving back and forth) or rotating (spinning like a whirlybird).

STORAGE & CARE

The best rest. Store garden tools in a dry, well-ventilated space—dampness promotes rust on metal tools. Wall-mounted metal or plastic clip holders keep long-handled tools off the floor and out of the way.

Quick cleanup. Clean tools after each use. To save time, keep a 5-gal. bucket of sharp builder's sand at hand—pump shovel and trowel blades up and down in the sand to remove caked-on mud. Add mineral oil to the sand and your tools will receive a light coating of rust protection in the bargain.

Lube job. Once a year, lubricate tools that have moving parts (such as hedge shears and hand pruners) by squirting lightweight machine oil on springs and pivot points.

Stay sharp. Sharpen trowels, spades, and other digging tools to maintain a keen edge. Hold the tool in a vise with the beveled edge facing you, then push a 10-in. mill bastard file in short quick strokes following the angle of the original bevel. Finish with a light filing on the back side of the blade. You can buy replacement blades for hand pruners if needed.

Rust buster. Remove rust buildup on tools with a wire brush or flexible sanding block. A medium-coarse wire wheel on a hand drill is speedier. For heavy rust deposits, use a sanding disc in the drill.

Handling handles. Protect wood handles from splitting by lightly wiping them down twice yearly with boiled linseed oil. When the oil dries, whisk the surface smooth with fine steel wool. To protect your hands, tape over small splinters. Replace badly splintered or cracked tool handles that can snap with use.

TOOLS FOR SPECIAL NEEDS

Long-handled trowels allow gardeners with limited reach to dig in the middle of wide beds and large containers. Some have telescoping handles and inter-changeable heads.

Step-on weeders pop shallow weeds out of the soil with a single, simple, no-bend motion. To pull a weed, place the tool head over the plant, push the blades down with your foot, and depress the trigger.

Watering wands reach up to 3 ft.; extend-ing your reach into beds and even overhead. They are best for containers, delivering a gentle stream that doesn't disrupt potting soil or expose roots.

Cut-and-hold shears do just that — they snip, then grasp flower stems or branches until released.

Arm supports attach to gardener's fore-arms to relieve pressure on the wrists without inhibiting finger mobility

Seed dispensers assist gardeners with limited fingertip sensitivity; they con-trol the flow of seeds through adjustable openings. Some are built into trowels; others are sold separately.

Rubber sponge grips with non-slip sur-faces offer gardeners with diminished arm or hand strength a cushioned surface to grasp. They come in standard and large sizes to fit most tool handles.

Kneeler stools have padded knee supports on one side and a stool on the other. In the kneeling position, the legs become handles, which support and guide a gardener's descent to ground level.

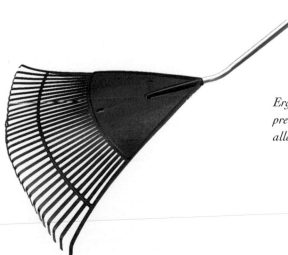

Ergonomic rakes help ease back strain and prevent injury. Their long, S-shaped handles allow gardeners to work without bending.

**ELIMINATING
ACHES & PAINS**

Be brawny. Use big muscles for big jobs. Lift with your legs (knees bent), not with your back. Power a trowel with your forearm and elbow, not your wrist and fingers.

Get down. Perform ground-level chores from a squatting or kneeling position. Bending from the waist is an invitation to backache.

Square off. When digging, face your shovel. Twisting or jerking your spine can cause injury. Inserting the blade vertically will increase your leverage when you pull back the handle.

Lighten the load. When shoveling amendments or soil, decrease the weight of each shovelful and increase the number of shovelsful.

Keep moving. When performing repetitive tasks, vary your wrist positions and change hands often.

Hold it close. To prevent shoulder and back aches, keep your tool as close as possible to your body.

Sun shade. In hot, sunny weather, wear a hat, and put sunscreen on all exposed skin.

Pace yourself. Quit *before* you feel really fatigued.

Feel your pain. Listen to your body. If something hurts, stop what you are doing and either get help or switch to a different tool or task.

SENSIBLE GARDENING

Digging, weeding, watering, and hauling around bags of yard supplies can all cause gardeners to work up a sweat, but backaches, strained shoulders, and stressed wrists need not be by-products of your labors. Many times a little planning—and a safety precaution or two—are all that is needed to prevent injury. Before gardening, make it a habit to warm up your body with a gentle ten-minute stretch. Once outdoors, try to vary activities; this will help you avoid the repetitive actions that can strain your muscles and tendons. Alternate ground-level tasks such as weeding with upright chores like digging or hoeing and reaching jobs such as pruning.

When creating new garden areas, plan to incorporate pathways wide enough to accommodate garden carts and don't make beds so wide that it's a struggle to reach into them. Install an automatic irrigation system, too, to eliminate the need for heavy watering cans. Hillside gardeners need steps and level "landing pads" where they can safely park their feet and tools.

Kids who are interested in gardening will work—and feel—better when they use tools in scale with their size. Check garden and home centers for small rakes and shovels, as well as gloves designed to fit little hands. Keep gardening tools of any size sharp and in good repair. There's nothing more frustrating, and more wasteful of energy, than trying to accomplish a job with a dull or malfunctioning tool.

THE SAFE GARDEN

Chemicals. Follow the manufacturers' recommended guidelines for the use, labeling, storage, and disposal of herbicides, pesticides, fungicides, and fertilizers. See p. 225 for more specific information on working with chemicals in the garden.

Electricity. For outdoor use, a GFCI (Ground Fault Circuit Interrupter) is essential—and it should be installed by a qualified electrician. Don't power permanent pond pumps, lighting, or other installations by means of an extension cord run from the house.

Walkways. Paths and steps can become slick in inclement weather. Use sand to provide traction on ice. In wet weather, nail strips of asphalt to steps. Rid surfaces of slippery moss by applying a moss-killer.

Water. Young children can drown in just a few inches of water, so make sure all ponds, pools, and spas are kid-proof. Your local municipality may have specific regulations, but fences, locked gates, or other secure barriers are absolutely essential.

Access. Anything on your property that might attract—and then injure—children can be legally considered an "attractive nuisance." If you have old equipment, cars, or other such items in your yard, you must keep them inaccessible to curious youngsters.

Tools. The tips on these pages guide you to the proper use and storage of hand tools. When using power tools, read the owner's manual for advice on extension cords, safety features, and proper operation.

Soil

acking fertile, well-drained soil, plants and lawns fall prey to every pest or disease in the vicinity. Although it can be a lengthy process—especially if the soil has a high clay content or the topsoil has been scraped off—even a modest soil improvement program is worth the effort.

A soil test may be in order if you're planning to put in a new lawn, vegetable plot, or ornamentals. Although some tests can be expensive when conducted by a lab, it's easy to test the texture of your soil yourself. Just pick up a handful of moist soil and squeeze it into a ball. If the soil easily breaks apart when you let it go, it has a high sand content. Clay soil will hold its shape. Garden loam will mold into your hand, but will crumble when poked. To see the effects of soil texture on irrigation, see page 191.

SOIL SAYINGS

Texture. The size of mineral particles in the soil.

Structure. The arrangement of mineral particles in the soil.

Clay soil. Dense structure of small, close-fitting particles. Drains slowly, and soil nutrients may be inaccessible to plants.

Sandy soil. Made up of large particles. Often drains too rapidly for water, nutrients, and fertilizers to be absorbed by plant roots.

Loam. The ideal mix of sand, clay, silt, and organic matter.

Salinity. A measure of salts in the soil; excess salinity commonly occurs in arid parts of the West.

pH. A measurement of a soil acidity or alkalinity on a scale of 0–14, with neutral being 7. A reading over 7 indicates alkaline soil; under 7 indicates acidic soil.

Hardpan. An impenetrable layer of hard soil or clay beneath the surface that prevents water drainage.

Topsoil. The top layer of native soil, usually best for plant growth. If buying topsoil, try to find material that approximates your existing soil.

Compost. A soft, crumbly brownish or blackish substance resulting from the decomposition of organic material. You can make your own compost from garden and kitchen waste (see p. 69).

Nutrients. Nitrogen (N), phosphorus (P), and potassium (K) are considered the main nutrients for plant health; other important minerals are termed "micronutrients."

Potting soil. A mixture designed for container plants. Most contain shredded bark, vermiculite, and forest materials or sphagnum peat.

Organic mulches such as pine needles should be renewed annually; 2–3 in. is the minimum, but you can lay it thicker if you like. Purchase only guaranteed weed-free material—straw, hay, and many manures, for instance, may contain weed seeds.

IMPROVING THE SOIL

If your soil is poor, you can grow plants that will tolerate it, garden in raised beds, or embark upon a soil improvement program. The quickest route to improvement is to order a delivery of topsoil from a reputable dealer, then mix the new soil with the old using a rotary tiller. The slowest (but probably easiest) path is to add organic mulch around plants as needed—as the mulch decays, it will gradually enrich the soil, enabling you to grow fussier plants. You can also add slow-release fertilizers to meet nutrient needs, adjust the pH (add lime to acidic soils, sulphur to alkaline soils), and mix a 2–4-inch layer of compost or other organic matter into the top 8–12 inches of soil.

MULCHING

On uncultivated land, spent plant materials accumulate and slowly decompose on the soil beneath plants. In cultivated gardens, the addition of such a layer, called mulch, not only improves the soil, it makes a garden look tidy, holds weeds and soil temperature down, and keeps clay soils from crusting. Pine needles, compost, raked leaves, gravel, shredded bark chips, and various agricultural byproducts all make good mulches, but make sure that any mulches you use are weed- and disease-free. To protect plants from insects and rot, which thrive in moist conditions, hold organic mulches a few inches back from the crowns and trunks of woody plants.

A 5- to 6-sheet layer of newspaper overlapped 4–6 in. at the edges is inexpensive and effective—plus newspaper doesn't harbor weed seeds, as some organic mulches do. Moisten the newspaper as you work to hold it in place, then top with a thin layer of decorative mulch such as wood chips.

Because they shed water and tend to break into smaller pieces, plastic mulches are less practical than landscape fabric (above). Available in different weights, the fabric allows water and air to penetrate. Like newspaper, fabric mulches should be covered with a more attractive (and weed-free) mulch.

Due to their rapid drainage, gravel and stone mulches eliminate muddy strolls through a garden. They are particularly suited to desert gardens. To prevent weeds, underlay with landscape fabric; to stop the gravel from migrating into adjacent areas, edge it with a commercial or homemade edging (see p. 53).

FERTILIZING PLANTS

Unless you garden exclusively with plants that thrive in poor soil, plan on feeding established flowers, trees, shrubs, and lawns at least every spring. Many plants, such as most roses, require additional feedings throughout the growing season—make sure you understand the nutrition requirements of a plant before you add it to your garden. Anything planted in a container will require fairly frequent fertilization, because nutrients quickly leach out of the potting mix. Prepare for new plantings by digging in slow-release granular fertilizers about a month before planting, so nutrients will be available to the roots when they are in the ground.

When shopping for fertilizer, read labels carefully. For general garden use, choose a "complete" fertilizer. These products contain nitrogen (N), phosphorus (P), and potassium (K), which are always listed on the label in that order. The numbers next to the element represent the percentage contained in the product. Unless you have special requirements, choose a balanced formula (for example, 10-10-10). Fertilizers with higher percentages of phosphorus and potassium (for example, 3-16-16) are often called "blossom boosters" because they improve flowering—they're especially useful for container-grown plants. Some fertilizers are packaged for specific types of plants. If you buy "camellia food," "rhododendron and azalea food," "bulb food," or "rose food," apply it exactly as directed on the label.

TWO COMMON FERTILITY PROBLEMS

For lawns, a fertilizer spreader distributes granular fertilizer and powdered amendments over the turf at an even rate. This model attaches to a mower.

Concentrated liquid fertilizers are quickly absorbed by a plant's roots or leaves but leach through the root zone rapidly if too much water is applied.

Without sufficient nitrogen, plant leaves yellow, from their tips toward the stem and from the bottom of the plant upward. The growth of the plant is also stunted by nitrogen deficiency.

Iron deficiency causes yellow leaves with green veins and stems. A chelated iron solution sprayed directly onto leaves ("foliar feeding") is usually quicker acting than one added to the soil.

Granular time-released fertilizers make nutrients available throughout the growing season, dissolving a little bit with each watering.

Irrigation

Watering can be the most time-consuming of all garden chores. And in many parts of the West, where summer temperatures soar and summer drought is a fact of life, supplemental water is essential to bountiful plants. Yet learning how much water your plants need—and the best way to deliver that water to them—can be perplexing. Unpredictable nature adds to the confusion, bringing twice as much—or half as much—natural rainfall from one year to the next.

Some experts counsel infrequent, deep watering. Others recommend more frequent, intermittent watering that maintains the soil at a constant level of moisture. Certainly, the worst kind of irrigation is frequent and shallow, which encourages roots to grow too close to the soil surface. Left unwatered for a few days during hot weather, these delicate roots can suffer severe damage. Ultimately, the health of your plants is your best guide. Verify the water needs of plants before you buy them, and read the following pages to learn the most time-efficient ways of meeting those needs. Without question, a controlled irrigation system that delivers moisture on a regular schedule according to your garden's needs is the most effective and time-saving method. With an initial investment of a few hours of time and a few hundred dollars, you'll be rewarded with a healthier garden and more time to enjoy it.

WHY SO THIRSTY?

What's the dirt? The ability of soil to absorb and retain water is closely related to its composition (see facing page). Clay soils, with their small, closely packed particles, absorb water slowly and drain slowly as well, retaining water longer than other soils. Sandy soils, on the other hand, have comparatively large particles; their composition allows water to drain much more quickly.

Plants are different. Plants have widely differing water needs. Those native to semiarid and arid climates have evolved features that allow them to survive with little water and low relative humidity. They may have deep root systems (such as *Acacia*, for example) or leaves that retain water (such as succulents). The majority of familiar garden plants, however, prefer reliably moist soil. And many annuals and vegetables require regular moisture throughout the growing season if they are to bloom well or produce a good crop of vegetables.

Better with age. Older plants have established root systems with plenty of small root hairs–the organs that collect the most water for the plant. Small plants have relatively small root systems and tend to dry out quickly. A mature plant's roots extend far out from its trunk (see facing page), at least to the "drip line," which is roughly equal to the extent of its leaf canopy. They also extend deep into the soil, giving them a greater soil reservoir from which to draw water.

How's the weather? When it's hot, dry, or windy, plants use water rapidly, and young or shallow-rooted ones cannot absorb water fast enough to keep foliage from wilting. During cool, damp weather, on the other hand, plants require less water.

Stuck in a pot. Container-grown plants dry out more quickly than those in the ground, because their roots fill out the container, and water drains more quickly. See pp. 148–149 for more information.

ONE GALLON OR TWO?

Plants that "need no supplemental irrigation when established" usually don't need to be watered by the second or third summer after planting.

"Drought-tolerant" plants can survive with 3 to 6 soakings during a dry summer.

"Regular irrigation" usually means weekly or bi-weekly for established plants. During very hot weather, however, plants may require more frequent, even daily, soakings.

Drip irrigation has been shown to increase agricultural crop yields by up to 50 percent.

Some cacti can live on less than 1 inch of water per year.

A ½-inch-diameter hose delivers up to 200 gallons per hour (gph); a ¾-inch-diameter hose up to 500 gph.

A single drip irrigation emitter delivers from ½ to 2 gallons of water per hour.

An 800-square-foot lawn needs 2,000 to 4,200 gallons of water a month, depending on the turf grass type and the climate.

Adding "1 inch of water" means 62 gallons of water for each 100 square feet of garden.

Because the same amount of water penetrates differently depending on soil type—from deep and narrow in sandy soil to wide and shallow in clay soil—drip emitters must be placed closer together on sandy soil and further apart on clay soils. This ensures that water penetration is both deep and wide.

Although a plant's roots may be widely distributed, the majority of water and mineral absorption (70%) takes place in the upper half of the root zone. For most perennials and small shrubs, that's about 2 ft. below the surface, and at least as wide as the drip line. You must keep this entire zone well-irrigated.

WATER SAVERS

Testing. To verify how moisture moves through your soil, water for 30 minutes, then wait 24 hours. Dig a hole or use a soil sampling probe (a long, hollow tube available at irrigation supply stores) to assess if the water has moved beyond the first few inches of soil. If not, you probably have poorly draining soil.

Dripping wet. A controlled irrigation system delivers water steadily and predictably (see p. 195).

Stay together. Group plants with similar water needs. You'll avoid under- or over-watering.

Mounds and swales. Whenever you raise a planting mound, you also create a depression, or swale, into which water will flow and pool.

Basins. Create a "moat" around large shrubs and trees, or new transplants. Build a doughnut-shaped ridge of soil several inches high around the plant's drip line. Fill the basin several times to ensure deep penetration of water. Don't let water remain in a pool around the plant's crown, however.

Mulch. Organic and inorganic mulches keep soil cool and reduce water evaporation (see p. 188).

Runaway. Faulty sprinklers, broken hoses, and loose faucet fittings all waste water; keep them in good repair. Slopes and swales may direct water away from the garden. Channel the water or, better yet, prevent runoff by installing a drip irrigation system on slopes.

Shade. Trees, overhead arbors, and buildings all block the sun's rays—and the resulting evaporation of water. You can create shade over critical areas, such as water features, with trees or structures.

Root irrigators. If you have trees or shrubs in paved areas where their drip lines cannot be watered, the needlelike probe on the end of this tool injects water into the root zone of the plant to a depth of 1 ½ ft. Work in concentric circles around the dripline of the canopy.

Eliminate lawn. Lawns can be the most thirsty planting in the garden. If your water usage is too high, consider installing a ground cover or woody shrubs instead.

HOSES & SPRINKLERS

Porous polyvinyl hose soaks soil when water is flowing from faucet at high pressure (shown); at low pressure, water slowly seeps out. To prevent clogging, install a drip filter and make sure holes are facing away from, rather than towards, the soil surface.

Some sprinklers offer different spray patterns: squares, circles, rectangles, and more. Simply move the sprinkler around by hand and rotate the spray dial for the pattern that matches the area you are watering.

Sprinklers are better for lawns or low ground cover, but hose-end sprinklers can deliver water in an uneven pattern. Measure this pattern by placing 5 identical straight-sided cups in the area of coverage; run sprinkler for 30 min. and see how cups of water differ. Move the sprinkler by hand so that patterns overlap. The hose-end sprinkler shown here has a dial to set sprinkling time.

Decorative device blends into garden beds. This one has a copper tube riser with a curled top that conceals a pop-up sprinkler head.

Ooze tubing (often made from recycled tires) has thousands of tiny pores so water seeps out slowly. Hose can be installed directly to faucet or with a pressure regulator and filter. Bury tubing 2–6 in. or cover with mulch.

Turn one watering device into four with a fitting that allows you to connect different hoses to a single faucet. Levers on each outlet let you control flow.

WATERING BY HAND

Watering with hoses is time-consuming and is best reserved for new transplants or containers. Buy hoses that make the job easier. Reinforced vinyl hoses are kink resistant and lightweight—important if you need to move the hose around a lot. Rubber hoses, which have dull surfaces, are the heaviest and toughest types; they kink in hot weather but work well in cold weather. Reinforced rubber-vinyl hoses are flexible, kink resistant, moderately heavy, and durable. Remember to flush hoses before connecting them to hose-end sprinklers; algae and mineral deposits can build up quickly.

DROUGHT STRESS

Many plants wilt during the day, but if plants are still wilted first thing in the morning, they may not be getting enough water. Plants suffering from drought stress usually recover within 24 hours after being watered; if they do not recover, suspect pests or another problem. Under long term stress, plants wilt or stop growing. Fruit and flowers drop. Leaves are lighter. Bare spots appear in ground cover or lawns. Weeds, pests, and diseases increase.

On the other hand, plants that are overwatered are also subject to diseases, particularly root and stem rots. Symptoms of excessive water include stunted, slow-growing and weak plants, and yellowed leaves. Symptoms of stem rot include blackened, drooping stems and branches.

To simplify connecting one hose to several devices—such as spray heads or hose-end sprinklers—install female brass quick couplers on the hose and a male quick coupler onto each device.

Gauge indicates moisture content of upper 6 in. of soil; insert probe (above); needle points to moisture level. Rain gauge (above, right) measures the amount of rainfall; use it to calculate whether additional irrigation is needed, especially during spring, when rains are tapering off. Fill lawn gauge (right) to "zero line;" when water level falls, it's time to irrigate lawn.

Toadstool-shaped guard prevents hose from cutting corners and damaging plants. Commercial models are available at garden centers, or fashion a homemade version from a sturdy stake.

DRIP DOINGS

Timer. Determines when and for how long system runs. Powered by electricity (battery or 110-volt) to activate system at specified times, or hand-operated, (much like an egg timer).

Backflow preventer. Plastic or brass hose-thread vaccum breaker prevents debris from the irrigation system from entering house water system. Must be above high point of irrigation system.

Filter. Keeps small drippers and emitters from clogging. Models include simple hose thread or Y-filter (both are shown below); both have mesh screen that can be rinsed and reused.

Pressure regulator. Controls flow of water to tubing.

Compression fitting. Connects tubing lines to each other and filter assembly to tubing.

Tubing. Shown below, right are ½-in. and ¼-in. sizes. Half-inch line has either in-line emitters or accepts punch-in emitters; attaches to faucet connection with compression fittings. Quarter-inch line runs to smaller plants.

Emitters. Inserted into holes in tubing; various models available. Release water onto soil at precise rates.

Micro-sprayers. Inserted into holes in tubing; various models available. Spray or mist water onto plants.

Punch. Special tool makes holes for emitters in tubing.

"Goof plugs." Close off emitter holes, if needed.

Fertilizer dispenser. Fits between timer and filter; alllows addition of water-soluble fertilizer.

CONTROLLED IRRIGATION

By far, the most efficient and time-saving way to water your garden is with an automatic or semi-automatic irrigation system. All such systems consist of four basic components: A system of delivery tubes or hoses; a pressure regulator and filter that fit between the tubes and the water source; emitters or sprayers that attach to the tubes; and a timer to automate the system.

There are two types of controlled irrigation systems currently available for homeowners. For lawns, a network of rigid underground pipes connected to sprinkler heads is typical. (Drip irrigation systems are being developed for lawns, but the sprinkler system is still the best option.) The sprinkler heads, which come in a wide variety of styles, are subject to breakage and must be carefully maintained. Installation is not complicated, but unless you are prepared to dig a series of trenches, hire a landscaper or irrigation specialist to install a sprinkler system before you put in the lawn.

DRIP IRRIGATION COMPONENTS

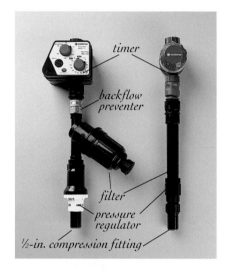

timer

backflow preventer

filter

pressure regulator

½-in. compression fitting

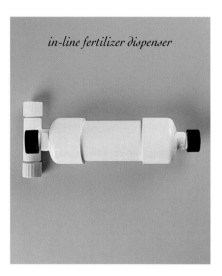

in-line fertilizer dispenser

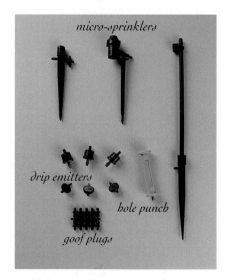

micro-sprinklers

drip emitters

hole punch

goof plugs

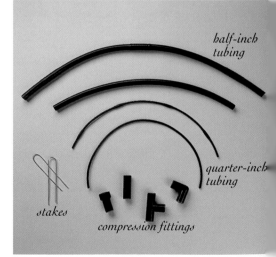

half-inch tubing

quarter-inch tubing

stakes

compression fittings

INSTALLING A DRIP SYSTEM

Drip irrigation delivers water through a system of flexible hose lines and small outlets called emitters (you can also hook up the tubing to micro-sprinklers). Drip systems are efficient and extremely flexible. You can tailor them to water individual plants or to distribute water over larger areas. Because the pliable plastic lines are above ground, you can move, add, or change them as needed. Water penetration depends on the time the system runs and the emitters' delivery capacity, rated in gallons per hour (gph).

Each drip irrigation system is individually designed; the basic components are shown on the facing page. You can design your own system, or seek the help of a qualified irrigation supplier (several are listed on pages 232–233) or a landscaping professional. To design the best route for the tubing, draw a rough sketch of your garden, including water and electrical outlets, and pathways or other obstructions. The spacing of emitters will depend on your soil type, climate, and the type of plants you are watering. If you have grouped together plants with similar water needs, you have created "zones"—areas that can be set on the same irrigation schedule—another reason to evaluate your plants' water needs when you are designing your garden.

POSITIONING EMITTERS

Place drip emitters depending on the type of plants you have. To supply the largest amount of water to the plant's roots, position emitters in a circle around the drip line of the tree, or in a spiral starting at the drip line and working in toward the trunk. Keep at least 1 ft. away from the trunk to prevent rot.

For borders and raised beds with well-draining soil, position parallel tubes running from a solid line. Tubes should have in-line or external emitters approximately 12 in. apart. Run water through a complete tubing circuit, or close off tubing, as shown.

Planting Techniques

It's tempting to quickly fill up a new garden. But gardening is not like indoor decorating. A new coat of paint can transform a room immediately—and that look won't change until you repeat the exercise. With a garden, things take a little more time. Before rushing out to the garden center and ending up with a hopeless jumble, take the time to do a little planning first.

If you want color right away, start by planting annuals in containers until you have a garden plan; move the pots around to get ideas for color schemes. While you are installing new paving or other hardscape, visit the nursery and evaluate perennials when they are in bloom: you can buy them in nursery containers for later planting but you will have to keep them well watered, and they can become rootbound.

After installing your irrigation system, transplant new trees and shrubs and install the lawns or ground cover—proper planting techniques are shown on the following pages; however, if you plan to hire professionals, these are the types of plants that benefit most from their expertise (they are also the most expensive and time-consuming to replace later). Finally, plant flower borders and fill raised beds.

PLANTING A MIXED BORDER

A low-maintenance mixed border follows the same design rules as the classic version. Select a color scheme, and choose your plants from the Plant Selection Guides in Chapters 4 and 5, noting their different seasons of bloom and their height and width at maturity. Mix different textures—spired plants, roundish flowers, and daisy types. Tall growers should be in the rear, and small creepers suit as edging. Be sure to include at least one shrub, rose, or large ornamental grass, and some evergreen plants for year-round interest. Don't crowd too many different plants into the area, and make sure that all plants in the border have similar cultural needs.

Prepare the planting area first, and build any mounds or position any rocks you have included in your design. Lay drip irrigation lines. Put in the "anchors"—shrubs, grasses, or roses. Then plant perennials in irregular groups (three or more), spacing them so each plant has room to mature. (Marking growing areas with string or chalk is helpful.) If plants are available in four-inch pots, buy them. Research has shown that they'll catch up to one-gallon-size plants within six weeks. Plants from six packs will be somewhat smaller, but are more economical.

Well-spaced perennials always look sparse at first, so cover the gaps of bare earth with a mulch, or quick-growing plants (see right) between the perennial groups; pull them out or replant them as the border fills in. When planting cacti or vegetables, use a piece of shade fabric for two weeks on the south side of the young transplants to avoid sunburn (see page 217).

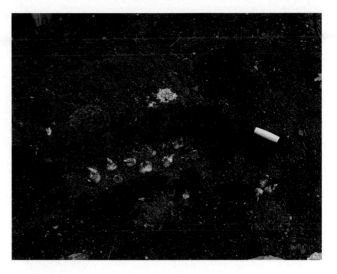

The roots of plants in nursery containers are often compacted into a tight mass (this is less true with smaller "plugs," which are deeper than they are wide). Before planting, tease the roots apart with your fingers, comb them out with a weeding fork, or — if they are truly impenetrable — slice into them lengthwise with a knife. (If you have recently purchased plants and they are very rootbound, return them to the nursery for exchange.)

Catalogs and garden centers usually indicate the correct planting depth for each bulb (generally about three times as deep as the bulb's greatest diameter). Dig a trench (as shown above) or use a bulb planter to make individual holes. Loosen the soil at the base of the hole, add bulb fertilizer according to the package directions, and place the bulb with the growth bud or pointed tip facing upward. Fill in with soil, and water well.

QUICK FILLERS FOR BARE SPOTS

Arugula

Dimorphotheca
AFRICAN DAISY

Erigeron karvinskianus
SANTA BARBARA DAISY

Kalanchoe

Lathyrus odoratus
SWEET PEA

Lobelia erinus

Lobularia maritima
SWEET ALYSSUM

Myosotis sylvatica
FORGET-ME-NOT

Nicotiana alata
JASMINE TOBACCO

Nigella damascena
LOVE-IN-A-MIST

Papaver rhoeas
SHIRLEY POPPY

Parsley

Salvia leucantha
MEXICAN BUSH SAGE

Swiss chard

Tropaeolum majus
NASTURTIUM

Viola tricolor
JOHNNY-JUMP-UP

WESTERN PLANTING SEASONS

Summer: Don't plant. Take advantage of the dry season to build patios, paved walks, decks, and other structures. Remove unwanted plants; decide on locations for shade trees.

Autumn: Prime time. Transplant most landscape trees, native shrubs, spring-blooming perennials. Put in new lawns. Plant spring bulbs.

Winter: Plant late. Transplant bare-root trees and roses in late winter.

Spring: Don't wait. Once danger of frost is past, transplant tender trees such as citrus, and flowering vines. Install lawns and ground covers. Plant warm-season vegetables.

PLANTING GROUND COVERS

Ground covers grow at different rates: refer to Easy-Care Ground Covers on pages 98–100 or ask a nurseryman how far apart to set each plant for cover within a year. When planting a slope with ground cover for erosion control, contain existing soil with erosion fabric, such as biodegradable jute netting available in rolls, or higher-weight erosion fabric (available at irrigation supply stores and some nurseries, or through mail-order, see pages 232–233). Install drip irrigation on slopes to minimize water runoff. To discourage weeds while the plants fill in, lay down a newspaper mulch (see page 188) or fabric (below) over the planting area. If one-foot spacing is recommended for your ground covers, use a 12-in. square floor tile as a template. Tilt the tile to a diamond shape, and set one plant at each of the four corners. Reset the tile at each plant, and work outwards to create a pleasing, rhythmic pattern while the ground cover fills in.

Secure landscaping material with U-shaped metal pins; cut holes in the fabric; insert seedlings, sprigs, plugs, or plants from nursery containers (left). Apply a thin layer of compost or wood chip mulch between the plants.

Thick, low-growing ground covers, such as this shade-loving baby's tears (Soleirolia soleirolii), *can crowd out weeds between stepping stones even when no fabric is installed (below). Edgings can prevent such aggressive ground covers from overstepping their bounds.*

PLANTING LAWNS

Most turfgrasses are sold as sod or seed, but creeping thyme, chamomile, and rustic pasture grasses such as buffalo grass and blue grama can be purchased as sprigs or plugs. The easiest and quickest installation is from sod—it's virtually an instant lawn. However, the strips of sod are also the most expensive. The disadvantage of installing plugs is that they take some time to establish, and you must prevent weeds from sprouting in the meantime. Follow the instructions here for best results.

Before planting a lawn, install any in-ground sprinkler system and edgings you've planned before preparing the soil. Then amend and smooth the soil several days before your sod or plugs arrive. After planting, water deeply, leaving a sprinkler on for several hours, then water every other day until the grass roots are firmly anchored into the soil (about 6 weeks).

Grade the soil with the back of a rake so that it slopes gently outwards from a raised center (far left); this improves drainage and helps prevent soggy spots later on. Moisten the soil.

Unroll strips in a brick-bond fashion along a straight edge, such as a pathway. Firmly press the edges together, and make sure all grass blades point in the same direction. Cut away excess sod around obstacles and edges with a serrated knife (left). Use a water-filled lawn roller (available at tool rental shops) to press down the sod.

For plugs, spread a layer of damp newspaper or other biodegradable paper over the planting area to prevent weeds from sprouting; mulch thinly for appearance. Plant at 8-in. intervals; the plugs will grow together in a year.

PLANTING SHRUBS & TREES

The difference between bare-root and container-grown nursery plants has little to do with plant quality. Bare-root roses, deciduous trees, and shrubs are usually sold from autumn to late winter when they are dormant and less bulky to handle. (Mail-order plants are usually shipped this way.) Bare-root specimens get an early start in your garden when they awaken and leaf out as the weather warms. Roses, citrus, Japanese maples, and some other plants are sometimes grafted (also called "budded") onto a hardy or more vigorous rootstock. Typically, own-root plants are a little smaller when purchased. Many shrubs and trees, including conifers, broad-leaf evergreens and shrubs with delicate root systems (such as *Bougainvillea*), are sold in containers.

PLANTING A BARE-ROOT SPECIMEN

Remove any packing material from the roots and soak the plant in a bucket of water. Dig a hole at least 2 ft. wide and 1½ ft. deep. Shovel some loosened soil back into the hole to make a cone-shaped mound. If the soil is sandy or heavy, add some additional organic material such as compost to your backfill mix.

Spread the roots of the plant over the soil cone. Trim any long roots with sharp shears so they will fit into the hole without bending. Prune off any torn or damaged roots as well. If you are planting a large tree, have a helper hold the trunk as you arrange the roots around the cone of soil.

Top *Bare root plants may be grafted onto a rootstock (left) or grown on the plant's own roots (right). Own-root plants usually start out smaller.*
Bottom *Plants in nursery containers (below) are actively growing in 1-gal., 5-gal., or larger plastic or wooden containers. You can evaluate leaf and flower color, fragrance, and other qualities.*

Lay your shovel handle across the hole to determine the soil level. Add or remove soil on the cone to set the plant so that the crown or bud union (the bump on the lower stem at the point of a graft) is just above the soil level. Where winter temperatures drop below 10°, place the bud union just below soil level.

Gently shovel backfill soil into the hole, firming it over the roots to stabilize the plant. Fill the rest of the hole with water to soak and settle the soil. After the water drains, finishing backfilling with more soil. Tamp the earth firmly and then water the planted area gently until it is well soaked.

PLANTING A
CONTAINER SPECIMEN

Always remove the nursery stakes at planting time so the tree can develop a strong trunk. Add support stakes if the tree will not stand by itself or if the root ball needs to be anchored. Set two or three sturdy stakes with soft and flexible ties 12 in. from the trunk and perpendicular to the prevailing winds (left). Remove support stakes within 6 to 12 months.

Leave landscape trees in their nursery containers until the proper planting time (see p. 197). Dig a hole as deep as the container but twice as wide, remove the plant from its pot, and lightly scratch the root ball with a trowel to loosen any tight or coiled roots. Place it in the hole and backfill with soil (far left), tamping down the earth. Water the plant deeply and frequently during its first year.

The bark of newly planted trees can be affected by sunscald, which splits the bark and can harm the tree. After transplanting, paint the trunk with white latex paint (left). If deer, rabbits, mice or other nibbling animals are a problem, protect the trunks of young trees with a white plastic tree guard. Unlike metal mesh, perforated plastic tree guards expand as the tree grows.

REMOVING PLANTS

Removing large landscape trees and shrubs with thick trunks (over 4 in.) is a job for a professional arborist or landscaper. But to remove an unwanted small tree or overgrown shrub yourself, first cut it back to the ground, using pruning shears and a hand saw. Chop the branches into smaller pieces as you cut to make it easier to remove the debris; branches less than ½-in. thick can be shredded into useful mulch with a motorized chipping machine (available at tool rental shops).

To kill the remaining roots, paint the cut stubs and any exposed roots with a herbicide containing glyphosate (see p. 226); the chemical will be absorbed into the roots and kill them. You may need to repeat the treatment a few times before you can easily loosen the soil around the dead roots with a spading fork and remove them. Commercial stump-killing products should be used only by licensed landscape professionals.

9

Maintaining Your Garden

No garden is completely effortless. Weather, growth, and wear and tear all take their toll on both structures and plants. Success depends on completing routine garden tasks at the proper time of year; regular maintenance done on a schedule will be better for your garden—and easier for you. Because pruning, spraying, and planting times depend on local climate conditions, refer to the Regional Guides on the following pages for specific advice for your area. Each Guide gives the essential tasks for each plant type; you'll probably find that your garden calls for just a few of the tasks listed for each month.

Even the most self-sufficient plants need occasional "cleanup"—removal of dead or unhealthy growth through selective pruning, shearing, or deadheading. Basic instructions are given on pages 212–217; if these seem too time-consuming or complicated, hire a professional for the most difficult once- or twice-yearly jobs.

Seasonal Maintenance Guide

California

🌿 *Trees, Shrubs & Roses*
🌱 *Flowers*
🌷 *Bulbs*
🌾 *Edibles*
🌿 *Lawns & Ground Covers*
✓ *General Maintenance*

JANUARY

🌿 Plant bare-root roses, shrubs, and trees (see p. 200), except in coldest mountain areas. Prune trees and shrubs while they are still dormant, but wait to prune spring-blooming shrubs until after flowers fade (see pp. 212–213). In mountain areas, keep snow from accumulating on branches. Spray established roses with dormant oil (see p. 224).

🌱 Plant annuals for midwinter bloom in zones 7–9 and 14–24.

🌾 In coastal and inland zones, plant cool-season crops (see p. 137).

🌿 Don't walk on lawns that are wet or frozen. If you're tired of maintaining a traditional lawn, plant an unthirsty ground cover such as shore juniper or low-growing rosemary (see pp. 98–100).

🌾 In the low desert, cut and dig in cover crop (see p. 188).

✓ Sharpen shovels and pruning tools, using steel wool to remove rust. Sand wooden handles and apply linseed oil to protect the wood plus a band of brightly colored, water-resistant paint to make tools easier to find if left in the garden. To keep long-handled tools rust-free, store them in a bucket filled with builder's sand saturated with mineral oil.

FEBRUARY

🌿 In mild zones, prune roses (see p. 215). If tree limbs have broken in winter storms, have them removed only if they pose a danger. Otherwise, wait until the weather warms to have them removed.

🌱 In zones 7–9 and 14–24, plant spring-blooming perennials such as common bleeding heart, catmint, and coral bells (see pp. 121–123). Slug and snail eggs begin to hatch now; keep after them by hand picking them at night, or use traps or commercial bait (see pp. 220–225).

🌷 In coastal and inland areas, plant summer-blooming bulbs such as montbretia and calla lilies (see p. 197).

🌾 In the low desert, plant warm-season vegetables (see p. 138).

🌿 In southern zones, keep lawns well irrigated (see pp. 190–195). Mow ground covers such as creeping lily turf and creeping St. Johnswort to the ground to encourage strong new growth.

✓ Start to control weeds such as oxalis now, while they are still small (see pp. 226–228). Slug and snail eggs begin to hatch now; hand pick them at night, or use traps or commercial bait (see pp. 220–225).

MARCH

🌿 Fertilize spring-bloomers with a complete fertilizer (see p. 189). Feed azaleas and camellias with an acid-type fertilizer after they bloom. Feed roses with a commercial rose food every 4–6 weeks until October. In zones 1–3, prune roses, unless temperatures dip below freezing at night (see p. 215).

🌱 In warmer zones, plant summer-blooming annuals and perennials (see p. 196). Water thoroughly and feed with a low-nitrogen fertilizer. When new growth appears on established perennials, cut back dead growth (see p. 217).

🌿 Give lawns an application of a high-nitrogen fertilizer (see pp. 101, 229) If desired, continue lightly feeding warm-season lawns until September. Mow and fertilize meadows (see p. 105).

🌾 Cut and dig in cover crop (see p. 188). In Southern California, feed citrus with high-nitrogen fertilizer.

✓ Check irrigation drip systems. Flush out or scrub sediment from filters and from the end of each line. Check screens for algae. Make sure all emitters are functioning; clean or replace clogged ones and check for and repair leaks in lines. Have the blades of your lawn mower sharpened, the oil changed, and the air filter cleaned.

APRIL

🌿 Feed trees and shrubs with a complete fertilizer (see p. 189). In zones 1–3, plant bare-root trees, shrubs, and roses (see p. 200).

🌱 Plant drought-tolerant perennials such as coreopsis, sea lavender, and yarrow (see p. 197). In warmer zones, continue planting summer-blooming annuals. Check new growth for aphids (see p. 200); blast them off with water from a hose.

🌷 Plant summer-blooming bulbs in colder zones (see p. 197). Water spring-blooming bulbs while the leaves are still green. Remove spent flowers but not the yellowing leaves.

🌾 In zones 1–3, cool-season crops can be planted, but wait until the danger of frost is past before planting warm-season vegetables.

🌿 In southern zones, plant sod or plugs of Bermuda grass, zoysia, or St. Augustine (see p. 199).

✓ Clean glass or plastic bird feeders by putting on top rack of dishwasher. Scrub wooden ones with hot, soapy water; allow to dry before refilling.

MAY

🌿 In windy areas, stake young trees (see p. 201). In southern zones, plant subtropicals such as cordyline and palms.

🌱 Plant perennials in colder zones after the last danger of frost (see p. 197).

🌾 In coastal and inland areas, plant warm-season vegetables (see p. 137).

🌿 In northern zones, plant lawns (see p. 199); use cool-season bent grass, bluegrass, or perennial ryegrass (see p. 103).

✓ To help control aphids, mealybugs, scale, and other soft-bodied insects, buy and release lacewings, a beneficial insect that feeds on a variety of garden pests (see p. 223).

JUNE

❀ Keep newly planted trees and shrubs well irrigated. Check roses for diseases or pests; treat with an all-purpose rose spray if needed (see pp. 224, 231).

✿ Deadhead annuals and perennials through the summer months to keep them blooming (see p. 216).

✦ Plant a last crop of cool-season greens such as spinach or mustard greens in coastal zones, and plant warm-season crops in all zones (see pp. 137–138).

♣ If you're damaging tree trunks with the lawn mower, remove the turf from the tree base and put down landscape fabric (see p. 228) and a layer of mulch.

✓ Use rain gauges to be sure sprinklers are delivering appropriate amounts of water (see p. 193).

JULY

❀ During hot months, check for spider mites (see p. 221) and treat with a miticide if necessary.

♠ Fertilize summer-blooming bulbs (see p. 189). Remove spent flowers, but don't remove foliage.

✦ Keep harvesting tomatoes to encourage continued fruit. Feed tomatoes with a moderate-nitrogen fertilizer. Pinch the growing tips of herbs (see p. 217).

♣ Keep the mowing height high during summer's heat; mow when the grass is about a third taller than the recommended height. Use a mulching mower that leaves clippings on the lawn. Aerate lawn if needed (see p. 229).

✓ If you have a compost pile, keep it moist during dry spells. If the compost attracts fruit flies, sprinkle lime on it.

AUGUST

❀ Give trees, shrubs, and roses a deep soaking.

✿ Keep annuals blooming by feeding them every 2 weeks (see p. 189).

♠ In southern regions, plant spring-blooming bulbs (see p. 129).

♣ Give turfgrasses a light feeding with a medium-nitrogen fertilizer (see p. 189).

✓ Take advantage of warm, dry weather to repair loose gate hinges or wobbly fence posts in preparation for fall and winter rains.

SEPTEMBER

❀ Fertilize established plants (see p. 189), except for California natives or drought-tolerant Mediterranean plants. In the low desert, fertilize and lightly prune roses.

✿ In warmer zones, plant perennials such as coreopsis and sage, as well as cool-season annuals such as calendula and annual larkspur.

♠ Plant spring-blooming bulbs (see p. 129).

✦ Plant lettuce, spinach, and other cool-season vegetables for a fall crop. Keep the soil moist until rains begin. Plant a cover crop if desired (see p. 188).

♣ If temperatures have cooled, lay new sod or plugs (see p. 199), and keep these areas well watered.

✓ Have the blades of your lawn mower professionally sharpened. Rake up fallen leaves; put them in the compost.

OCTOBER

❀ Plant trees and shrubs from nursery containers (see p. 201).

✿ If perennials are crowded, divide them; if they are straggly, cut them almost to the ground (see p. 217). Feed growing annuals with a high-nitrogen fertilizer.

♠ Continue to plant spring-blooming bulbs. Overplant them with cool-season annuals such as calendula and lobelia for a colorful winter show (see pp. 119–120).

✦ Plant garlic in zones 14–24. Pull up and dispose of spent tomato plants or other vegetables past their prime.

♣ Scatter grass seed on bare spots in lawn and keep well watered until winter rains begin.

✓ Make a complete inspection of your porch, patio, or any other exterior wooden structure that is subject to damage caused by moisture or insects.

NOVEMBER

❀ In colder regions, place or replenish mulch around young trees and shrubs (see p. 188).

✿ Plant perennials in zones 14–24.

♠ In cold regions, mulch newly planted bulb beds.

✓ Clean up garden debris. Go shopping — containers, landscape fabric, garden tools, and irrigation systems are on sale now at garden centers.

DECEMBER

❀ In coastal and southern zones, plant bare-root roses (see p. 200). Evergreens such as juniper, silver spreader, Australian tea tree, and atlas cedar can be lightly pruned; you can use the cut branches for holiday decorating.

♣ Mow only in warmest areas. Consider purchasing one of the new cordless electric mowers; most have a mulching feature that leaves finely shredded grass in place on the lawn, so no raking or bagging is necessary.

✓ Moss on pathways, decks, and stairs can be dangerously slippery; use moss-killer to eliminate it. If wooden steps or ramps are very slick, nail thin strips of asphalt roofing material on them to provide better traction.

Seasonal Maintenance Guide

Pacific Northwest

🌿 *Trees, Shrubs & Roses*
🌱 *Flowers*
🌷 *Bulbs*
🌾 *Edibles*
🌿 *Lawns & Ground Covers*
✓ *General Maintenance*

JANUARY

🌿 In zones 4–7, plant bare-root shrubs, trees, and roses as soon as the ground is workable (see p. 200). Apply a dormant oil spray to established roses (see p. 224).

🌱 Plant midwinter annuals, such as calendula and cornflower, in containers for instant color (see pp. 148–149).

🌿 Avoid walking on the lawn when it's wet or frozen.

✓ Bring containers indoors or into a sheltered spot (see p. 148) to protect them from freezing.

FEBRUARY

🌿 In zones 4–7, give roses their annual pruning when temperatures have risen well above freezing (see p. 215). For climbing roses, a light thinning is all that's needed.

🌱 In zones 4–7, inspect early blooming perennials, such as basket-of-gold, and shear dead leaves and flowers. This will encourage another round of bloom.

🌿 In mild coastal regions, prepare planting areas for grass sod; choose a tough, drought-tolerant type (see p. 103). See p. 105 for information on installing a meadow with ornamental grasses.

✓ Sharpen shovels and pruning tools, using steel wool to remove rust. Sand wooden handles and apply linseed oil to protect the wood plus a band of brightly colored, water-resistant paint to make tools easier to find if left in the garden. To keep long-handled tools rust-free, store them in a bucket filled with builder's sand saturated with mineral oil.

MARCH

🌿 Feed spring-blooming trees and shrubs with a complete fertilizer (see p. 189). Feed azaleas and camellias after flowering; use an acid-type fertilizer. Feed roses with a commercial rose food every 4–6 weeks until October. Check for branches that were damaged in winter, and remove or cut them back (see p. 213). If they pose a danger, consult a professional arborist.

🌱 In zones 4–7, divide overcrowded summer- and fall-blooming perennials such as maiden's wreath and sedum, and divide spring-blooming plants whose flowers have faded (see p. 216).

🌷 In zones 4–7, plant summer-blooming bulbs such as montbretia after mid-month (see p. 197).

🌿 Lay sod or plugs (see p. 199). To encourage ground covers such as creeping lily turf and St. Johnswort to produce strong new growth, mow them to the ground. Mow and fertilize meadow grasses (see p. 105).

🌾 Cut and dig in cover crop (see p. 188).

✓ Have your lawn mower blades sharpened, the oil changed, and the air filter cleaned. Start to control weeds while they're still small (see pp. 226–228). Slug and snail eggs are beginning to hatch; hand pick them at night or use barriers, traps, or commercial bait (see p. 220–225).

APRIL

🌿 Plant bare-root roses in zones 1–3 (see p. 215). Feed conifers (except for pines) and deciduous shrubs and trees with an all-purpose fertilizer (see p. 189). Shear flowering trees and shrubs after their blooms fade (see p. 216).

🌱 Plant drought-tolerant perennials such as coreopsis and sage. Apply a balanced fertilizer to established perennials (see p. 189). In zones 1–3, plant perennials and divide those that are overcrowded (see pp. 197, 216).

🌷 After spring-blooming bulbs have faded, remove the old flowers but leave the yellowing foliage; plant annuals, such as love-in-a-mist, as cover.

🌾 Plant cool-season vegetables from nursery packs (see p. 137).

🌿 Begin mowing turfgrass to recommended height (see p. 103).

✓ Before potting plants (see pp. 148–149), clean the pots with a solution of one part bleach to nine parts water.

MAY

🌿 Trim hedges (see p. 214). In zones 1–3, fertilize roses with high-nitrogen plant food (see p. 189).

🌱 Plant summer annuals such as lobelia and cosmos (see p. 119–120). Deadhead to encourage new growth (see p. 216).

🌷 In zones 1–3, plant summer-blooming bulbs such as ornamental onion and montbretia (see p. 197).

🌾 In western regions, plant warm-season vegetables from nursery packs (see p. 138).

🌿 Feed lawns with a high-nitrogen fertilizer (see pp. 189, 229).

✓ Check drip irrigation systems; flush out sediment from filters and check screens for algae. Clean or replace clogged emitters and check for and repair leaks in lines. To help control aphids, mealybugs, scale, and other soft-bodied insects, buy and release lacewings, a parasitic insect that feeds on a variety of garden pests (see p. 223).

JUNE

🌿 Keep new plantings of trees and shrubs well irrigated (see p. 191–195). Check roses for diseases or pests; treat with an all-purpose rose spray if needed (see p. 224).

🌱 Keep flowers well watered throughout the summer until fall rains begin.

In zones 1–3, plant warm season vegetables (see p. 138).

Mow often enough that you never have to remove more than a third of the grass blade at one time. Aerate lawn if needed (see p. 229).

✓ Clean glass or plastic bird feeders by putting on top rack of dishwasher. Scrub wooden ones with hot, soapy water; allow to dry before refilling.

JULY

Check for spider mites and treat if necessary (see p. 221).

If the foliage of earlier-blooming perennials such as lady's-mantle or daylilies is tattered, cut it to the ground and water well; fresh new growth will emerge within a few weeks.

Water summer-blooming bulbs and feed them with a liquid fertilizer to keep them blooming (see p. 189).

Keep harvesting tomatoes to encourage continued fruit production. Feed tomatoes with a moderate-nitrogen fertilizer. Pinch tips of herbs (see p. 217).

Keep lawns well irrigated (see pp. 191–195).

✓ If you have a compost pile, keep it moist during dry spells. If it attracts fruit flies, sprinkle lime on it.

AUGUST

Make sure plants are well irrigated, especially camellias and other evergreens (see pp. 191–195).

Feed annuals every 2 weeks with liquid fertilizer (see p. 189). If lobelia or sweet alyssum looks spent, shear to 1 in. above the soil and water well; it will revive and bloom again (see p. 216).

Plant fall-blooming crocus as soon as they are available.

To keep flowering ground covers compact, shear them after they've bloomed (see p. 216).

✓ Take advantage of warm, dry weather to repair loose gate hinges or replace a wobbly fence post. Inspect your porch, patio, or any other exterior wooden structure that is subject to damage caused by moisture or insects.

SEPTEMBER

Shop for trees and shrubs, such as beautyberry, Western redbud, and Amur maple, now that you can evaluate their ornamental fruits or colorful fall foliage. Plant them as the daytime temperatures cool (see pp. 200–201). Keep them well watered until fall rains begin.

When the weather cools, plant cool-season annuals. Plant new perennials such as coreopsis or astilbe (see p. 197) and divide any overcrowded ones (see p. 216)

Plant spring-blooming bulbs such as glory-of-the-snow and snowdrops (see p. 129).

Plant lettuce, spinach, and other cool-season vegetables from nursery packs. Keep the soil well irrigated until rains begin. Plant a cover crop, if desired (see p. 188).

If temperatures have cooled, lay new lawns (see p. 199), and keep well irrigated until rains begin. Fertilize lawns with a moderate-nitrogen fertilizer (see p. 101).

✓ Have the blades of your lawn mower professionally sharpened.

OCTOBER

Before freezing weather arrives in zones 1–3, remove weeds from around trees and shrubs and spread a layer of mulch (see p. 188). Stake newly planted trees and protect their trunks with paint (see p. 201).

Spring-blooming perennials are being sold now at reduced prices in garden centers. In zones 1–3, plant as soon as possible.

In warmer zones, plant cool-season annuals, such as lobelia, over planted bulbs.

✓ Test your soil if you suspect it is deficient in nutrients or that the pH may require adjustment (see p. 187).

NOVEMBER

Cut back perennials and annuals as frost kills the foliage (see p. 216).

In zones 1–3, mulch newly planted bulbs (see p. 188).

If slopes planted with turf are eroding during heavy rains, replace lawn grass with ground covers that have dense root systems, such as rosemary, bearberry, or low-growing juniper (see pp. 98–100).

✓ Go shopping. Containers, landscape fabric, garden tools, and irrigation systems are on sale now at many garden centers and nurseries.

DECEMBER

Evergreens such as juniper, glossy abelia, and Oregon grape can be lightly pruned (see p. 214) and the trimmings used for holiday decorations.

If calendulas or nasturtiums are still blooming in your garden, harvest some flowers to sprinkle on your winter salads—these flowers are edible.

Consider purchasing one of the new cordless electric mowers; most models have a mulching feature that leaves finely shredded grass in place, so no raking or bagging is necessary. The mowers are quiet, energy efficient, and easy to maintain.

✓ Moss on pathways, decks, and stairs can be dangerously slippery; eliminate it with a product that kills moss. Nail thin strips of asphalt roofing material on wooden steps to provide inconspicuous traction.

Seasonal Maintenance Guide

Southwest

🌿 *Trees, Shrubs & Roses*
🌱 *Flowers*
🌷 *Bulbs*
🌾 *Edibles*
🌼 *Lawns & Ground Covers*
✓ *General Maintenance*

JANUARY

🌿 In zones 10–13, plant bare-root trees, shrubs, and roses (see p. 200) and apply mulch (see p. 188).

🌱 In zones 10–13, plant early blooming perennials such as bleeding heart and winter-blooming bergenia (see p. 197).

🌾 In zones 10–13, plant cool-season vegetables from nursery packs (see p. 137).

🌼 In zones 1–3, avoid walking on lawns when the ground is wet or frozen. If you're tired of maintaining a lawn, consider planting drought-tolerant ground covers such as bearberry or low-growing rosemary (see pp. 98–100).

✓ Sharpen shovels and pruning tools, using steel wool to remove rust. Sand wooden handles and apply linseed oil to protect the wood plus a band of brightly colored, water-resistant paint to make tools easier to find if left in the garden. To keep long-handled tools rust-free, store them in a bucket filled with builder's sand saturated with mineral oil.

FEBRUARY

🌿 In zones 10–13, prune roses (see p. 215). In zones 11–13, keep trees and shrubs well irrigated (see pp. 190–195). In mountain areas, clear snow from trees and shrubs. Have cold-damaged limbs pruned only if they pose a danger. Otherwise, wait until weather warms to have them pruned (see p. 213).

🌱 In zones 12 and 13, when new growth appears on perennials, cut back dead growth (see p. 217).

🌷 Plant summer-blooming bulbs such as ornamental onion and montbretia in

zones 10–13 (see p. 197). Feed established bulbs with a complete fertilizer late in the month (see p. 189). Mulch new and established beds (see p. 188).

🌼 In zones 11–13, fertilize winter rye lawn with ammonium sulfate and then water well. Treat lawn for broadleaf weeds if necessary (see p. 226).

✓ Have the blades of your lawn mower sharpened, the oil changed, and the air filter cleaned. Start to pull or treat weeds while they are still small (see pp. 226–228).

MARCH

🌿 Cut back winter-damaged branches (see p. 213). In zones 10–13, fertilize roses, trees, and spring- and summer-blooming shrubs (see p. 189).

🌱 In zones 10 and 11, plant cool-season annuals such as calendula and cornflower; in zones 12 and 13, set out warm-season annuals such as marigolds and cosmos (see pp. 119–120). Plant perennials and ornamental grasses. Divide overcrowded perennials (see p. 216) and cut back established ornamental grasses (see p. 217).

🌾 In zones 10–13, feed cool-season vegetables and plant warm-season ones (see pp. 137–138). In zones 12 and 13, feed citrus with high-nitrogen fertilizer.

🌼 Plant a new lawn (see p. 199). Mow ground covers such as creeping lily turf and St. Johnswort to the ground to encourage strong new growth. Mow and fertilize meadow grasses (see p. 105).

✓ Check drip irrigation systems. Flush out or scrub sediment from filters and the end of each line. Check screens for algae. Clean or replace clogged emitters and repair leaks in lines.

APRIL

🌿 In zones 1–3, plant bare-root trees, shrubs, and roses. Deadhead early blooming trees and shrubs (see p. 213), and fertilize them (see p. 189). In zones 1–3, prune roses (see p. 215).

🌱 In zones 1–3, plant cool-season annuals such as calendula and cornflower, and shear perennials to encourage new growth (see p. 216). In other zones, deadhead annuals.

🌷 In zones 1–3, plant summer-blooming bulbs such as ornamental onion and montbretia (see p. 197). Water spring-blooming bulbs while the leaves are still green. Remove spent flowers, but not yellowing leaves, which can be hidden by planting tall, lacy-leaved annuals such as cosmos.

🌾 In zones 1–3, plant cool-season crops, but wait until the danger of frost is past to plant warm-season vegetables. In zones 10–13, feed warm-season vegetables (see p. 189).

✓ Clean glass or plastic bird feeders by putting on top rack of dishwasher. Scrub wooden ones with hot, soapy water; allow to dry before refilling.

MAY

🌿 In the low and intermediate desert, water roses deeply and mulch them (see pp. 188, 190–195). In windy areas, stake newly established trees (see p. 201).

🌱 Deadhead annuals and perennials. In high elevations, plant warm-season annuals such as marigold and cosmos after the danger of frost is past.

🌷 Remove spent flowers but not foliage from spring-blooming bulbs.

🌾 In dry areas, water and mulch vegetables regularly. In zones 1–3, feed cool-season crops with a balanced fertilizer (see p. 189).

🌼 Feed lawns with a high-nitrogen fertilizer (see pp. 101, 229). If desired, continue until September.

JUNE

🌿 Check roses for diseases or pests; treat with an all-purpose rose spray if needed to control fungal diseases or insects (see pp. 224, 230). Keep newly planted trees and shrubs well watered.

🌿 Deeply irrigate flower borders, raised beds, and containers.

🌱 Plant warm-season crops in all zones (see p. 138).

🌿 In mountain zones, adjust the mower blades to cut grass to 2–3 in. tall. Mow every 7–10 days. In warmer areas, set the mower to cut at about 1½ in. for Bermuda, St. Augustine, and zoysia grass.

✓ Before replanting containers, rinse or scrub away traces of old soil or fertilizer build-up (patches of white film on the outside of pots).

JULY

🌿 Have top-heavy trees trimmed to protect them from strong winds (see p. 213). Replenish mulch (see p. 188). Check for spider mites and treat if necessary (see p. 220).

🌿 If the foliage of perennials such as lady's-mantle or bergenia looks tattered, cut it to the ground and water well.

🌱 Fertilize summer-blooming bulbs (see p. 189).

🌱 Keep harvesting tomatoes for continued fruit. Feed tomatoes with moderate-nitrogen fertilizer. Pinch growing tips of herbs to encourage bushy foliage (see p. 217).

🌿 Stop fertilizing lawns during the hottest part of summer. Aerate lawn if needed (see p. 229).

✓ Keep your compost pile moist—but not soggy—during dry spells. If it is attracting fruit flies, sprinkle lime on it.

AUGUST

🌿 When weather cools, water established trees and shrubs well and feed them with a half-strength application of a complete fertilizer (see p. 189). In zones 1–3, stop fertilizing woody plants by the end of the month. In zones 12–13, keep roses well watered even though they may be dormant in hottest weather.

🌿 Keep deadheading annuals, and feed plants every 2 weeks with a liquid fertilizer (see p. 189).

🌱 In zones 10–13, keep fertilizing and watering warm-season crops.

✓ Inspect your porch, patio, fence, and any other wooden structures that are subject to damage caused by moisture or insects. Footing or pier settlement can also cause damage. If you are concerned about structural damage, call a professional for an evaluation.

SEPTEMBER

🌿 In zones 10 and 11, plant trees and shrubs from nursery containers; in windy areas, support newly planted trees with stakes (see p. 201). In zones 12 and 13, feed and lightly prune roses.

🌿 Plant perennials; they're often on sale at garden centers now. Apply or replenish mulch (see p. 188).

🌱 In mountain and high-desert zones, plant spring-blooming bulbs such as narcissus and spring star flower (see p. 129).

🌱 In zones 10 and 11, plant lettuce, spinach, and other cool-season greens from nursery packs (see p. 137).

🌿 In zones 11–13, overseed warm-season lawns with cool-season grasses (see p. 103). Fertilize lawns with medium-nitrogen fertilizer (see p. 101, 229). Don't fertilize Bermuda grass if you plan to overseed it with annual winter ryegrass in October; otherwise, feed it with a high-nitrogen fertilizer and water well.

✓ Have the blades of your lawn mower professionally sharpened.

OCTOBER

🌿 In zones 12 and 13, plant trees and shrubs from nursery containers (see pp. 200–201). In windy areas, support young trees with stakes (see p. 201). In northern zones, mulch roses.

🌿 In southern zones, plant cool-season annuals such as nasturtium and calendula once the weather has cooled; divide crowded perennials (see p. 216).

🌱 In zones 10–13, plant spring-blooming bulbs (see p. 129).

🌱 Pull up and dispose of crop plants past their prime. In zones 11–13, plant cool-season crops (see p. 137). In cold areas, pick tomatoes before frost hits. They will ripen in a paper bag indoors.

🌿 In zones 11–13, mow Bermuda grass to about ½ in., overseed with annual ryegrass, and water deeply.

✓ Test your soil now if you suspect it is deficient in nutrients or that the pH may require adjustment (see p. 187).

NOVEMBER

🌿 In desert regions, keep newly planted trees and shrubs well irrigated. Native desert plants don't need extra irrigation. In zones 12 and 13, prune and fertilize roses (see pp. 189, 215).

🌿 If weather is still mild in your region, plant perennials.

🌱 In high-elevation regions, mulch newly planted bulbs (see p. 188).

✓ Containers, landscape fabric, garden tools, and irrigation systems are available at reduced prices at garden centers.

DECEMBER

🌿 In zones 1–3, protect the trunks of young trees from sun scald (see p. 201). Apply a dormant oil spray to established roses (see p. 224).

🌿 Consider purchasing one of the new cordless electric mowers; most models have a mulching feature that leaves finely shredded grass in place, so no raking or bagging is necessary. The mowers are quiet, energy-efficient, and easy to maintain.

✓ Replenish mulch if needed (see p. 188).

Basic Pruning

ost woody plants require some pruning if they are to look and grow their best, but pruning can be an intimidating subject. Certainly, unless you feel confident and have experience, large trees are best pruned by a professional arborist with the right tools. Most homeowners, however, can easily manage the necessary pruning of smaller trees, shrubs, hedges, and roses.

In pruning, timing is everything and late winter or spring tend to be when most pruning tasks are carried out. In general, you prune flowering shrubs after flowering (spring or summer, depending on bloom time), roses and deciduous trees in late winter, conifers in early spring, and tender or semi-tropical shrubs in late spring. To identify when to prune different plants, consult the Regional Maintenance Guides on pages 204–211, and follow the guidelines given here.

Non-woody plants, such as many perennials and grasses—and even herbs and vegetables—also benefit from periodic grooming. Pinching, deadheading, cutting back, and other routine tasks are discussed on pages 216–217.

Terminal bud

Outward-facing lateral bud

Inward-facing lateral bud

Terminal bud

Flower bud

THE KINDEST CUT

Pruning encourages a plant to stop growing in one direction and start growing in another. How—and when—you prune depends on two factors: the effect you wish to achieve (such as prolonged bloom) and the growing characteristics of the plant. For the least maintenance, let plants grow according to their natural patterns. Prune young trees and shrubs just enough so they develop strong, shapely forms; prune flowering shrubs to produce more blossoms; and prune older shrubs to remove unhealthy or unwanted branches.

The illustration above shows the main points of growth on a typical branch—even though the terms may seem technical it's worth learning a little about them. Learning to recognize "growth buds" will help you identify where to make cuts, especially if you keep in mind one simple rule: cutting a *terminal bud* forces the branch to develop in the direction of other growth buds. The result will be healthier, bushier, more long-lived plants.

It's also helpful to observe a plant's growth patterns. Most deciduous shrubs and some evergreens produce new stems from the plant's base. Others, mostly evergreens, form a permanent framework of branches. Conifers have their own patterns; instructions for pruning them appear on page 214.

Finally, if you are still not confident about pruning, ask a nurseryman or a Cooperative Extension agent about pruning schedules in your region for the plants in your garden, or hire a garden consultant to do a once-yearly pruning of your plants or to train you to do it properly yourself.

MAINTAINING YOUR GARDEN

Thinning cuts remove overcrowded branches and any weak or old stems. Cut to where a side branch joins the main stem; no new shoots will be produced below the cuts.

Heading cuts—removing the terminal buds—force the branch to produce a cluster of new shoots from buds below the cuts. Do this to growing plants to make them more bushy.

Removing the terminal buds of a growing plant (far left) forces it to fill out and become bushier.

Removing, or pinching, the spent flower heads of blooming shrubs (left) prevents the plant from putting energy into seed production. For rhododendrons, the effect is bushier growth or side branching.

Rejuvenate shrubs by removing a third of oldest basal growth annually for 3 years (left). For shrubs that tolerate hard pruning (such as barberry and oleander), cut to a few stubs (right).

Clean up small trees by cutting off branches that are awkwardly crossed, diseased, broken, or damaged.

TRIMMING HEDGES

To maintain formal hedges, shear back new growth (usually recognized by lighter or softer foliage) by one-half or two-thirds in the spring after the first flush of growth has stopped. Always cut sides wider at bottom than at top, so sun can reach all foliage. Prune bare spots while the plant is actively growing to encourage more branching. For small hedges, use shears (left); power hedge trimmers (above) are handy for larger hedges.

PRUNING EVERGREENS

Prune most broad-leafed evergreens after flowering. Needle-leafed evergreens need less pruning, as their dense foliage is part of their charm. Young conifers sometimes form U-shaped or double trunks; cut away the weaker stem if you want a classic pyramid. For "random-branching" conifers (including arborvitae and juniper) make thinning cuts well into the shrubs (left) so the remaining branches conceal the cuts. To control size and shape of "whorl-branching" conifers (pines) remove their growth candles (right).

PRUNING ROSES

Although it may seem like it, there's no mystery to pruning roses. Wait until late winter, as new leaf buds begin to swell on the branches, and you'll have an easy time finding the right places to cut. Make cuts at a 45-degree angle, always just above an outward-facing lateral bud. During the blooming season, help form new flower buds by cutting lanky stems and spent blossoms just above any five-leaflet leaf (below, left).

Arching shrub roses, rugosas, and climbers usually require only simple thinning (see page 213). To prune bushy roses quickly, use sharpened hedge clippers to cut off the top of each plant by as much as one-third. Then use pruning shears to snip out the oldest, grayish canes and any that cross, look dead or diseased, or are thinner than a pencil. The stout stems of hybrid teas can be pruned back harder, 6 to 12 inches from the bumpy bud union or graft.

Remove dead wood and all weak, twiggy branches (darker ones shown here). Make these cuts flush with the bud union (the swelling at the base of the plant).

Cut out all branches that cross through the center of the plant. This opens up the bush and encourages it to grow into a vase shape.

If you deadhead roses, or cut them for display, always cut above a five-leaflet leaf. Dotted lines show best place to cut at different times during the growing season.

In mild climates, shorten the remaining healthy growth by one-third. In cold climates, remove any stems that were injured or killed by winter freeze damage. (This may result in a shorter bush.)

OTHER ROUTINE MAINTENANCE

Shear repeat-blooming perennials, such as lavender, or low-growing perennials, such as the basket-of-gold shown here, after bloom. Use hedge shears, scissors, or sheep shears. Do the same for loose-stemmed annual flowers, such as alyssum, in midseason to induce a fresh round of bloom.

Deadhead long-blooming perennials and annuals, such as daylilies, coreopsis, zinnias, marigolds, and geraniums (above) by snipping off the spent flowers with shears. The result will be a longer period of bloom. For a repeat show on foxglove, cut faded stalks down to 4–6 in.

Divide overgrown iris clumps by digging out their shallow rhizomes in fall. Snap or cut them apart at their joints and discard any rhizomes that do not have a fan of leaves. Dust the cut ends with a fungicide, trim the leaves to 4–6 in., and replant.

To create more plants from a multiple-stemmed perennial such as red hot poker, dig up the entire root ball and split it with a sharp shovel or a fork. Take sections that contain both roots and green stems, trim the stems to 4–6 in., and replant.

Pinch the growing tips of annual herbs and vegetables a few times early in the season to create sturdy branching at the base of plants. Pinch the tips of tomatoes (above) to keep their growth compact and encourage fruiting.

Shade delicate seedlings from hot sun with a bit of lattice, window screen, or shade cloth (above)—this protects them until their roots have developed. To keep the growing roots of young vegetables moist and cool, mulch between plants.

Cut back ornamental grasses, salvias, lavender (above), and deciduous perennials to 4–6 in. above the ground to make room for new growth. Do this job in late winter, when dead plant parts can easily be pulled from the ground.

Cut off browned, blackened, or damaged fern leaves near the center of the plant when you see new growth in spring (above). Comb your fingers through foliage of ornamental grasses to remove old leaves.

10
The Healthy Garden

By selecting pest- and disease-resistant plants and keeping them healthy and well watered you substantially reduce the potential for problems in your garden. You're even less likely to be bothered if you clear out favorite overwintering locations for eggs, pupae, and spores; an annual fall cleanup belongs on every maintenance calendar.

Still, no matter how many precautions you take, slugs and snails will always find their way over from the neighbor's garden or weeds will drift in from neighboring fields or be brought by birds. But you needn't call up an arsenal of deadly poisons at the first sign of trouble. First identify the particular insect or disease; then, only if the infestation is extensive or the damage severe should you try to eliminate it, always starting with the least-toxic method. If the same problem returns to your garden over and over, review the prevention methods shown here, or consider removing the problem host plant altogether.

LIVE!
In This Box
...Live Nematodes

BENEFICIAL NEMATODES

Effective against more than 230 kinds of garden pests,
including cutworms, corn root worms, strawberry weevils,
gypsy moth larvae, cabbage root maggots, white grubs, and
many more.

BRING YOUR GARDEN TO LIFE!

Orcon
A Division of
Organic Control Inc.
Los Angeles, CA

Problem Pests

When you choose the right plants, water and feed them on a regular schedule, and give your garden an annual cleanup in fall, you'll find that few plants will be lost to insect and animal pests. But every garden is subject to attack by creatures that find your plants as attractive as you do. Where you live, and your climate, will determine your worst pest problems. Gardeners on the borders of wild land may find that deer and gophers are a constant menace; in foggy coastal climates, snails and slugs are likely to be ever-present. Many pests multiply during the onset of warm weather, only to recede as nature's balance readjusts and beneficial predators reduce the harmful pests' population. Some pests are happy to feast on a single plant type; certainly most have favorites—but even this varies from place to place. Your local Cooperative Extension agent or a good nurseryman can tell you the most prevalent pest problems and solutions in your area.

Not only is the pest population diverse, but some pests cause different kinds of damage at different stages of their lives. Many pests are nocturnal, so a weekly check during the evening hours can often help you determine the culprit of a particular kind of damage. Before you treat a pest, identify it correctly. Again, your Cooperative Extension service and local garden center can help, especially if you bring them an example of the pest or the damage it has caused.

Oakmoth caterpillars eat the leaves of oak trees—they can defoliate entire trees. Healthy trees usually bounce back from infestation. In summer, if you see more than 2 dozen caterpillars at a time, hand pick them or spray with carbaryl or acephate. Bacillus thuringiensis (Bt) may control smaller larvae. Large trees should be treated by an arborist.

Mealybugs mass in powdery colonies on the leaves or stems of many ornamental plants. Although mealybugs are related to aphids, their waxy coating protects them from most pesticides. Natural predators—green lacewings and ladybugs—are the best defense. If badly infested, spray ornamentals with acephate.

Snails and slugs eat the leaves and stems of all plants. They feed at night and on overcast or rainy days. Trails of silvery slime between plants signal slugs—stop them with barriers of copper edging (see p. 222), wood ashes, or diatomaceous earth (from a garden center, not the pool-filter type). Hand pick at night, when the pests are active—after 10 p.m. is best. For chemical control, use bait or liquid containing metaldehyde.

Aphids are soft-bodied sucking insects that reproduce quickly and attack a variety of garden plants, particularly feeding on new growth. Control them with regular washings with strong bursts of water from a hose, and by spraying with insecticidal soap. Control ants, which feed on the aphids' sticky honeydew. Spray badly infested plants with an insecticide containing pyrethrin, diazinon, malathion, or acephate.

Weevils feed on roots as larvae and leaves, flowers, and bark as adults. Shrubs, trees, and flowers are all targets. Adults can be trapped or deterred with sticky traps, or treated with rotenone, neem, pyrethrum, or acephate. Beneficial nematodes, applied in fall, can kill larvae. Diazinon or chlorpyrifos kill other types of beetle "grub" in lawns.

You may be able to keep tunneling moles, gophers, and ground squirrels out of your garden by surrounding it with underground fencing 3–4 ft. deep. Or, use barriers for raised beds and plant bulbs in baskets (p. 223). A noisy dog can be a good deterrent. As a last resort, try traps or poison baits, following the manufacturer's instructions.

Cutworms chew leaves and can sever the stems of seedlings or recently transplanted vegetables and flowers. Protect seedlings with paper collars (p. 222) or diatomaceous earth (the type for gardens, not pools) sprinkled in a ring around each plant. Treat infested lawns with a lawn-specific insecticide containing diazinon or chlorpyrifos.

Gypsy moths attack—and kill—many landscape trees, including coniferous evergreens. To prevent adult females from climbing up a tree to lay eggs (and to keep larvae from traveling down), wrap the trunk with a sticky barrier (see p. 222). Hand-pick and destroy egg masses and caterpillars; severe infestations call for an insecticide containing neem, carbaryl, or acephate.

Scales cling to evergreen and deciduous landscape trees like barnacles, protected by a crusty, fuzzy, or bubbly exterior that resembles disease more than insect infestation. Pesticides are more likely to kill the beneficial insects that feast on scales. Instead, scrape scales off leaves and bark with a plastic scouring pad. Control ants, which can cultivate scales for their honeydew.

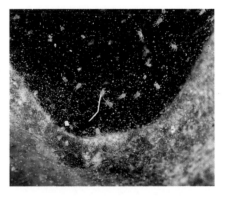

Mites attack a variety of flowers, vegetables, shrubs, trees, and house plants. They're nearly invisible, except when they cluster together to suck juices from leaves, stems, and flower buds. You can blast mites off plants with a stiff jet of water or use an insecticidal soap formulated for mite control. Most insecticides don't kill mites—buy a miticide formulated for use on the infested plant instead.

To stop snails and slugs, enclose vegetable and flower beds with sections of 3-in.-high copper banding. The copper discharges a small electrical shock when touched by a snail or slug, making it beat a hasty retreat.

MANAGING PESTS

When it comes to low-maintenance gardening, prevention is always better than cure. Choose your plants wisely, selecting those known to be resistant to common diseases as well as unpalatable to animal and insect pests. The Plant Selection Guides in "The Ornamental Garden" and "The Edible Garden" (starting on page 76) will get you started; your local garden center, the Cooperative Extension service, and your neighbors can all offer valuable recommendations for plants that work in your area.

Because stressed plants are especially susceptible to pest infestation and disease, keep your garden healthy by providing fertile soil along with the right amount of fertilizer, water, and sun or shade for each plant. If you do encounter problems, act immediately—it's far easier to deal with pests and diseases before they take hold. Try simple solutions first. Barriers, blasts of water, and sprays made from common household substances will often do the job and are safer for people, pets, and the environment than chemicals.

It's increasingly common to find "beneficial" insects for sale in nurseries and catalogs—bugs that will do the work of pest control for you. Beneficial insects can be very useful, but before you bring home a bag of ladybugs, read the tips given at right.

Gauze row covers protect young, tender vegetable leaves from flying and crawling insects while letting sunshine and air through. Mail-order catalogs and garden centers carry a variety of row covers of different weights.

Trap adult weevils and other insects that crawl up the trunks of trees and shrubs by spreading a thick layer of sticky material around the trunk of affected plants. To trap flying insects, spread the product on a yellow card and hang it up.

To keep out crawling insects surround newly transplanted seedlings with collars made from bottomless paper cups or plastic containers. As the plants grow, they'll be better able to withstand the insects' attentions.

Buying in. Mail-order suppliers and garden centers offer many beneficial insects to help you manage garden pests—ladybugs, praying mantis, and lacewings are the most common. No matter which species of insect you buy, determine in advance whether you need just a few—to "seed" your garden—or larger numbers to manage a pest population that has gotten out of control.

Be a good host. Offer beneficial insects appropriate food to eat at all stages of their lives. Adults need flowering plants for pollen (see right), nectar, and shelter; some, such as parasitoid wasps, need pest eggs, or the metamorphosing form of the pests, in which to lay their eggs. Even with your best attempts, beneficials may move on or die out when their food or host supply runs low.

Favored flowers. Many beneficial insects are attracted to flowering plants from the carrot *(Apiaceae)*, daisy *(Asteraceae)*, and pink *(Caryophyllaceae)* families. Perennials such as yarrow and coreopsis are inviting to many beneficials, as are easy-to-grow annuals such as cosmos and sweet alyssum.

Fly away home. Ladybugs consume many unwanted pests, so purchasing them may seem to make sense, but ecologists point out that we don't yet know the long-term effects of introducing them to the garden. And since most are sold before they're ready to feed and lay eggs, there may not be much reason for them to hang around your garden, even if it's brimming with pests. To increase your chances of success, buy "preconditioned" ladybugs from specialty suppliers.

If a neighborhood cat decides to turn your garden beds into litter boxes, commercial repellents or chili powder may keep it at bay. If not, deter the creature by placing sections of chicken wire or hardware cloth between the plantings, then conceal the wire with a thin layer of mulch.

Gophers, moles, and ground squirrels tunnel through the ground to eat tender bulbs and shoots. Protect bulbs from gophers by setting their root balls into wire cages in the soil (right) or lining planting holes with barriers of hardware cloth. As an alternative, build raised beds and line them with hardware cloth (left) or chicken wire. A wire mesh size of ½ in. will stop all pocket gopher species found in the West.

Deer fencing should be 7–9 ft. high. Add reflective tape, or install a horizontal extension or second fence in front of the first if needed. Protect tender, young trees in wire cages, and sprinkle or spray deer repellents around beds and borders.

SOLVING PEST PROBLEMS

When prevention and simple pest-management techniques don't work, pesticides are the obvious choice. But shop carefully—try to pick a product that will solve the problem with the least risk to beneficial creatures, people, and the environment. Insecticidal soaps and dormant and summer oils, for example, kill a variety of insects but are relatively nontoxic. When buying a stronger insecticide, choose single-purpose, rather than broad-spectrum, products to protect the beneficial insects that inhabit your garden. (An easy way to distinguish between products is to count the number of insects the product claims to kill. Shorter lists are more likely to be found on single-purpose pesticides.) When possible, avoid broad-spectrum systemic pesticides. Since systemic pesticides are absorbed by the plant's living tissue, they won't wash off or dissipate into the air. Therefore, every insect that ingests part of the plant could be affected. When spraying vegetables, check the product label to be sure the pesticide is safe to use on edibles.

Oils smother insects, larvae, and eggs, and help prevent diseases. Light oils, called summer oils, can be used year round. Heavy oils, called dormant oils, should be used when plants are dormant. For large areas, use a pressure-pump applicator.

If the problem is limited to one or several plants, use a hand sprayer to direct an oil mixture or a pesticide right where you want it. Many manufacturers offer premixed pesticides in convenient small-size containers.

Beneficial nematodes are effective against some grubs, including weevils and Japanese beetles. Mix with water and apply in fall, according to the manufacturer's directions. Most can be applied from a simple watering can or a hose-end sprayer.

To protect your tastiest plants from slugs and snails, encircle them with a liquid barrier. But don't use this type of product —or snail and slug baits—where it will be accessible to children and pets.

PEST CONTROLS

Active Ingredient	Brand Names/ Manufacturers	Controls	Comments
acephate	Orthene	aphids (large infestations) mealybugs, adult weevils, thrips, oakmoth caterpillars	for ornamental flowers and woody plants, including oak trees; not for edibles
Bacillus thuringiensis (Bt)	many	caterpillars, budworms, gypsy moth caterpillars	for ornamental flowers and woody plants; edible crops
carbaryl	Sevin	aphids, beetles, moths, cutworms, mites, ticks, gypsy moth caterpillars	for woody ornamentals including roses and rhododendrons; lawns
carbaryl/metaldehyde	many; available as granules and bait	slugs, snails, ground-dwelling insects	for ornamental flowers and woody plants; lawns
chlorpyrifos	Dursban; available as spray and granules	ants, fleas, grubs, cranefly larvae, weevils, caterpillars, wasps, mites, ticks, cutworms	for woody ornamentals; lawns; some edibles
diatomaceous earth	many	ants, fleas, earwigs	for ornamentals and edible plants
diazinon	many; available as spray and granules	aphids, cutworms, fleas, beetles, grubs, mites, cranefly larvae	for ornamental flowers and woody plants; some edibles
diphacinone	Green Light gopher killer	pocket gophers	for burrow entrances; soil beneath affected plants
fatty acid soap (repellent)	Hinder	mammals, rodents	for ornamental and edible plants
insecticidal soap	many; concentrated or pre-mixed liquid	aphids, thrips, whitefly, scale, mites, ticks	for many ornamental and edible plants
malathion	many	whitefly, scale, aphids, weevils, caterpillars, mites, ticks	for ornamental flowers and woody plants; lawns; some edibles
metaldehyde	many; available as liquid, granules, and bait	slugs and snails	for ornamental flowers and woody plants; lawns; edibles
methyl nonyl ketone	Dexol Dog & Cat Repellent	mammals	for soil beneath affected plants
neem oil	many	aphids, whitefly, scale, weevils, moths, mites, ticks, thrips	for ornamental flowers and woody plants; some edibles
potassium nitrate/sulfur	Dexol Gopher Gasser	gophers, moles, ground squirrels	for animal burrows; soil beneath affect plant
pyrethrin	many; available as spray and powder	mealybugs, whitefly, scale, weevils, caterpillars, mites, ticks, beetles, spider mites, ants, budworms	for ornamental and edible plants
resmethrin	many	aphids, whitefly, scale, mites, ticks	for many ornamental plants
rotenone	several; available as spray or powder	aphids, ants, scale, mites, weevils	for many ornamental and edible plants

SAFETY TIPS

Under lock and key. Protect kids and pets from accidental poisoning by storing chemicals in locked cabinets or on high shelves.

For good measure. Mix pesticides exactly as specified on the label, never stronger. Keep a magnifying glass with your chemicals to make it easier to read the label. To ensure accuracy, store a set of measuring spoons with your applicators.

Protect yourself. Wear long sleeves, long pants, closed shoes, a hat, and gloves when mixing and applying pesticides. If you're using a pesticide whose label carries a "warning" rather than a "caution," add goggles and a face mask to your outfit.

Make a label. Label spray bottles with the product name and the date. Mix only small amounts at a time, so you know the product is fresh.

No dumping. Never pour a liquid pesticide—even if it's diluted—onto the ground or into a drain of any kind (including a sink). Don't use up leftover pesticide by spraying healthy parts of the garden. And never throw pesticide powder or granules into the trash. Instead, call your local recycling center, garbage company, or water agency and find out where you can drop off pesticides.

Worst Weeds

Weeds are wild plants (and some invasive cultivated plants) that compete with your garden plants for water, nutrients, and space. They're inevitable, but you can control them. Prevention—mulches, landscape fabrics, and blanketlike ground covers—is the first line of defense. Hand-weeding before weeds set seed is also critical. If you're vigilant for a few years, you'll be rewarded with a sharp decline in your weed population.

Because they develop extensive root systems, perennial weeds are more difficult to manage once they've grown past the seedling stage—to get rid of the plant, you have to dig out the roots. Hasten their demise by repeatedly cutting back the tops, which stresses the plants, but it may take several seasons to eradicate the plants. Annual weed seeds can be windborne or delivered by birds, arrive in nursery containers, or be present in certain mulches (only use mulches that are certified weed-free).

Herbicides are powerful chemicals that can damage desirable plants and contaminate water and soil. Before buying a herbicide, always read the label to ensure you have the correct product for the weeds in your garden.

Some ornamental plants can become invasive in good growing conditions and may eventually overpower your garden or invade wild areas. At right is a list of some of the worst offenders in Western gardens.

USING HERBICIDES

There are two main types of herbicide, or weed-killer: pre-emergents prevent seeds from germinating; post-emergent "contact" types kill weeds on contact; slower-acting 'translocated' post-emergents interfere with the weed's metabolism (they are best for perennial weed control). Most herbicides are further specified as selective or nonselective; the latter kill any plant with which they come in contact. Brand names vary from place to place; look for the "active ingredient" to determine which chemicals a herbicide contains, and how it should be applied.

For lawns, common pre-emergents contain one or more of the following ingredients: atrazine, dithiopyr, isoxaben, oryzalin, pendimethalin, and trifluralin. Post-emergents for control of broadleaf weeds include dicamba, MCPP, and 2, 4-D. For crabgrass, use MSMA or DSMA. For nutsedge in lawns, use bentazon.

In ornamental plantings, long-lasting pre-emergent products include dichlobenil (Casoron) and trifluralin (Preen) granules, and oryzalin spray (Casoron for woody ornamentals only). For established weeds, first try glyphosate (Roundup) or herbicidal soap; both must be sprayed directly—and only—on the target weed. Selective chemicals for grassy weeds include fluazifop-butyl and sethoxydim. For brush control, try glyphosate, triclopyr, 2,4-D or glufosinate.

TOO MUCH OF A GOOD THING

Bamboo, golden and black
Phyllostachys aurea and *P. nigra*

Bellflower, creeping and Siberian
Campanula

Calla lilies
Zantedeschia

Dame's rocket
Hesperis matronalis

English ivy
Hedera helix

Fountain grass
Pennisetum setaceum

Four o'clocks (Pacific Northwest)
Mirabilis jalapa

Giant Burmese honeysuckle
Lonicera hildebrandiana

Horsetail
Equisetum hyemale

Japanese anemone
Anemone hybrida

Jubata grass
Cortaderia jubata

Mint
Mentha

Morning glory
Ipomoea tricolor

Pampas grass
Cortaderia selloana

Purple loosestrife (Northwest and Mountain states)
Lythrum virgatum

Sweet violet
Viola odorata

Trumpet vine
Campsis radicans

Blackberry

Mallow

Thistle

Creeping bellflower

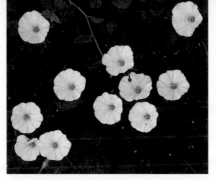

Bindweed

Nutsedge

Purslane

Groundsel

Oxalis

Thicket- and Grove-forming Weeds

Blackberry. Perennial, spreads by underground stems, canes can grow 20–30 ft. in one season.

Deep-rooted Weeds

Bindweed. Perennial, spreads by rhizomes, but seeds can lie dormant for 50 years before sprouting. Roots can penetrate 10 ft. into soil.

Dandelion. Perennial, reproduces by seed and roots, forms deep taproot.

Mallow. Annual or biennial, reproduces by seed, forms deep taproot.

Nutsedge. Perennial, spreads on tubers as deep as 18 in.

Thistle. Annual, biennial, and perennial, reproduces by seed, grows from deep, wide-spreading roots.

Shallow-rooted Weeds

Purslane. Annual, spreads by seed or reroots from stem fragments. Easy to pull or hoe.

Spurge. Annual, spreads by seed. Easy to pull or hoe.

Rampant Reseeders

Creeping bellflower. Spreads by seed and deep-seated creeping rhizomes.

Groundsel. Annual, spreads by seed, often several generations in a year.

Yellow oxalis. Perennial, reproduces by above-ground runners and seeds. Seed capsules can shoot seeds as far as 10 ft. away.

Annual Grasses

Bluegrass. Annual (some perennial), sets seed rapidly in cool weather, often before plants can be pulled.

Crabgrass. Annual, spreads by seeds and rooting along the stems.

Perennial Grasses

Bermuda grass. Perennial, spreads by rhizomes, above-ground runners, and seed.

Kikuyu grass. Perennial, spreads by rhizomes, above-ground runners, and seed. Few chemical controls effective.

PREVENTING & CONTROLLING WEEDS

Space fast-growing annuals and ground covers closely together and they will eventually shade out weeds as they grow. Staggered, intensive planting is most natural looking; set plants an equal distance from one another in all directions. But restricted air flow and trapped moisture can invite insects and disease.

Fabric weed barriers trap perennial weeds underneath, but seeds of annual weeds can sprout and grow in the mulch above. Use landscape fabric in permanent plantings around perennials and shrubs, or in pathway construction (see p. 46). Cover the fabric with 2 or 3 in. of mulch to disguise it.

Pre-emergent herbicides are available in granular form, and as soluble liquids that can be applied with a hose-end sprayer (above). Apply them to the soil or lawn early in the season before weeds germinate. Read the label to learn which weeds the herbicide controls best and whether it can be used on a lawn.

Spot sprays kill weeds that have already sprouted. But because they don't distinguish between valued plants and weeds, you must apply these products carefully. In close quarters, use a paintbrush rather than a spray applicator.

Long-handled weeding hoes let you remove weeds without bending. Pincer-type tools have a forked blade that makes it easy to pop the long root out of moist soil with minimal disturbance to the surrounding area. For other weeders, see pp. 182–184.

Sweep a propane-powered flamer a few inches above weeds in pathways or along curbs. Rather than burning up, the cells of the weed actually burst and it quickly dies. Take care with the flamer in dry, fire-prone areas.

THE HEALTHY GARDEN

CULTURAL PROBLEMS

Plants deprived of the essentials they need often take on symptoms of disease or insect damage, when in fact their health is being damaged by conditions that exist in your garden. Lack of water (or too much water) can cause yellow or mottled leaves. Temperature swings during pollination can make blossoms fall from vegetables, trees, and flowers. A lack of iron in the soil can make leaves lose their green color (called chlorosis), but so can a nitrogen deficiency (see page 189). In the fight against cultural problems in a low-maintenance garden, your best defense is information. Talk to neighbors, nursery staff, and your local Cooperative Extension agent to learn the types of problems that are typical in your area and the steps for dealing with them that have proved most helpful. Then use the Plant Selection Guides in "The Ornamental Garden" to choose plants that can tolerate the environment you offer, be it dry, smoggy, shady, poorly drained, or windy.

Compacted soil and hardpan limit the ability of the roots to obtain nutrients and oxygen. Try to improve drainage (see p. 63), or plant in raised beds and containers filled with good soil.

Moss is made up of thousands of tiny, rootless plants. It signals acidic, poorly drained soil, and inadequate sunlight. Improve drainage (see p. 63), raise soil pH, or treat with moss-killers.

Scorched leaf tips and margins are signs that a plant is not receiving adequate water due to drought, wind, sun, salt burn, or root damage. Some plants, such as the Japanese maple shown here, also suffer when given overhead water that has a high salt or mineral content.

Thatch is a layer of intermingled dead roots, partially decomposed grass stems, and debris that has accumulated below turf grass blades and above the soil surface. Thatch ¼–½ in. is normal. To avoid thatch, keep the lawn well fed, well watered, and mowed to the correct height.

LONG-LIVED LAWNS

So sweet. Lime raises the pH of acidic soil and improves drainage through clay soil. Add powdered lime in fall at a rate of 40 lbs. per 1,000 sq. ft.; granular products at a rate of 25 lbs. per 2,000 sq. ft.

Fresh air. A core-aerator removes thin, cigar-shaped plugs of turf. Use it once a year in early spring or fall. Power types can be rented.

I'm hungry. In spring, turf grass needs nitrogen for leafy growth, so use a high-nitrogen fertilizer. In fall, it needs both nitrogen and potassium, which encourages root growth, so feed with a fertilizer such as 12-4-8.

I'm thirsty. Water your lawn with an automatic sprinkler system so you control delivery—for most lawns 1 in. per week is sufficient. Don't let soil get saturated.

"Grasscycle." Use a mulching mower that leaves clippings on the lawn. They'll provide nitrogen and mowing goes faster without bags to empty.

Less moss. Moss can overpower lawns because it likes bad conditions (see left). Treat in late winter.

What's thatch? If your lawn has thatch (see below, left), dethatch in spring with a rented power dethatcher or hire a landscaping company to do it for you.

Barely there. Overseed bare spots in spring or late summer. Use grass seed specified for overseeding.

Let the light shine. Few turf grasses thrive in shade. Keep overhanging branches well pruned.

Weed out. Control grassy and broad-leaf weeds with the herbicides listed on p. 226. Try to remove likely sources of weed seed (don't put a bird feeder over the lawn, for instance).

Grub be gone. Treat for insect larvae as needed (see p. 225).

Darn dog. Train household pets not to use the lawn as a rest room.

Plant Diseases

Populate your low-maintenance garden with plants known to be resistant to common diseases. Good gardening practices can go a long way toward preventing disease. Fungi and bacteria, for instance, need moisture to thrive. It therefore makes sense to avoid overhead watering. If it's not possible to water from underneath, water during full-sun hours so leaves can dry fully before dusk. Following the additional cultural tips on the next page will also help keep disease down.

Many fungicides control a variety of fungal diseases; the chart on the facing page will help you decide which one to use to treat diseases on your plants.

If you grow roses, you might wish to try all-purpose fungicide/insecticide products. These systemic sprays control a variety of diseases and pests.

Powdery mildew fungi appear as white or gray patches on leaves and flowers, never stems. Infected leaves eventually turn yellowish green to brown. New growth may be stunted or distorted.

Oak root fungus can live for many years in old tree roots, so watch for it when planting on newly cleared land. The disease is initially characterized by yellowing and wilting leaves. Later on you'll see white fans of feltlike fungus growing at ground level. If oak root fungus is a problem in your soil, plant resistant species — your local Coopertive Extension can give you suggestions.

In the early stages of disease, rust fungi are characterized by powdery pustules on the undersides of lower leaves. As the disease progresses, upper leaf surfaces develop spots, then turn yellow.

The black spot fungus, which targets roses, starts as small black circles that eventually widen to about ½ in. Look for irregular margins — that's how you can distinguish black spot from other fungi and spotting caused by cold or chemicals.

Damping off disease is caused by various fungi that cause young seedlings to grow to about an inch high before wilting and toppling. Container plants grown in garden soil rather than potting mix are more susceptible.

The aster yellows bacteria turns plant foliage yellow, stunts and distorts growth, and prevents flowering. The disease is spread by leafhoppers and affects edibles, such as lettuce, and ornamentals such as cosmos, marigolds, and petunias.

PREVENTING DISEASES

Diseases often thrive where plants don't get enough light or air circulation. Space plants generously to encourage air to move and moisture to evaporate.

Practice good garden hygiene. Discard infected plants promptly. Clean up fallen plant debris and discard it, especially in fall, to prepare for wet weather.

When working with or around infected plants, disinfect the tools you've used in a solution made with 1 part household bleach to 9 parts water.

DISEASE CONTROLS

Active Ingredient	Brand Names/ Manufacturers	Controls	Comments
chlorothalonil	many, including Daconil	gray snow mold, dollar spot on lawns; anthracnose, powdery mildew, black spot	for use on roses, tomatoes, lawns, ornamental flowers, and woody plants
copper sulfate, basic	many, often called Bordeaux Mixture	downy mildew, anthracnose, late blight	for use on ornamental flowers and some edibles
lime sulfur (calcium polysulfide)	several	leaf spot, powdery mildew, rust; also controls some insects	for use on ornamental flowers and woody plants; can be used as dormant spray
thiophanate-methyl	several	powdery mildew, black spot	for use on roses; systemic
triforine	Funginex	powdery mildew, black spot, rust	for use on roses, maple, oaks, and fruit trees; systemic
triadimefon	several, including Bayleton	rust, powdery mildew; lawn diseases	for use on roses, lawns; systemic
myclobutanil	several	powdery mildew, rust, leaf spot	for use on roses and other ornamentals
sulfur	several; available as dust or wettable powder	powdery mildew, rust, scab	for use on ornamental flowers and shrub and edibles

Finding Help

MAIL ORDER SUPPLIERS

ROSES

Jackson & Perkins Co.
One Rose Lane
Medford, OR 97501-0745
(800) 292-4769
Call for free catalog

High Country Roses
P.O. Box 148
Jensen, UT 84035
(800) 552-2082
Old garden roses, hardy shrub &
species roses; catalog

Heirloom Old Garden Roses
24062 Riverside Dr. NE
St. Paul, OR 97137
(503) 538-1576
fax (503) 538-5902
Wide selection of low-maintenance
roses; 124 page color catalog

Petaluma Rose Co.
P.O. Box 750953
Petaluma, CA 94975
(707) 769-8862 fax (707) 769-0394
www.sonic.net\~petrose
Wide variety of roses; catalog

Weeks Roses
430 East 19th St.
Upland, CA 91784
(800) 992-4409
Broad selection of roses; catalog

OTHER PLANTS

Greer Gardens
1280 Goodpasture Island Rd.
Eugene, OR 97401-1794
(800) 548-0111
fax (514) 686-0910
Rhododendrons, Japanese
maples, perennials, conifers,
ornamental grasses, books

Garden Escape
www.garden.com
Gardening website with on-line
marketplace

Canyon Creek Nursery
3527 Dry Creek Road
Oroville, CA 95965
(530) 533-2166
Uncommon perennials; sizable
salvia collection, hardy geraniums,
euphorbias

ForestFarm
990 Tetherow Rd.
Williams, OR 97544
(541) 846-7269;
fax (541) 846-6963
Native plants, ferns, grasses, common and uncommon perennials,
shrubs, and trees

Heronswood Nursery Ltd.
7530 NE 288th St.
Kingston, WA 98346
(360) 297-4172
Call for catalog

A High Country Garden
2902 Rufina St.
Santa Fe, NM 87505-2929
(800) 925-9387
Specializing in plants for the
Western Gardener;
64-page mail order catalog

Plants of the Southwest
Agua Fria, Route 6, Box 11A
Santa Fe, NM 87501
(800) 788-7333 (mail order)
Native & drought-tolerant plants;
call for price list

Greenlee Nursery
301 E. Franklin Ave.
Pomona, CA 91766
(909) 629-9045
Large selection of ornamental and
native grasses. Catalog includes tips
on planting and care

Wayside Gardens
1 Garden Lane
Hodges, SC 29695
(800) 845-1124
Unusual perennials, bulbs (including
daffodils, lilies), grasses, ornamentals, shrubs, trees, and vines

Yucca Do Nursery
Route 3, Box 104
Hempstead, TX 77445
(409) 826-4580
Many plants adapted to the
Southwest and Southeast; catalog

GENERAL PRODUCTS

A&L Western Laboratories, Inc.
1311 Woodland Avenue, Suite 1
Modesto, CA 95351
(209) 529-4080;
fax (209) 529-4736
A&L tests soil samples by mail

**Harmony Farm Supply &
Nursery**
3244 Gravenstein Hwy, N
Sebastopol, CA 95472
(707) 823-9125;
fax (707) 823-1734
Natural chemical controls, beneficial organisms, sprayers and
dusters, and soil care products.

Peaceful Valley Farm Supply
P.O. Box 2209
110 Springhill Drive
Grass Valley, CA 95945
For orders call:
(888) 784-1722
Hugh seed selection, quality tools
and equipment, and irrigation and
watering supplies; catalog

Gardens Alive!
5100 Schenley Place
Lawrenceburg, IN 47025
(812) 537-8650
Natural pesticides, weed killers,
fertilizers, animal repellents,
pheromone traps, floating row
covers, beneficial insects

Natural Gardening Company
217 San Anselmo Avenue
San Anselmo, CA 94960
(707) 766-9303
Composters, tools, earthworms,
beneficial insects, animal repellents,
pheromone traps, drip-irrigation
kits, and heirloom tomatoes

Gardener's Supply Company
128 Intervale Road
Burlington, VT 05401
(800) 955-3370
www.gardeners.com
Plant labels, tools, watering supplies, floating row covers, water timers, garden ornaments, composters, containers, and greenhouses.

Smith & Hawken
(800) 766-3336
Upscale garden ornaments; teak, wicker, and other furniture; clothing, accessories; high-quality tools

John Oldani Pop-Up Irrigation Sculptures
16530 County Rd. 63
Brooks, CA 95606
(530) 796-4143
Sculptural alternative to standard irrigation heads

The Urban Farmer Store
2833 Vicente St.
San Francisco, CA 94116
(415) 661-2204;
(800) 753-3747
Irrigation products; outdoor lighting; ponds & pumps; garden tools

LOCAL GOVERNMENT REGULATIONS

To find out what permits are required, consult your local building department, which is located at the town hall or municipal center in your region. You can find the phone number in the Government ("Blue") pages of the phone book under "Building & Planning" or "Planning." Permit requirements and codes vary from region to region and can include the following:

Building permits. Required for structural projects such as decks, fences, and swimming pools.

Utilities and easements. Areas that must be left accessible to someone other than the property owner, such as utility workers. Often specified on the property deed.

Setback. The minimum distance between a building (including decks and garden sheds) or other structure and the property lines.

Lot coverage. There are limits on the allowable structural coverage of residential lots.

Tree removal. In many areas, heritage trees of significant age or beauty are protected.

Water courses. Protected watercourses, creeks, streams, ponds, and reservoirs.

Height limit. The maximum height for structures

GARDEN PROFESSIONALS

Landscape Architect. A state-licensed professional who can produce detailed working drawings of the site and who usually supervises all installation.

Landscape or Garden Designer. Offers the same services as a landscape architect, but often more focused on residental projects. May have the same academic credentials as the landscape architect, but not a state license.

Landscape Contractor. Installs landscapes; hires subcontractors as needed; installs irrigation systems, structures, and plants.

Structural Contractor. Specialist in a particular field such as fencing or masonry.

Structural and Soils Engineers. A licensed professional responsible for reviewing the stablity of a structure. An engineer's stamp may be required by the city or county if the structure is to be built on an unstable or steep lot.

Planting Help. A responsible gardener willing to help with extra tasks such as planting or general maintenance. A good recommendation can often come from your local retail nursery.

Horticulturist. A specialist in the care and selection of plants. Often has training in garden design.

Arborist. A specialist in the care of trees and woody plants; pruning, shaping, and removal if needed.

Cooperative Extension Service. The Cooperative Extension Service is organized by county or region and is usually associated with a local college or university. Your local horticultural agent or Master Gardener is a valuable resource. To find your local office, look in the Government ("Blue") pages of the phone book under "Cooperative Extension."

Index

Italic page numbers refer to relevant photographs or illustrations. **Boldface** page numbers refer to Plant Selection Guides.

Photo Credits

For pages with 4 or fewer photographs, each image has been identified by its position on the page: left (L), center (C), or right (R); top (T), middle (M), or bottom (B). On pages with more than 4 photographs, images are identified by their position in the grid (shown at right).

	L	C	R
1	1	1	1
2			
3			
4			
5			

End papers, hardcover edition: Fiona Gilsenan

Archadeck: 59 B. Frank S. Balthis: 18 TR. Patrick Bennett: 65 R. Botanika: 28 B. Marion Brenner: 25 BL; 88 C; 89 C; 125 L, R; 130 L; 140 R; 144 R. Ralph S. Byther: 230 C3. David Cavagnaro: 141 C. Peter Christiansen: 188 BC; 193 TR. R. Cowles: 189 C1. Rosalind Creasy: 134. Claire Curran: 18 BR; 18 L; 34; 38; 88 L, R; 127 L; 130 R; 131 L; 140 C; 145 R. Thomas Eltzroth: 230 C2, L1, L2, R1. Derek Fell: 131 R; 214 TR. William E. Ferguson: 220 C1; 221 C1. Charles Marden Fitch: 220 L; 221 L2. Gardener's Supply Co.: 192 R1, R3. Fiona Gilsenan: 1 B; 40; 109 L, R; 115 L; 118 TL, TR; 124; 126; 127 C, R; 133; 139 C; 139 L; 140 L; 142 TL, TR; 144 C; 156 B; 159 B; 178; 202; 220 R2; 227 L1. David Goldberg: 226; 227 L4, R2; 229 BL. Harold Greer: 89 R. Ali Harivandi: 229 BR. Lynne Harrison: 14; 25 M; 26; 35 TR; 36 TR; 59 M; 76; 113 L; 116 L; 117; 128 BR; 152 T; 160 R1. Philip Harvey: 103; 229 TL. Lisa Herbert, H & H

Horticulture: 8; 10; 12. High Country Gardens: 188 BR. Saxon Holt: 30 TL; 33 B; 42; 45; 54 BR, TL; 58 BR; 60 T; 94 C; 96 M; 105 T; 214 BR, TL. Sandra Ivany: 80 T. Roz Joseph: 39 T. judywhite/New Leaf Images: 25 T; 31 BR; 32 B; 72 BL; 104 TL; 106 BL; 136 TC, TL; 155 TL; 160 R3. Mark Luthringer: 43 B. Ray Maleike: 189 L1. Charles Mann: 16; 20; 22; 27 B, T; 29 T; 30 TR; 35 B; 54 TR; 61 B; 64 TR; 66 L; 67 B; 89 L; 125 C; 153 BL; 154. David McDonald: 29 B; 31 TL; 32 TR; 43 T; 44; 58 TR; 60 B; 70; 73 BL; 101; 102; 115 C, R; 130 C; 144 L; 145 L; 155 TR. William T. Molin: 227 L2. Terrence Moore: 65 L. Arthur N. Orans: 131 C. Jerry Pavia: 1 T, M; 6; 27 M; 30 B; 32 TL; 33 T; 35 TL; 37 TR; 39 B, M; 50; 52; 56 TR; 72 R; 73 TR; 74; 90; 91 T; 96 B, TL, TR; 105 B; 106 TR; 112 MR, TR; 113 R; 136 B; 142 BL; 161. Pamela K. Peirce: 221 L1; 227 R1, R3, R4; 229 TR. Norman A. Plate: 118 BR; 141 R; 142 BR; 150 TL; 188 TL; 189 R1, R3; 192 R2; 193 BR; 198 T; 200; 214 BL; 218. Suzanne Porter: 192 L2. Ian Reeves: 48; 62; 180; 182;

183; 184; 185; 187; 188 BL; 189 R2; 192 C1; 193 BC, L; 194; 196; 197; 198 B; 212; 216 BL, TR; 217. Bill Ross: 116 R. Richard Shiell: 36 TL; 91 B; 110 B, TL, TR; 112 BR, TL; 146; 227 L3, R5. Steve Sibbett: 230 C1. Chad Slattery: 28 T. K. Bryan Swezey: 216 TL. The Center for Universal Design, North Carolina State University: 47 BL. Michael S. Thompson: 2; 36 B; 37 TL; 47 R; 68; 79; 94 L, R; 97; 106 TL; 109 C; 128 TL, TR; 136 TR; 139 R; 151 T. Mark Turner: 24 L, R; 57 L; 58 TL; 59 T; 61 M; 73 BR; 110 TC; 158 B; 159 T; 160 R2; 220 C2. Visions: 141 L. Andy Wasowski: 56 BR; 78; 80 B; 158 T. Darrow M. Watt: 190; 192 L1. Ron West: 220 R1; 221 C2, R1, R2. Peter Whiteley: 61 T; 152 LB. Russ A. Widstrand: 216 BR. Tom Woodward: 145 C. Cynthia Woodyard: 25 BR; 47 TL; 67 T; 72 TL; 106 BR; 132; 148; 150 B, TR; 155 B; 156 M; 157; 160 L2; 162. Linda Younker: 37 B; 56 L; 57 R; 64 BR, TL; 66 R; 104 BR, TR; 151 B; 152 BR; 153 BR; 156 T. Thomas A. Zitter: 230 R2.

Our thanks also to the following:

Archadeck
Kathleen Brenzel
Michael Berger
Bruce and Gloria Burgener
Tom Christopher
Archie Days
J.T. Dimmick (Maxsea Soluble
  Seaweed Plant Foods)
Marcia Donahue
Philip Edinger
Richard Elmore
Daniel Forest
Tony Gilsenan

Ellen Hatfield
Jay Hawkinson
Mary Jane Hofmeister
Sara Jamison
Guy Johnson
Landscaping by Andre
Mark Leeper
David Lovro
Dorothy Mockus Lubin
  (University of California
  Forest Products Laboratory)
Frank Mainzer
Steve Martino

Todd Menard
  (Artisan Landscaping)
Cathy Nelson
John Oldani
Rex Pace (The Center for
  Universal Design, NCSU)
Tishana Peebles
Thais Powers
Tim Psomas
Rob and Julie Reis
Tina Rousselot
Pam Ryan
Anita Sanders

Deborah Slater
Smith & Hawken
Britta Swartz
Christine Ten Eyck
Craig Thomson (The Garden
  Grow Company)
Urban Farmer (San Francisco)
Nancy E. Wagner
Carolyn West (New York
  Botanical Garden)
Lonnie Zeweren